Integrating Diversity

Being

Papers given to the Family Justice Council's Interdisciplinary Conference for judges, directors of social services, mental health professionals, academia, guardians ad litem, panel managers and other professions, held at the Dartington Hall Conference Centre, Dartington Hall, Totnes, Devon, between 28 and 30 September 2007, together with Resolutions arising from the discussions in small group sessions.

Edited by

The Rt Hon Lord Justice Thorpe

and

Samantha Singer
Barrister

Family Law

Published by Family Law
a publishing imprint of
Jordan Publishing Limited
21 St Thomas Street
Bristol BS1 6JS

British Library Cataloguing-in-Publication Data

A catalogue record for this book is available from the British Library.

ISBN 978 1 84661 080 6

Typeset by Letterpart Ltd, Reigate, Surrey

Printed in Great Britain by Antony Rowe Limited, Chippenham, Wiltshire

Contributors

Dr Bode Adesida
Consultant Child and Adolescent Psychiatrist, Dartford Child Mental Health Service

Dr Nick Banks
Chartered Consultant Clinical Psychologist, Child & Family Psychological Assessment Services

Professor Ravinder Barn
Royal Holloway, University of London

Dr Julia Brophy
Senior Research Fellow, Oxford Centre for Family Law and Policy, University of Oxford

Dr Aggrey Burke
Consultant Psychiatrist and Senior Lecturer, St Georges University, London

Nicholas Crichton
District Judge, Inner London Family Proceedings Court

Nadine Finch
Barrister, Garden Court Chambers

Professor Susan Golombok
Centre for Family Research, University of Cambridge

Dr Sally Hodges
Clinical Psychologist, The Tavistock Centre

Nadira Huda
Child Protection Coordinator, London Borough of Tower Hamlets

Julia Isikwe Hughes
Independent Social Worker, Trainer and Children's Guardian

Dr Jagbir Jhutti-Johal
Research Associate, Oxford Centre for Family Law & Policy, Universit'

Dr Ravi Kohli
Head of Applied Social Studies, University of Bedfordshire

Sherry Malik
Corporate Director (Strategy and Performance), CAFCASS

Dr Sue McGaw
Consultant Clinical Psychologist, Director, Special Parenting Service, Cornwall Partnership Trust

Professor Ann Phoenix
Faculty of Social Science, Open University and Institute of Education, University of London

Dr Neela Shabde
Consultant Paediatrician, North Tyneside General Hospital

Dr Claire Sturge
Consultant Child Psychiatrist, Alexandra Health Centre

Lennox K Thomas
Consultant Psychotherapist, Refugee Therapy Centre

Dr Kate Ward
Consultant Paediatrician, Airedale General Hospital

Dr Elspeth Webb
Senior Lecturer, Department of Child Health, Cardiff University

Foreword

By Sir Mark Potter
President of the Family Division

My second Dartington conference, with its theme of 'Integrating Diversity', had high expectations to meet in the light of the high standard set by the first conference which I attended in September 2005. I am happy to say that it amply achieved these expectations.

The contributions of a programme of exceptional speakers, drawn from leading members of the medical, legal, academic and social work professions, have resulted in the thought-provoking content of the papers which make up this volume.

The work of both delegates and speakers in the invaluable small group discussion sessions which took place has been consolidated by the drafting committee to produce 14 resolutions under the title, 'Neither Blind to nor Blinded by Culture'. These resolutions represent, in succinct form, the collective thinking of the members of the inter-disciplinary community who made up the conference.

It is to be hoped these resolutions will be well received by government and that they will inform and benefit future practice in family law.

Sir Mark Potter
January 2008

Editorial Introduction

We live in an uncertain and rapidly changing world. I therefore find it reassuring to know that in the autumn of each year that ends with an odd number there will be a Dartington Conference. This institution had its first beginning in September 1995 and this is the 6th volume in the series published by Jordans to disseminate the papers, the discussion and the decisions taken at the Conference itself. (With the publication by Jordans of 'Re-Rooted Lives' in July 2007, a return to the themes explored at our first Dartington Conference, it is perhaps more properly the 7th volume in the series).

In this our latest volume we break new ground. We have never before focussed on a single distinct topic. I am in no doubt that the decision to do so was a wise one. The more diverse our society, the more important it becomes to ensure that what we dispense as family justice can be accepted as such by all communities, including those whom the legislators and judges did not have in mind, when passing statutes and construing the law.

This was the second of the Dartington Conferences to fall under the auspices of the Family Justice Council. Its planning and delivery was overseen by an enthusiastic planning group which was hugely assisted by Khatun Sapnara and the Diversity Committee of the Family Justice Council that she chairs. Her experience and enthusiasm, and that of the members of the Committee, identified and attracted our eminent expert contributors. Learning from past experience we resisted the temptation to cover too much ground thereby exhausting the delegates and stifling innovation. Indeed, some of the liveliest debate emerged towards the end of the Conference.

For the first time at this Conference we were able, through the work of a drafting committee, to produce proper resolutions. This new development proved extremely successful and will be a permanent feature of future conferences.

The issues covered and the lessons to be learned are of particular importance to all who work in our courts of trial from (and perhaps particularly so) the Family Proceedings Courts to the High Court. I therefore hope that what we publish will be widely disseminated and read by all whose work takes them into our family courts. Once more the Family Justice Council will distribute copies to its local branches, providing them with material for events in their own areas in the coming year.

I would like to express my thanks to the Family Justice Council Secretariat whose administration both before and during the conference was of the highest standard, and to the staff at Dartington Hall who demonstrated their usual hospitality and professionalism.

The true editor of this work is Samantha Singer who has been impressively effective as a rapporteur in addition to making a real impact at the Conference with her lively personality.

Rt Hon Lord Justice Thorpe
January 2008

Contents

Seventh Dartington Conference Opening Address

Lord Justice Thorpe

Court of Appeal

The Dartington Interdisciplinary Family Justice Council Conference is no longer an event. It is now an institution. Many of us assembled this afternoon are regulars; some of us were at the first Conference in 1995 and some of us have yet to miss a Dartington Conference. Others are here for the first time. This is particularly so as this year we are tackling a theme never tackled before. It is one of obvious and growing importance. Those who have been before can see with hindsight that the Dartington Conference has made an enormous contribution to the developing Family Justice System. We now take the interdisciplinary approach for granted; it was not so 15 years ago. Particularly dedicated legal minds thought that there was no place for other disciplines, other sciences or other practices. To get funding for the first Conference was a great struggle. Eventually it was achieved and that Conference generated the impetus which created the President's Interdisciplinary Committee. Although now delivered by the Family Justice Council, there has been no perceptible break in the continuity of success. A number of dedicated individuals have made enormous contributions to the planning which is an essential precursor to each Conference. Planning for the next starts at the close of the last Conference and is equally divided between members and non-members of the Council. We are enormously grateful to them.

One can prejudge the quality of the Conference from a reading of the papers. It is expected that delegates will have read the papers in advance and will know what is to come. There is a lot of novelty in these papers for me. In my current roles, I regard myself as shielded from many of the highly important issues which the papers address. Thus it is going to be an unusual Dartington Conference for me in the sense that the territory we are surveying is new. I do not expect I will have much contribution to make other than to sit attentively and to learn.

There has been great support for the Conference: finance from the Government and from Jordans Family Law, commitment to publish the papers. Greg Woodgate, from Jordans, is here and will be hosting the reception this evening. The Conference publications, through Jordans, have varied in quality as a result of the choices made for Conference themes. We have to choose 18 months in advance the subject we will tackle and we may find that a topic loses appeal. We have chosen some duds in the past: the Family Law Act 1996 was selected and shortly before the Conference the Government abandoned the fundamental reform that Parliament had sanctioned.

The first publication, edited by Nicholas Wall, entitled *Rooted Sorrows*, has proved the most enduring and best-selling of all the publications. And so under Richard Hudson's distinguished leadership, a return to the theme of 'Rooted Sorrows' was commissioned focusing particularly on legal and psychoanalytic thinking. The series is not just seven volumes covering each of the alternate years' Conferences; it is now augmented by an extra volume entitled *Re-rooted Lives*. I commend the book to you. You may think I am not entirely impartial given one of the editors is an old friend and the other is my wife. Unashamed I do commend it to you. Do look at it before you go.

In 2005, at the last Conference, there was a botched attempt to produce some resolutions at the end of the Conference. I go to a lot of international family law conferences where drafting of resolutions is absolutely standard practice. This is particularly so with the conferences arranged by the Hague Permanent Bureau where importance is attached to the emerging resolutions. They have an impact on governments' policies and on governments' funding for the Permanent Bureau. So, I endeavoured to see whether we could generate messages that would be heeded by Government departments and major players in the family justice system but failed for want of preparation and planning. I want to do it more professionally this Conference. Yvonne Brown is to chair sessions to draft carefully worked up and relatively succinct resolutions which, as a Conference, we can either approve or reject. Khatun Sapnara has had great influence in that she chairs the Diversity sub-committee and has attracted to it people who are not members of the Family Justice Council. She is, in a sense, one of the parents of this Conference. If you have ideas about possible resolutions please take them to her. I have filled my allotted 15 minutes which means we are still running 5 minutes late. We will need speakers for the first sessions to take their places swiftly at the table.

PLENARY 1

WHAT IS DIVERSITY AND HOW DOES IT IMPACT ON THE FAMILY JUSTICE SYSTEM?

Diversity at the Inner London Family Proceedings Court

Nicholas Crichton

District Judge, Inner London Family Proceedings Court

SUMMARY OF THE PAPER

District Judge Nicholas Crichton introduced his paper by explaining that his aim was to offer a glimpse of life on the 'bottom branch of the tree' of family justice at the centre of the capital. The Inner London Family Proceedings Court at Wells Street sees approximately 4,000 cases each year, approximately 1,700 of which are public law cases. The principal focus of his paper is public law. However, the case examples listed in his paper are to be seen as a microcosm of the types of cases dealt with at Wells Street on a daily basis. The examples give a hint of the wide ranging issues coming before the court.

District Judge Crichton's intention in introducing his paper was to touch on one or two of the topics raised in the paper.

District Judge Crichton has heard that in the South East of England 800 languages and dialects are spoken, 150 of which are spoken within a five-mile radius of his court. This demonstrates the huge problems dealt with in the courts every day. Although interpreters are by and large excellent, there is a real concern whether they are truly able to interpret the concepts. What do 'core assessment', 'parental responsibility', 'special guardianship', 'placement' and even 'contact' mean to the interpreter? What do these words mean in court users' own languages? Judges have to rely on lawyers to explain and make sure that their clients understand the concepts because there is little opportunity to check they have been understood when in court.

District Judge Crichton recalled that on Wednesday of the previous week, he had met four representatives from the Legal Aid Group from the Ministry of Justice. Together they saw a number of cases where serious, professional negotiation had led to resolution. The cases resolved in this way would have taken a day each to deal with in court had it not been for the efforts of the lawyers involved.

District Judge Crichton considered the meaning of 'good enough parenting'. It is a wholly subjective concept. He took the view that we should seek to uphold the concept but warned that we do need to address it with a degree of flexibility. He explained that he had in the past worked for some time in the former Soviet Union, and he had just come back from Ethiopia. In those countries District Judge Crichton had seen levels of poverty and deprivation beyond anything experienced in the UK. There are no systems in place for removing children, even in cases of gross sexual abuse. Indeed, in Eastern Europe, some societies are only gradually coming out of denial that such abuse exists.

District Judge Crichton considered example 4 in his paper. That case involved a Nigerian father who had a child with a woman with whom he had no relationship. He visited mother and child in hospital and then stood back. He understood that an assessment would be carried out, but did not wish to be a part of it. In the event, the mother failed and the father stepped up and put himself forward to look after the child. Social services asked him where he had been. He explained that it did not occur to him that the mother would fail.

In Nigeria you might see a blind beggar with a child on her hip and no one would dream of removing the child as there is nowhere to remove the child to. The father has gone on to do a splendid job looking after his son.

Finally, District Judge Crichton touched upon the issue raised in the final paragraph of his paper. He is alarmed by recent pronouncements suggesting that we can no longer afford to give 'hopeless' parents their day in court. Who is to say that they are 'hopeless'? How can it be suggested that they should not have a voice? He noted that the English and Welsh family justice system is rightly renowned for its sense of justice and fairness, and concluded with three thoughts – the 'three Vs'.

- *Vulnerability: people and children are often extremely Vulnerable; they are deserving of particular patience and understanding.*

- *Values: in the Family Justice System we have a responsibility to demonstrate that our Values can and will be maintained.*

- *Victimisation: if we ride roughshod over people this will leave them resentful and their resentment will spread through their families and be conveyed to children who will in turn feel they are Victims.*

THE PAPER

Introduction

I hope that it is not too glib to say that diversity is the daily business of the Inner London Family Proceedings Court at Wells Street. Diversity is the norm. We do not only have to deal with problems arising from drug and alcohol misuse, mental health and learning disability. Historically and currently London has been and is a melting pot, a vast cauldron of different races, nationalities and cultures. Some are long established, others are trying to establish themselves, yet others are merely passing through. Some are here legally, some illegally, but whatever their status their children are entitled to the protection of the law. I am told that there are some 150 languages spoken within a five-mile radius of my court. Travelling on the London Underground confirms that impression. What it means for us as a court serving the City of London and the 12 inner London Boroughs, and receiving work from a number of the outer London Boroughs, is a fascinating glimpse into the cultures and mores of the different societies – fascinating, but also difficult and challenging. Perhaps the best way of illustrating the variety of problems that come before the court is to give examples of just some of the cases which come before us on a daily basis, examples both specific and general.

PUBLIC LAW

1   A Croatian family who almost certainly entered the country illegally. Six children, the eldest two being 14 years 11 months and 14 years 1 month. Father was prostituting them in the Kings Cross area. The girls were going to school with large sums of cash in their pockets. The police became involved and care proceedings were started. The girls were placed in a residential unit. Mother remained at home with her four younger children and father was subject to a bail condition not to return home. One night the entire family disappeared, including the two girls, and they have not been heard of again. To us the prostitution of such young girls is deeply shocking. To this family and arguably to the girls themselves, it was normal practice and an accepted way of life.

2   Two children aged 12 and 10. Bangladeshi parents. Mother 35 years younger than father, who had died. Mother spoke no English. Isolated even within her own community.

Over-feeding the children to the point where both were overweight to a life-threatening degree. Risks to the children's emotional, social and psychological welfare.

3   Child of 2 from a village in the Congo, which had been attacked and razed to the ground by rebel troops. Parents feared dead, although mother subsequently surfaced. Child brought to this country by a priest and placed with a maternal uncle. Uncle unable to cope. Mother subsequently contacted in a village near Kinshasa. Wanted child returned, but unwilling to submit to any kind of social work assessment. Uncle assessed by social workers in this country according to standards that were completely foreign to him.

4   Child of 6 months born to Nigerian father and alcoholic Scottish mother, as a result of a 'one night stand'. Mother failed residential assessment. Social workers believed father to be incapable of caring for the child, since he had seen the child just once, at 6 days old, and had then stood back. Father explained that in Nigeria nobody would ever consider removing a child from its mother. Blind beggar women would be seen beside the road with children on their hips. There is no machinery for removing such children into state care. He assumed that his child's mother would be found suitable to care for him. When she was found unsuitable he asked to be considered. Social services were dismissive. They were directed to conduct an assessment and father went into a mother and baby unit for 3 months. A Nigerian child and adolescent psychiatrist referred to him as having 'innate parenting skills'. He passed with flying colours.

5   A Pakistani family with eight children, one of whom was severely handicapped both physically and mentally. Mother entirely dependent upon father, who misused alcohol and was violent to her and the children. Eventually mother agreed to seek occupation and non-molestation orders, although these were contrary to her cultural beliefs. Once those orders were properly enforced the other children rallied round and the family were able to start functioning.

6   Father from Jamaica and mother from Sierra Leone. Three older children said to be the subject of a voodoo curse, which could be lifted only by the sacrifice of a baby's vital organs. Witch doctor in London recommended that the parents take their fourth child, a baby of 6 months, to the Gambia to swim in alligator-infested waters in order to lift the curse.

7   A Nigerian grandmother who brought her granddaughter to the UK for a 4-week holiday to visit relatives. While here her own father, a Chieftain, died. As the oldest child she took on his title and duties and it was her responsibility to arrange his funeral. She returned to Nigeria in a hurry, intending to return for her granddaughter in 2–3 weeks when all had been dealt with. She was refused an entry visa because her granddaughter was on her passport and she could not produce her. She complained of dismissive and racist treatment by immigration officials. The situation took several months to resolve.

8   Zimbabwean mother, West Indian father. Mother an overstayer, but since she had a child she was granted leave to remain provided that she remained living with father. He was extremely violent. She was terrified of leaving him for fear that she might be sent back to Zimbabwe, with or without her baby. She was of limited intelligence and had difficulty comprehending what the proceedings were about.

9   Physical Chastisement:
    - Families from West Africa, notably Sierra Leone and Angola who whip their children with electric flexes and sometimes rub chilli pepper into the wounds; also rub chilli pepper into the private parts of their daughters who appear to be taking an interest in boys.

- West Indian father who held a hot steam iron to the leg of his teenage son for 8–10 seconds by way of punishment.
- Iraqi family who branded 12-year-old daughter with a hot knife for theft of £1.50 – branded on lips, hand and inside of thighs. Cautioned by police!
- Chinese family, who chained teenage daughter to radiator without food for days, just because she had been seen holding hands with a boy.
- West Indian father who chained stepson in garage at night to sleep on sacks while his own children slept in comfort.
- Well-to-do American family from bible belt deep south who regularly beat their children, believing it to be their responsibility to produce respectful and law-abiding citizens. In this case the significant harm was more emotional than physical as there was an unpleasant ritual involved.

10 Home Alone:

Children being left alone at home is a common occurrence. In one case a child of one year old had been left alone in his cot for 2–3 hours every day, one parent having gone to work early in the morning, and the other parent not arriving home from night shift until 2–3 hours later. Complete astonishment that anybody thought that this was wrong. We learn that such arrangements are very common in many parts of the world.

PRIVATE LAW

1   Two boys, aged 8 and 6, the sons of an easy-going, not particularly well-educated mother from Mauritius and a Jamaican Rastafarian father, who places a very high value upon education and strict discipline. When they separated mother and father agreed that the boys should alternate between their parents week by week. Another judge, mistakenly in my view, decided that a shared residence order was the way forward. If such orders can ever work they certainly will not work if the parents cannot agree about anything. The boys were saying that they were afraid of their father and did not wish to spend so much time with him. Eventually I made a residence order in favour of mother with a fairly flexible order for contact with their father who also shared parental responsibility.

2   A 6-year-old child of Russian mother and Moroccan father. Child autistic. Long waiting list for treatment in the UK, but first class treatment available in Moscow. Father resisting mother taking child back to Moscow for 3 months every summer for treatment. Unable to understand child needs to be treated in familiar surroundings – demanded he should be treated in France, where father had relatives. Mother terrified that according to Islamic law, when child reached the aged of 7 he should be handed over to father.

3   A 6-year-old child of English mother and West Indian father. Father in prison. Mother suffering from terminal cancer. Mother placed child with old family friend who happened to be in a homosexual relationship, although he had children of his own from a previous relationship. Friend provided excellent care, emotionally as well as physically, but father's family were homophobic and put pressure on mother and on the placement.

4   Many domestic violence cases requiring Re L hearings in which mothers allege that Muslim fathers claim it is their right to beat them. One young mother, not a Muslim, was made to wear the hijab or she would not be accepted by father's family. Beaten if she did not do so. Child taken from her and handed to father's family, all in the name of Islam.

5   Lesbian partners. One has been three times impregnated with the sperm of an unidentified donor, the same donor on each occasion. Each time when the child is 18 months to 2 years old they come to court to seek a shared residence order – the only way for the mother's partner to obtain parental responsibility.

ADOPTION

The whole issue of adoption of same-sex couples is in the public arena at the moment. There are probably as many different views as there are people who think about the issue. There are probably few, if any, who would disagree that the best way to bring up a child is within a household of a mother and father. However, many children do not have that option available to them. Values and attitudes have changed considerably within the last 40–50 years, and it is now difficult to reach a consensus on social and ethical matters. Some have strongly held religious views that adoption by a same-sex couple is wrong. However, increasingly in my court we see same-sex couples providing loving homes for children who might not otherwise have that experience. I have dealt with several such adoptions. One in particular sticks in the mind. Two boys from a very troubled background. Went through several foster homes unable to cope with them. Eventually fostered by two gay men who provided them with the stability and security they needed. At the adoption hearing the boys, now aged 12 and 10, were clearly extremely happy as were their adopters, two committed men who had adapted their lives to meet the needs of the boys. Obviously there may be difficult years ahead, but there was a strong feeling this was a group which had the strength and the commitment to come through.

COMMENTS AND CONCLUSIONS

When people come to this country they are subject to the laws of this country. Sometimes they come with such a completely different cultural background and understanding of a child's needs that the standards which we seek to uphold are difficult for them to understand and adhere to. I believe that we are entitled to expect them to try to come to an understanding of those standards. At the same time in many cases we also need to have an understanding of why they have done what they have done and try to establish whether they have begun to understand our standards and have the capacity to observe them. The cases of which I have referred to above represent a very small section of the kind of challenges we face on a daily basis in my court. There are no simple answers. In some cases there appear to be no answers at all. In the case of the boy who was quite seriously injured by his father holding a steam iron to his thigh, we were lucky enough to have an extremely articulate Rastafarian social worker. She said that her own children felt 'victimised' by herself and her husband because they felt they had been treated differently from their peers. However, her children were able to 'gang up' against their parents in their resistance to the stricter regime they experienced at home. This boy had been singled out and scape-goated by his parents and felt isolated. The level of punishment to which he had been subjected was not acceptable in any culture or society. That message coming from her made it easier for the parents to accept than if it had come from a middle-class English social worker.

One of the problems we encounter is the difficulty which people from different races and cultural backgrounds have in believing that social services and the courts do not exist to remove children from families. Many come from backgrounds where there are no social services and where the police are corrupt and/or violent. When told by their new neighbours in this country that social services want to take their children away, why would they not believe them? It is not surprising therefore, that they are disinclined to provide information requested and to be open and to place their trust in social workers or the courts. As the number of experienced family law lawyers diminish, and with it the provision of independent legal advice, the situation can only deteriorate yet further.

While it is important to have an understanding of cultural diversity and of the different approaches of people from different backgrounds, we should not seek to compromise our own standards, which we have arrived at over a long period and which continue to evolve. Are we too 'nannyish', or have we become sophisticated in our understanding of child development? On the whole I believe it to be the latter, although sometimes I worry a little about the former.

Other issues

There is still a difficulty in obtaining suitable representation of ethnic minorities on the bench, both in terms of judges and magistrates. I do worry about what is the perception of people from ethnic minorities coming before the court and feeling that they are being judged by people who live by completely foreign standards and who often give the impression that they do not understand the standards of the people whom they seek to judge.

There is probably a greater diversity in the ranks of social workers, but I do sometimes get the feeling that white English social workers of 25 or 30 years' experience have considerable difficulty understanding the backgrounds of the people whom they seek to assess. On the other hand we see social workers from many other countries, some from commonwealth countries and some not. The standard of their work, of their written reports, and sometimes of their spoken English, can be extremely variable.

In my court we are served by a large number of interpreters of many different languages. Most are extremely competent. I have little doubt that they are accurately translating the words, but I wonder how far the concepts are translated.

Disability

I have not touched upon the various forms of disability that we have to cope with in our court. The physically disabled are catered for on the ground floor of the building. We have all the usual equipment to enable us to cope with the problems with those with hearing disabilities.

And finally …

I feel that I cannot conclude without some comment upon the beginnings of a doctrine that we can no longer afford to provide 'hopeless' parents with their 'day in court'. I could not disagree more fundamentally. There is of course a crucial human rights issue to be considered. In addition, the Children Act requires us to consider every aspect of the best interests of the children whose cases come before our courts. If we deny parents the right to be heard, however inadequate their cause those parents will leave the court with strong feelings of resentment that they have not been allowed to have their say. If they have any kind of future contact with their children, either consciously or unconsciously, they will feed that resentment back into their children's lives in a way that can only be destructive for the children, and therefore contrary to everything which we seek to achieve for them.

The Mundane and the Manageable: Diversity and the Family Justice System

Dr Julia Brophy

Senior Research Fellow, University of Oxford

and

Professor Ann Phoenix

Faculty of Social Science, Open University and Institute of Education, University of London

INTRODUCTION

The ethnic composition of the UK is in flux. In particular, the number of ethnic groups represented among residents and citizens is increasing through EU enlargement and other migrations (ONS, Census, 2001). Partly because of this, outside of the family justice arena, debates about racial, ethnic and cultural diversity and multiculturalism are moving at a greater pace than is generally evident in literature about issues of diversity in family proceedings.

Researchers and writers in a range of disciplines including anthropology, psychology, sociology, criminology and globalisation studies are engaging in wide-ranging debates about multiculturalism, identities, citizenship, ethnic and cultural practices. These debates include discussion of the concepts, terms and definitions used to describe the field of 'race', ethnicity, culture, religion and language (Ansell and Solomos 2007; Murji and Solomos, 2004; Rattansi, 2007). It is generally agreed that ways of thinking about these issues have changed and that it is important to recognise that there is no universal 'minority' or 'white' experience (eg Modood 1997; Garner 2007). Globalisation is increasingly recognised as creating transnational families and global care chains (Lutz, 2007a, b; Williams and Gavanas, 2007) so that people from minority ethnic groups have continuing primary relationships outside the nation in which they live. This means that there are important differences between people from the same ethnic backgrounds as well as similarities between them. At the same time, some debates on multiculturalism currently conceptualise differences from the British nation and so multiculturalism as problematic (eg Goodhart, 2004) – an idea that is much disputed (eg Modood, 2007). In addition, racism has an impact on the experiences and life chances of people from minority ethnic groups and, at least partly, contributes to their social exclusion (Barn et al, 2005; Chahal and Julienne, 1999; Enneli, Modood and Bradley, 2005; Rattansi, 2007).

As a result of these debates and contestations, this area is one in which practitioners find it difficult to keep up with current thinking on diversity. And it is not perhaps surprising that there is some anxiety about discussing these issues in the family justice arena.

Key concepts such as identity, ethnicity and 'culture' can be difficult and contested. For example, identity is increasingly recognised to be a dynamic and negotiated territory. Ethnicity is characterised among other things by a sense of belonging and by group identity and according to Fernando (1991) influenced by social pressures and psychological needs and perceived as partially changeable. According to Karner (2007), ethnicity has dual characteristics; it can be a source of meaning and solidarity but it can also underscore discrimination and social exclusion. For example, adults and children sometimes treat children from different ethnic groups differently (eg Connolly, 1998; Ogilvy et al, 1990, 1992).

An international review of research and writing from cultural anthropologists and others, suggests that 'culture' is defined as characterised by behaviours and attitudes, usually determined by upbringing and some choice and perceived as changeable through, for example, processes such as 'assimilation' and 'acculturation' and economic and social contexts and choices (Brophy, 2000). According to such research, 'culture' not only guides and motivates certain behaviours but also can provide specific meanings through which behaviours and events can be constructed and understood (Brophy 2000). It is, however, not a static set of ideas, beliefs, values and perspectives but rather a dynamic and contested phenomenon.

The following quote indicates that young people from minority ethnic groups themselves recognise that their cultures are changing and see differences within their ethnic group for example, as a result of gender:

> Yamail: I think that things are changing in Bangladeshi home, yes, some more than others. But going to university gives us ... big opportunities, for boys as well as girls. But the way I see it the girls are taking advantage of this more than the boys. And people outside the community talk about tradition holding them back. But the thing is, they have learnt all this macho stuff in this society, our fathers aren't like that (Mac an Ghaill and Haywood, 2005, p.33)

WHY IS IT RELEVANT FOR PROFESSIONALS IN THE FAMILY JUSTICE SYSTEM

It may seem unnecessary to consider why issues of diversity are relevant to the Family Justice System (FJS) since law and Guidance make it an unavoidable area for practitioners. Policy and Guidance under the Children Act – Parts III and IV – demonstrate its relevance at many stages in the investigation and assessment process and in the delivery of services for families.[1] The Race Relations (Amendment) Act 2000 also imposes a duty on public bodies to ensure that they actively establish that they are not discriminating on the grounds of 'race' and 'ethnicity'.

This section aims to clarify why addressing diversity makes for good and helpful practice rather than simply being a matter of compliance with law and Guidance. Notions of 'cultural practices' and 'cultural relativism' in the context of children's rights are debated in legal discourse (eg Freeman 1998). And while forced marriage and female genital mutilation are illegal in Europe, many struggle with a range of issues and more subtle nuances about, for example, what constitutes 'normative' familial behaviours and child rearing practices – in multicultural, multiracial Britain. Thus, busy practitioners (children's guardians, childcare lawyers and others) have expressed a need for a source of information/quick reference about 'cultural practices' in diverse communities (Brophy et al, 2005).

---

[1]   For example, Children Act (CA) 1989, s 22(5)(c) – in the case of looked-after children, the local authority has a duty to consider a child's background; s 61(3) – Duties of voluntary organisations to address child's background when making decisions; s 74(c) – Day care should meet additional needs arising from diverse backgrounds; Sch 2, para 8 – local authority has duty to provide relevant cultural activities as part of family support services; Sch 2, para 11 – Attention to diversity when recruiting day carers and foster carers.

WHY IS IT SO DIFFICULT TO TALK ABOUT DIVERSITY?

First, what is the evidence that there is a problem in talking about diverse backgrounds and cultural contexts? There are several sources: evidence from the Inquiry into the abuse and murder of Victoria Climbié (Laming 2003), interviews with solicitors acting for minority ethnic parents in care proceedings, and interviews with minority ethnic parents themselves (Brophy et al, 2005). Moreover, practitioners in a range of settings, such as mental health and counselling services on both sides of the Atlantic have reported they feel ill-trained and ill-prepared to work with minority ethnic clients in predominantly white communities (eg Lafromboise and Foster 1992: Mintzet et al 1995: Allison et al, 1996; Echemendia et al, 1997; Sue 1997). Relatively few clinicians in England and elsewhere continue to argue that practitioners must come to terms with how racism and culture mediate their clinical work with minority ethnic families (eg D'Ardenne and Mahtani 1999; Fontes 1995; Keating, 2007; 2005; Littlewood 1992; Lau 1998: Lau and Bond 2000; Maitre 1995; 2005). However, Williams and Keating (2005) argue that mental health practitioners need to make connections between a person's lived experiences, their behaviour and their distress. They found that mental health professionals were fearful about discussing issues of 'race' and culture.

There are recurrent themes in child protection and mental health arenas. Some practitioners are fearful about starting a dialogue about 'race' and what might be termed 'ethno-cultural' contexts,[2] they are concerned about being seen as racist, are fearful of 'getting it wrong', being uninformed either in the tenor of the questions asked or their ability to understand and integrate accurately information obtained from a client. Some are concerned about using the wrong terms or offending people simply by raising diversity in backgrounds and contexts for discussion. Thus, unless unavoidable some professionals may 'sidestep' this area of discussion altogether – or may make assumptions about behaviours and motivations. Moreover, some minority ethnic solicitors and experts also avoid discussing this area with clients or patients (Brophy, Jhutti-Johal and McDonald 2005; Brophy, Shabde and Ward 2007).

There are ongoing debates about whether professionals intervene too early in minority ethnic households (misunderstanding behaviours and motivation or simply failing to check perceptions), or too late (leaving children in high risk situations where, had the child been white, professionals would have acted earlier). The Inquiry into the murder of Victoria Climbié (Laming, 2003) illuminates some of these issues. For example, Part five of the Report (Working with diversity) identified:

> 'There is some evidence to suggest that one of the consequences of an exclusive focus on 'culture' in work with black children and families, is [that] it leaves black and ethnic minority children in potentially dangerous situations, because the assessment has failed to address a child's fundamental care and protection needs.' (Ratna Dutt, director, Race Equality Unit)

Lord Laming stated: 'Victoria was a black child who was murdered by her two black carers. Many of the professionals with whom she came into contact during her life in this country were also black. Therefore, it is tempting to conclude that racism can have had no part to play in her case. But such a conclusion fails to recognise that racism finds expression in many ways other than in the direct application of prejudice'.[3] It is in the *assumptions* made by professionals that Lord Laming placed some responsibility for Victoria's death. Those he took issue with were (a) that racial 'matching' necessarily equated with [better] informed evidence-based practice, and (b) that matching of itself ensured accurate information about what constitutes 'normative' child

---

[2] In practice, diverse backgrounds and contexts to family life and parenting may link traditions and practices with both an ethnic group and a culture; in certain instances values and practices may also be determined by religious beliefs.

[3] Laming, 2003, para 16.1.

rearing practices in diverse cultural contexts.[4] He reported that he had considered during the Inquiry whether a failure by a particular professional to take action to protect Victoria, may have been partly due to that professional losing sight of the fact that her needs were the same as those of any other 7-year-old girl, from whatever cultural background'.[5]

Lord Laming argued that professionals lost sight of Victoria's needs because warning signs were not fully explored – some of these signs were 'read' by professionals as representing culturally appropriate behaviour. Thus, for example, a social worker thought Victoria's 'regimented' behaviour in front of her carers was appropriate for an Afro-Caribbean (sic) child – but no evidence was offered for that view.[6] A pastor made erroneous assumptions that Victoria's behaviour resulted from her recent arrival from Africa (she had been in Europe for almost a year at that point).[7] In addition, medical practitioners who noticed marks on Victoria's body considered the possibility that children reared in Africa may be expected to have more such marks than those raised in Europe.[8]

The Report noted that fears about being accused of racism operated on a number of levels. For example, it stopped professionals acting in circumstances where otherwise they would have done, and it affected the thinking and practices of 'same race' professionals who were fearful of being thought unsympathetic to someone of their own race. Lord Laming concluded there were so many instances of bad practice that it was not possible to say which were due to prejudice and which were due to incompetence or a lack of attention (Laming 2003 para 16.6-7).

While research in this area is not extensive, the studies available demonstrate some problems. For example, while research found very few cases where there was any indication that professionals had delayed proceedings too long, or moved in too quickly, there was a lack of attention to issues of diversity in some statements and reports (Brophy et al, 2003).

Subsequent research revealed anxieties by some solicitors about raising diverse backgrounds with some parents in case they were considered racist. Equally, research indicates that some parents have been dissatisfied because reports/statements did not provide information for courts on their diverse backgrounds and contexts (Brophy et al, 2005).

HUMAN RIGHTS AND 'POLITICAL CORRECTNESS'

The right to respect for private and family life (Article 8 of the European Convention on the Protection of Human Rights and Fundamental Freedoms (ECHR)) is of course a qualified right.[9] However, it is interpreted to require the involvement of parents/carers and children in decisions that impact on their family life. Parents and children should be consulted throughout the process and services offered should take account of the diverse background of families.[10]

---

[4]   The murder of Toni Ann Byfield in 2003 raised similar questions about whether social workers took for granted unwarranted assumptions about the family structure and responsibilities of African Caribbean families (NAGALRO, 2004).

[5]   Laming, 2003, para 16.2.

[6]   For example, a black social worker said when she heard of Victoria standing to attention before Luao and Manning (latter found guilty of her murder) she concluded this type of relationship was one that can be seen in many Afro-Caribbean (sic) families because respect and obedience are very important features of the Afro-Caribbean family script (Laming, 2003, para 16.4).

[7]   Laming, 2003, para 16.4.

[8]   Laming argued this assumption, regardless of whether it is valid or not, may prevent a full assessment of those marks being made.

[9]   The State may intervene where the law permits if this is necessary to protect a child's rights and freedoms, for example where it is necessary to protect a child from significant harm (Horowitz, Kingscote and Nicholls, 1999).

[10] Section 22(5)(c) – in the case of looked-after children, local authority has a duty to consider a child's background; s 61(3) – Duties of voluntary organisations to address child's background when making decisions; s 74(c) – Day care

Outside of the family justice system a human rights framework is often seen as at best an extension of 'political correctness'. In the current political climate the Equalities and Human Rights Commission is often the recipient of much 'bad press' at least in the 'red top' press. This is also the case with some discussions about diverse family values and practices.[11] For example, Brophy et al (2005) found that some solicitors express exasperation at experts who did not understand that things might be done differently in some minority ethnic households and in some circumstances solicitors felt parents had not been 'heard and understood'.

Moreover, the best interests principle is often seen – at least by lay audiences – as somewhat nebulous, while 'significant harm' is a complex concept to explain. The notion that the State might be interested in parenting practices and that courts might presume to know better than a parent what is harmful to a child or in his/her best interests can be anathema to many parents, especially some who are newly arrived in the UK. Research indicates this is often a major hurdle for lawyers to overcome prior to engaging a parent's cooperation in proceedings (Brophy et al, 2005).

The task of engaging with some minority ethnic families – both newly arrived and British born Black and Asian British – and demonstrating that professionals have addressed and understood diverse backgrounds and contexts can be demanding. Nevertheless part of the immediate challenge to the work of professionals and courts is to make attention to issues of 'diversity' more transparent – primarily to the parties involved in proceedings – but also to wider communities.

This means enabling more professionals to become *culturally competent* and thus more confident in routinely discussing this area with parents and young people and where necessary improving documentation. Practitioners need to be able to address both issues of racism and accusations of 'political correctness' while keeping a clear focus on the welfare and needs of children. These issues are not mutually exclusive.

A FRAMEWORK FOR ADDRESSING AND DOCUMENTING ATTENTION TO ETHNIC AND CULTURAL DIVERSITY

As already argued (Brophy, 2007) notions of cultural relativism and cultural pluralism and 'emic' and 'epic' modelling of behaviours[12] (to determine whether these fall within the parameters of what would be considered acceptable in a given ethnic group) share common shortcomings. They tend to treat 'culture' as a static phenomenon, minority ethnic groups as homogeneous, and sometimes determine whether parenting behaviour falls within a cultural 'norm' by seeking explanations in the 'country of origin'.

As we argue above, outside of the legal arena ways of thinking about identity, and ethno-cultural contexts are changing as globalisation increasingly creates transnational families. Thus, the family justice system is likely increasingly to address people from minority ethnic groups who have points of reference that take them beyond the borders of the nation in which

---

should meet additional needs arising from diverse backgrounds; Sch 2, para 8 – local authority has duty to provide relevant cultural activities as part of family support services; Sch 2, para 11 – Attention to diversity when recruiting day carers and foster carers.

[11] Lord Laming stated 'political correctness' has no place in child protection (2003, para 16.11).

[12] This is a term used in cultural anthropology (borrowed from the natural sciences) to assist in determining whether actions constitute child 'abuse' when assessing 'cross culturally'; it is suggested (eg Korbin, 1980) that professionals should be familiar with the viewpoint of members within the culture in question (the 'emic' perspective) and those of people outside of culture in question (the 'epic' perspective). One must then distinguish child-rearing practices viewed as acceptable by one group but generally unacceptable by the other – and then determine 'idiosyncratic departures' from culturally accepted standards.

they live; thus notions of acculturation and assimilation may have a limited currency. However, as also identified above, there are important differences between people from the same ethnic backgrounds as well as similarities between them, including by socio-economic status, education and changing gender roles (eg Reynolds, 2005). Any understanding of parenting practices within the country from which clients or their parents come cannot be sufficient to explaining parenting practices in the UK. This is particularly the case since people from the same place who migrate to different places may well behave in different ways (Bauer and Thompson, 2006). Equally – and we have not touched on this issue here – there are an increasing number of inter-racial, inter-ethnic and inter-religious partnerships and little work has been done on the implications of this for legal practice. Finally, the approaches available have not offered an analysis of power or a 'space' to examine issues of racism in professional practices. Research identifies that racism remains a reality in the lives of some parents and young people, and in contemporary social and political economy it has a shifting agenda and 'agency', some racism is overt some is covert and more difficult to unearth (Bhavnani, Mirza and Meetoo, 2005).

In terms of improving dialogue about these issues, it may be helpful to consider what might be called 'paradigms of intersectionality'. In sociological and cultural studies literature important intersections are identified as 'race and social class', 'race and gender' and 'race and nationalism' (eg Phoenix and Pattynama, 2006). In the child protection arena the key questions are: what are the important stages – the important intersections – and how can practitioners facilitate the exploration of issues of diversity at each intersection? It is no longer sufficient simply to focus on relevance in relation to threshold – although that of course remains important. In the current climate of 'openness, transparency' and the duty on public bodies to prove that they are not discriminatory, the family justice system needs to be able to demonstrate that parents from diverse backgrounds are 'heard and understood'.

Key findings (Brophy et al, 2003; 2005) indicate we should focus on concerns and allegations that result in failures of parenting, addressing intersections of diverse culture/religious/linguistic frameworks at the juncture of:

- the delivery of family support services to families;

- non-cooperation of parents with welfare and health professionals;

- mental health problems and appropriate services – especially for mothers of South Asian origins;[13]

- assessments of potential for change and methods of engaging with minority ethnic parents about what is required.

These are not the only junctions at which there should be dialogue about issues of diversity but research findings indicate they are likely to be crucial points. In an endeavour to make diversity 'mainstream' we suggest this approach offers a theoretical and practice 'space' in which the significance of cultural and religious diversity as well as racism can be addressed and assessed.

REFERENCES

Allison, K W, Echemendia, R J, Crawford, I and Robinson, W 1 'Predicting cultural competence: Implications for practice and training' (1996) 27(4) *Professional Psychology-Research and Practice* 386–393

---

[13] Including services for drug and alcohol abuse.

Ansell, A and Solomos, J *Race and Ethnicity: Key Concepts* (London: Routledge, 2007)

Barn, R, Andrew, L, and Mantovani, N *Life After Care: A study of the experiences of young people from different ethnic groups* (York: JRF/The Policy Press, 2005)

Bauer, E and Thompson, P *Jamaican Hands Across the Atlantic* (Jamaica: Ian Randle Publishers, 2006)

Brophy, J 'Child maltreatment in diverse households: Challenges to child care law, theory and practice' in S Meuwese, S Detrick and S Jansen et al (eds), *100 years of Child Protection* (The Netherlands: Wolf Legal Publishers, 2007)

Brophy, J 'Child Maltreatment and Cultural Diversity: A critical review of "race" and culture in clinical writing and research' (London: research report for the Nuffield Foundation, 2000)

Brophy, J, Brown, L, Cohen, S and Radcliffe, P *Child Psychiatry and Child Protection Litigation* (London: Royal College of Psychiatry (Gaskell), 2001)

Brophy, J, Jhutti-Johal, J and McDonald, E *Minority ethnic parents, their solicitors and child protection litigation, Research Series 5/05* (London: Ministry of Justice, 2005)

Brophy, J, Jhutti-Johal, J and Owen, C *Significant Harm: child protection litigation in a multi-cultural setting* (London: Ministry of Justice, 2003)

Brophy, J Shabde, N and Ward, K *Integrating 'diversity' into paediatric practice: Message for the family justice system* (forthcoming, 2008)

Bryne, B White *Lives: The Interplay of 'Race', Class and Gender in Everyday Life* (London: Routledge, 2006)

Chahal, K and Julienne *"We can't all be White" Racist victimisation in the UK* (York: Joseph Rowntree Foundation, 1999)

Connolly, P Racism, *Gender Identities and Young Children: Social relations in a multi-ethnic, inner-city primary school* (London: Routledge, 1998)

Culley, L 'A critique of multiculturalism in health care: the challenge for nurse education' (1996) 23 *Journal of Advanced Nursing* 564–570

D'Ardenne, P and Mahtani, A *Transcultural Counselling in Action* (London: Sage, 2nd edn, 1999)

Echemendia, R J, Harris, J G, Congett, S M, Diaz, M L and Peunte, A E 'Neuropsychological training practices with Hispanics: A National Survey' (1997) 11(3) *Clinical Neurophyschology* 229–243

Enneli, P, Modood, T and Bradley, H *Young Turks and Kurds: A Set of 'Invisible' Disadvantaged Groups* (York: Joseph Rowntree Foundation, 2005)

Fernando, S *Mental Health, Race and Culture* (London: MacMillian, 1991)

Fontes, L Aronson 'Culturally informed interventions for sexual child abuse' in L A Fontes (ed), *Sexual abuse in nine North American cultures: Treatment and Prevention* (Thousand Oaks CA, USA: Sage, 1995) 259–266

Freeman, M 'Cultural Pluralism and the rights of the child' in J Eekelaar and T Nhlapo, *The Changing Family: Family Forms and Family Law* (Oxford: Hart Publishing, 1998) 289–304

Garner, S *Whiteness* (London: Routledge, 2007)

Goodhart, D 'Too Diverse? Is Britain becoming too diverse to sustain the mutual obligations behind a good society and the welfare state?' *Prospect* (February 2004)

Horowitz, M, Kingscote, G and Nicholls, M *The Human Rights Act 1998 – A Special Bulletin for Family Lawyers* (London: Butterworths, 1999)

Karner, C *Ethnicity and Everyday Life* (London: Routledge, 2007) A Race Equality Foundation Briefing Paper

Korbin, J 'The cultural context of child abuse and neglect' (1980) 4 *Child Abuse and Neglect* 3–13

Laming, Lord 'Working with diversity' The Victoria Climbié Inquiry. Report of an Inquiry by Lord Laming. Part five: 16 Cm 5730 (London: The Stationery Office, 2003). See www.victoria-climbie-inquiry.org.uk/finreport/4working.htm (accessed 26 June 2007)

Lau, A 'Cultural and ethnic perspectives on significant harm: its assessment and treatment' in M Adcock, and R White, *Significant Harm* (Croydon: Significant Publications, 2nd edn, 1998) 101–114

Lau, A and Bond, A 'Children and families involved in Children Act Proceedings' in A Lau (ed), *South Asian Children and Adolescents in Britain* (Whurr publishers (now, West Sussex: Wiley), 2000)

Littlewood, R 'How universal is something we can call therapy?' in J Kareem and R Littlewood (eds), *Intercultural Therapy Themes Interpretation and Practices* (Oxford: Blackwell Scientific, 1992) 38–56

Lafromboise, T and Foster, S 'Cross Cultural Training: Scientist-Practitioner models and methods' (1992) 20(3) *Counselling Psychologist* 471–489

Lutz, H Vom Weltmarkt in den Privathaushalt. Die neuen Dienstmädchen im Zeitalter der Globalisierung (proposal) From the world market into the private household. The new maids in the age of globalisation (2007a) (published in German as Vom Weltmarkt in den Privathaushalt. Die neuen Dienstmädchen im Zeitalter der Globalisierung)

Lutz, H (ed) *Migration and Domestic Work: A European perspective on a global theme* (Aldershot: Ashgate, 2007)

Mac an Ghaill, M and Haywood, C *Young Bangladeshi people's experience of transition to adulthood* (York: JRF, 2005)

Maitra, B 'Giving due consideration to the family's racial and cultural background' in P Reder and C Lucey (eds), *Assessment of parenting: psychiatric and psychological contributions* (London: Routledge, 1995) 151–165

Maitra, B 'Culture and child protection' (2005) 15 *Current Paediatrics* 253–259

Mintzet, L B, Bartels, K M and Rideout, C 'Training in counselling ethnic minorities and race-based availability of graduate-school resources' (1995) 26(3) *Professional Psychology – Research and Practice* 316–321

Modood, T, Berthoud, R, Lakey, J, Nazroo, J, Smith, P, Virdee, S and Bersham, S *Ethnic minorities in Britain: diversity and disadvantage* (London: Policy Studies Institute, 1997)

Modood, T *Multiculturalism: A Civic Idea* (Oxford: Polity, 2007)

Murji, K and Solomos, J 'Introduction: Racialization in Theory and Practice' in K Murji and J Solomos (eds), *Racialization Studies in Theory and Practice* (Oxford: Oxford University Press, 2004)

NAGALRO Birmingham Area Child Protection Committee Review of the Case of Toni-Ann Byfield (2004). See www.nagalro.com/docs/SH%20Vol%2014,%20issue%202,%20NEWS.doc (accessed 31 August 2007)

Ogilvy, C M, Boath, E H, Cheyne, W M, Jahoda, G, and Schaffer, H R 'Staff attitudes and perceptions in multicultural nursery schools' (1990) 64 *Early Child Development and Care* 1–13

Ogilvy, C M, Boath, E H, Cheyne, W M, Jahoda, G and Schaffer, H R 'Staff–Child Interaction Styles in Multi-ethnic Nursery Schools' (1992) 10 *British Journal of Developmental Psychology* 85–97

ONS 'Census 2001 – Ethnicity and religion in England and Wales' (2003). See www.statistics.gov.uk/census2001/profiles/commentaries/ethnicity.asp (accessed 25 February 2007)

Phoenix, A and Pattynama, P (eds) 'Intersectionality' (2006) 13(3) *Special issue of the European Journal of Women's Studies*

Rattansi, A *Racism: A Very Short Introduction* (Oxford: Oxford University Press, 2007)

Reynolds, T *Caribbean Mothers: Identity and Experience in the UK* (London: Tufnell Press, 2005)

Sue, D 'Multicultural training' (1997) 21(2) *International Journal and Intercultural Relations* 175–193

Williams, F and Gavanas, A 'The intersection of child care regimes and migration regimes: a three-country study' in H Lutz (ed), *Migration and Domestic Work: a European Perspective on a Global Theme* (Aldershot: Ashgate, 2007)

Williams, J and Keating, F 'Social Inequalities and Mental Health' in A Bell and P Lindley (eds), *Beyond the Water Towers: The unfinished revolution in mental health services* (London: Sainsbury Centre for Metal Health, 2005)

Diversity Perspectives, the CAFCASS Journey

Sherry Malik

Corporate Director (Strategy and Performance), CAFCASS

SUMMARY OF THE PAPER

Sherry Malik introduced her paper, by using her allocated time in a slightly different way to the other speakers. She put back to the floor an issue Professor Phoenix had raised about culture. She invited members of the floor to get up and find someone they had not met before and did not know well and find out about the culture in which he or she grew up as a child. She then asked that members of the floor describe to one another, in their pairs, the culture in which they are now living and one thing they had brought with them from childhood and one thing they had left behind.

Sherry Malik asked that people call out things that they had talked about with their partner in the discussions. The answers included:

- _Roots_

- _Values_

- _Urban/rural_

- _Class_

- _Language_

- _Religion_

- _Etc._

This list, she pointed out, was dynamic: no one single thing makes up culture; it means different things to different people. Culture is changing and it is dynamic. Some things we grew up with are still important to us whereas others are not.

As adults, we mesh our culture with our partner's and form another culture that our children then grow up in. In our work with families, we need to be able to use this knowledge – being 'Asian' or 'Chinese' or 'Somali' is not something that can be learnt from books because each family's culture will be unique to them.

Sherry Malik referred to a piece of research undertaken by Beverley Prevatt Goldstein, who, sponsored by Cafcass, is looking at how well we serve black and minority ethnic families in private law and from which research she drew some preliminary recommendations.

The early recommendations included ditching the practice of 'learning about cultures', as this just strengthens stereotypes whereas culture is dynamic and does not stand still. Sherry Malik asked that we say to families 'these are the theories I am using in my work' be it attachment theory or presumption of contact with father, etc and ask 'what does this mean for you? How does it fit with your culture?' as the answers to these questions can give common ground to form an assessment. In essence, she advocates promotion of service users as the experts on their own culture.

Another finding from Beverley Prevatt Goldstein's research was that a team culture of talking honestly and openly about diversity issues and also having 'passion' in the team were key factors where the practice was found to be good. She added finally that those who receive training in anti-discrimination are doing much better in dealing with issues of diversity in practice.

THE PAPER

If I were to ask you to reflect on the culture that you grew up in and then on the culture you are living in now, you would tell me that there are many aspects of your childhood culture that you have brought with you into your life today and others that you have left behind. We grow and evolve and our culture changes over time. The way you celebrate Christmas or Eid or Diwali now may be different to how you celebrated it growing up as a child, because your partner's traditions merge with yours and these then form a new culture that you and your children live in and so it goes on.

Culture, and we all have one, is dynamic and constantly changing over time. Fans of Richard Dawkins[1] might even want to argue that culture takes on a life of its own constantly evolving as it interacts with its environment. Culture is made up of many different components: food, language, music, history, geography, clothes, values, discipline, tradition, rituals, festivals, religion, collective memory, etc.

In Cafcass, we want our staff to start from this perspective. The values and beliefs that people have are shaped by personal and unique circumstances, which cannot be stereotyped by simply being Indian or Pakistani, Iranian or Turkish, Welsh or English, Scottish or Irish. The 'Molly Misbah' case in Scotland is a prime example of how globalised and complex the issues in our work have become.

Today's Britain is a melting pot of these components, be it food, dress, values or moral dilemmas. It is the families we work with, who are the experts on their own cultures. Open questions such as 'how do you celebrate birthdays in your family?'; 'what happens at meal times?'; 'who makes what decisions in the family?' etc, can tell you so much about how things are done in different families, what traditions and values are important to them, how hierarchies may operate. In our work to safeguard children, this can be used to explore many issues in detail from the family's perspective.

For families in the UK, 'culture' has changed dramatically over the last generation – a massive decline in membership of churches, political parties and other social institutions, a massive expansion in social networking of one sort or another, the continuing marginalisation of people with disabilities of one kind or another, the continuing lack of joined-up services for children whose parents have mental health problems. The patterns of family life throughout England are

---

[1]   Richard Dawkins is the Charles Simonyi Professor of the Public Understanding of Science at Oxford University. His books about evolution and science include *The Selfish Gene, The Extended Phenotype River out of Eden* and most recently, *Unweaving the Rainbow.*

ever changing and complex, with divorce, reconstituted families, dual culture marriages and children and migration and in our work we can no longer make assumptions about culture. We just have to take the time to find out.[2]

Cafcass is on a journey, one of self-assessment, the desire for continuous improvement and becoming a learning organisation. Put simply it means that we don't want service users to complain about the same things year on year and not change, we don't want to wait for inspectors to tell us what we aren't doing well. We do, however, want to ask those whom we work with, including children, 'how was it for you?' and learn from this. We want to review how well we are doing on an ongoing basis and be more open and transparent about our work. Above all, we want to keep the unique stories of the families we work with at the very centre of our work, considering each of these within the context of their unique identities and their diverse cultural experiences.

Our self-assessments and inspection reports have been telling us that our reports do not always address diversity issues meaningfully. One judge told me about a report he had just received and how he challenged the practitioner that: 'simply acknowledging that the father was black African Caribbean does not address diversity issues: it's how everything then relates to that issue, how it impacts on the care of the children is what I want to know more about. It's the "so what?" question and the answer was missing.'

Whether someone has a disability, is gay or is an asylum seeker, what we must seek to do is to explore how that may impact on the issues before the court. Simply stating it does not mean anything. Over the years many social workers I have worked with have said, the family's race or gender or sexuality is not an issue here, why raise it? How can the essence of *who someone is* not be an issue?

UN Secretary, General Kofi Annan, said:

> 'It is one thing to bemoan the persistence of prejudice and quite another to actually do something about it. All too often when faced with bigotry, institutional prejudice and discrimination, organisations and individuals are silent and complacent. This passivity masquerades as tolerance but in reality this is complicity, since it emboldens the intolerant and leaves victims defenceless. True tolerance is more assertive, more active.'

So as an organisation and working within a larger Family Justice System what are *we* actively doing to ensure that our services are relevant and meaningful? When we are working with someone who does not speak English, when we employ someone who is gay or a lesbian, when someone with a disability visits us, are we being fair? Are we providing the same service as we do to others? What is the experience of our diverse service users when they come into contact with us? Indeed *who* are our service users?

The return of diversity monitoring forms currently stands at over 76% (as at the end of June 2007) and we are optimistic that this will continue to improve as it has year on year (from a low base of 20% in 2004) This is a statutory duty that we must comply with and which we are taking seriously. These returns tell us that around 18% of our service users are not White British, that Asian families are more likely to be represented in our private law work (around 8%) than Black families (3.1%). In public law proceedings this is reversed although the difference is less pronounced (4.3% Black Families, 3.1 % Asian families). Mixed parentage families formed nearly 5% of public law proceedings and 3% of private law proceedings. Nearly 6% of our private law service users and over 8% of our public law service users say they have a disability. We need to understand the gaps in our services and we can only do that through proper monitoring which

---

[2]   The increased number of immigration-related care cases, in teams like Leicester can take up to three times as long to resolve.

is understood and carried out by all staff as an *essential* part of the work we do. We now expect all our teams to routinely consider such information along with the management information they use to monitor their work.

When I have visited offices across the country, staff still ask questions such as: 'What is the purpose of these? What do I tell service users who want to know why I am asking questions about their ethnicity or disability?'

Here are some examples of how we are using this data to help us provide a better service.

WORKFORCE PLANNING

A significant proportion (54%) of our workforce is over 55 and may choose to retire at 60. This presents us with an opportunity to plan for the future composition of our workforce, so it is more representative of the communities we serve. If we don't understand the makeup and needs of our service users through monitoring, we are simply guessing and not making informed decisions.

Case example: workforce planning

Each local area will, as part of its annual business planning cycle, set out its workforce plans. This means understanding past demand and future projections, carrying out an analysis of need within the context of our remit, and matching this against existing skills, the profile of staff[3] and services available in the organisation.

WORKING WITH FAMILIES WHO DO NOT SPEAK ENGLISH

Many teams face issues in working with interpreters and sometimes dealing with several community languages in a single area. This is a resource planning issue and we propose to use the data to back up local business cases to recruit first language workers, be they family support workers or Foster Care Associates (FCAs), receptionists or to commission an interpreting service.

Case example: working with a diverse community in Bradford

Bradford has a very diverse population, with a large Asian Muslim community. Strong partnerships have been developed with a growing range of voluntary groups, in particular with Muslim faith advisers.

It is estimated that approximately 25% of S7 reports prepared by the office involve members of the Asian community. In recognition of this there are two posts designated as Cafcass Support Worker/Interpreter, but who are a regional source. The office has also a full-time receptionist with Asian language skills.

TRANSLATING OUR MATERIALS

We currently translate our leaflets into other languages on demand, but through accurate data gathered from diversity monitoring we can more routinely consider the translation and

---

[3] We are better at monitoring the diversity of our employed staff at 98%; 5.5% of our staff are disabled although unseen disability is higher, 9.2% of all staff and 8.3% of our FCAs are from BME communities (Cafcass Annual Report 2006/07).

interpreting needs of our materials into the principal languages among our service users. Similarly, we need to know the requirement for information presented in the form of audiotape or Braille, and accessibility issues for our website.

Case example: translation

Over the past year we've had several requested for leaflets in Kurdish and Polish, which demonstrates shifting demand and the need for ongoing monitoring of which languages our service users use.

ASYLUM AND IMMIGRATION ISSUES

We know we are dealing with increasing numbers of *asylum and immigration issues* which have added to the complexity of the work we are doing, but until recently we have been unable to pull together a coherent response at a national level because we did not know the scale of the work in this area. We need to be able to ask the right questions early on to support children through the additional issues they encounter as a result of immigration and asylum status.

Case example: BIA protocol

Cafcass and the Border Immigration Agency (BIA) are developing a protocol on how to work together effectively to ensure the welfare of children and young people involved with both agencies. The strict rules of confidentiality that govern our work result in particular steps needing to be taken to ensure we share information appropriately, without breaching this confidentiality. We are developing guidance, along with two standard letters to ensure a consistent organisational response to these queries.

RELIGIOUS BELIEFS AND CULTURE, COMMUNITY LINKS

What links should we make within our communities, with whom and for what purpose? We can only act on this with purpose when we understand more about our service user base. By knowing the communities we serve, we can ensure that partnerships and training for FCAs reflect and benefit the service users. For example, in London where 13.6% of service users are Muslim, the second largest belief after Christianity, we are acting on this information to forms links with this section of the community within London and to provide suitable training to staff.

Case example: working in partnership

The Southampton team set up a multi-disciplinary working group with statutory and voluntary organisations to improve outcomes for children from minority ethnic communities. That same team reports 100% returns on diversity monitoring and has developed effective dialogue with religious leaders and groups linked to the minority ethnic community served by Cafcass including asylum seekers.

LEARNING AND DEVELOPMENT NEEDS

These cannot be targeted if we do not know the makeup of our service users. We have built in criteria for all our course specifications to include issues of diversity as well as to be child-centred. We are also supporting training at three other levels, depending on job role and development needs:

- an online Equality and Diversity certificate which covers legislation and duties for all staff and which is offered at a very nominal fee or in some cases is free in collaboration with local colleges;

- team based diversity training, which helps each team to recognise local issues and resolve these. Several regions have rolled out a dedicated programme of team based diversity training;

- training for FCAs to support practice issues. Examples include Working with African Caribbean fathers, Working with Black Families, Parental Mental Health.

Case example: culturally competent training

Dr Begum Maitra, Consultant Child and Adolescent psychiatrist, is helping us to deliver a programme of training nationally between January and March 2008 to our FCAs to:

- *understand how larger group beliefs (cultures) influence individual parent's beliefs, parenting behaviour, and ideas about 'children's needs';*

- *develop skills at observing, interviewing and drawing influences from cross-cultural assessments;*

- *integrate a theoretical understanding of culture and culture practice with a consideration of the best interests of an individual child.*

As an organisation we have signalled our commitment to have Equality and Diversity integral to our developments by providing leadership at Board and Executive level. Harry Marsh, who is a Cafcass Board Member, and I provide this lead and ensure that all our colleagues are actively considering the impact of our policies and developments on all groups of staff and service users.

The case for why the Family Justice system and the various agencies in it need to start to work together has been established very clearly by the work carried out by Julia Brophy and her colleagues[4] who describe the experiences of Black and Minority Ethnic families in the family courts. I have recently started to attend the FJC Diversity subcommittee chaired by Khatun Sapnara and pay tribute to the commitment and expertise of its members. This is an arena to work together and I look forward to both sharing the work of Cafcass and to work on new developments with the Committee. In particular I believe the Family Justice System needs to develop a comprehensive strategy, which sets out how it will deal with Equality and Diversity issues and the National FJC can look to its Diversity Committee to lead on it.

Cafcass has made good progress in establishing frameworks: In the past 2 years we have developed a 5-year Equality and Diversity Strategy, a Service User Diversity Policy, which sets out our promise, our new Disability Equality and Gender Equality Schemes and along with our Race Equality Scheme we have put together a comprehensive work programme, which is built into every strand of our 3-year Strategic Business Plan. We are routinely carrying out impact assessments on all our new developments, have developed a practice resource guide covering themes such as working with interpreters, diversity and welfare checklist, race and child protection and gender and sexual orientation.

I started by stating our intention to provide every service user, including children, an opportunity to give us some feedback about their experience of our work with them. Currently we have a Quality Assurance system, which has a feedback form for adults, and children and we

---

4   Brophy, J, Jhutti-Johal, J and McDonald, E *Minority ethnic parents, their solicitors and child protection litigation* (2005); Brophy, J, Jhutti-Johal, J and Owen, C *Significant Harm: Child Protection Litigation in a Multi-Cultural Setting* (2003).

also use Viewpoint. However, we are developing an online feedback system which will allow individual password protected feedback, linked to our Case Management System (CMS). This will in time allow us to analyse the outcomes for service users and their experiences in a much more robust way. Our needs, wishes and feelings packs is another example of how we seek to ensure individual needs are identified and presented to the court.

But we don't want to stop there. We want to move from consultation to participation.[5] Focus groups, participation boards, sharing of reports before filing them, engaging with those who are complaining: it takes courage to open ourselves up and to work in a more open and transparent way. Our Young People's Board, a very energetic and diverse group of young people, have helped us on this journey enormously, for example being part of recruitment panels, developing policies, informing consultations such as the one on transparency in the family courts. It is only by walking this road that we will begin to provide a meaningful and relevant service which is based on a better understanding of the context of our service users' lives.

As an organisation we are beginning to talk and raise issues of diversity in our practice. For me this is the most positive sign, for none of us know all the answers. By asking, talking, discussing and sharing we will gain the knowledge and confidence to develop our practice models in working with some very complex issues. Around the country there are some fantastic examples of how individuals and teams within Cafcass are working with complex issues of diversity and we need to more routinely learn from these.

We have made good progress, but much more needs to be done. We need to develop better partnerships, both internal and external. All complex legislation, like specific equalities legislation, requires partnership working for it to be successful. The key to this will be for Cafcass to be less structurally isolated and to face outwards more, and to learn from other organisations just as they can learn from us. Diversity is a corporate responsibility for all of us in the Family Justice System.

QUESTIONS FOR CONSIDERATION

1   The local authorities monitor their service users diversity, as does Cafcass. Currently the family justice system does not collect diversity statistics. The service user therefore has to give information at various points, which from their perspective, is tiresome. Should we not think this through collectively as a system, understand the value of the information we may gather and then collect diversity monitoring information at the point of application? We can then more usefully share this information across the system to help with planning services.

2   What two things could you do at a local level, which would improve the experience of BME service users?

---

5   Cafcass Service User Engagement and Participation strategy 2006.

PLENARY 2

HUMAN TRAFFICKING AND ASYLUM SEEKERS

Human Trafficking as Modern Day Slavery and the UK Government's Response

Nadine Finch

Barrister, Garden Court Chambers

SUMMARY OF THE PAPER

Nadine Finch mainly considered children who have been trafficked when presenting her paper. She explained that trafficking in human beings means bringing someone across an international border to use him/her as a commodity; something which is now more profitable than drugs trafficking and more widespread.

She noted that although this year we have been commemorating the 200th anniversary of the abolition of slavery, in reality slavery has never gone away. Slavery takes place on a significant local level in certain parts of the world; children are trafficked across Saudi Arabia and parts of Africa in order to compete in camel racing. Many of these children die.

Nadine Finch explained that there is frequent movement of children across internal borders in Africa, especially from the Democratic Republic of Congo. Children in these situations are mainly picked up on the street and put to work in plantations. In parts of Asia children are sent to work in sweat shops.

Nadine Finch noted that globalisation has led to the export of the trade of human trafficking. Gangmasters will be involved in bringing people into countries in the way that we know to have happened with the Morecombe Bay cockle pickers. Sometimes in these situations the traffickers are part of the same community as those they traffic.

In the case of the children that went missing from the care of West Sussex social services, referred to in the paper, it is thought that the children were removed by very sophisticated Nigerian trafficking rings. The children are often initiated by animistic ceremonies, for example, where chickens are killed, and are then too terrified to alert others to what has happened to them.

Few of the children who are freed from the influence of the traffickers feel able to 'go public' with their experiences. Nadine Finch recalled one girl, who was around 15 years of age and who had initially felt secure in a good children's home, who fell down the stairs and believed this to be a sign that the traffickers would get to her and that she was no longer safe.

Nadine Finch raised the particular problem of cannabis houses. Vietnamese gangs are known to bring children to work in such houses to grow the cannabis plants. The working conditions in the cannabis houses are extremely unhealthy for the children. An additional problem is that, when discovered by the authorities, some children are charged as accessories to drugs offences and can end up in Young Offender Institutions.

Many child prostitutes are trafficked by Albanians from all over the Balkan states. Globalisation has meant that not only do the traffickers know that there is profit to be made in this trade but also where there is demand; in which areas to operate and how to go about it. In other words, there is not just a 'pull' factor.

To suggest that gangs are behind trafficking operations can be an exaggeration. Nadine Finch noted that there are a lot of one-woman trafficking operations, by women who themselves may have been trafficked. A favoured route is known to be Nigeria to Italy. However, the previously trafficked individual may initiate her own route.

Families are often implicated in trafficking, for example by selling a child at the start of the process. It can be considered better to use one child to raise cash so that other children can be sent to school. This can be very difficult for trafficked children to face up to.

Nadine Finch posed the rhetorical question why this issue is important. The reason, she suggests, is because the existence of trafficking is often not picked up on when cases come to court. Many children are bought for domestic slavery as servants though they are here ostensibly under private fostering arrangements and may even be registered in school. It can often be quite difficult to find out where the child has come from. A complicating factor is that families, particularly in West Africa, send children to the UK to gain social or economic advantages. There can be major differences, however, between children who have to do some housework during their stay and those who are exploited.

In one case involving a Vietnamese family, a child aged 10 was required to sleep on the floor, unlike the other children. The reality of the situation was uncovered when the child mentioned to other adults that he was not allowed to play with the other children.

Nadine Finch stressed that nobody really knows how many children may be involved in trafficking. Although some of the general characteristics are recognisable, there is often huge confusion about the variety of relationships when families of asylum seekers come before the family courts and complicated versions of how children came to be with them are given. Sometimes the children are not children of the particular family and will say that they came here as the adults needed children in their household to access public housing and local authority support in this country. There is a minority of children who are not getting protection as the authorities do not recognise what is happening to them.

Nadine Finch noted that these children cannot be protected until they are identified. In her view, more training is needed for immigration officers, social workers, teachers and others.

It is very difficult for unaccompanied children to get to the UK. Children cannot be sent to school here without being accompanied unless they attend a private school and have the appropriate visa. While other children may be sent here for benign reasons, such as to get better education or employment, we must question whether this is what is actually going on or whether the children are being brought here to be exploited.

Nadine Finch informed the Conference that next month, October 2007, a child trafficking advice and information telephone line is to start. This has been set up so that professionals can receive advice. It is run by the NSPCC and is partially funded by the Home Office and by Comic Relief.

She referred the Conference to the various other resources and organisations which have been developed to deal with human trafficking which are summarised in the paper.

Nadine Finch concluded by summing up the message of her paper: we must recognise that trafficked children are the victims of some of the worst child abuse and give them permanency and stability so that they can recover from the abuse they have suffered.

THE PAPER

Human trafficking is one of the gravest violations of fundamental human rights involving the loss of liberty, the control of one's own dignity and bodily integrity and the imposition of physical, sexual, emotional and mental abuse. Many of those trafficked never regain the physical and mental health they previously enjoyed and may contract serious and life-threatening illnesses and infections.[1]

It is the view of the Joint Committee on Human Rights[2] that human trafficking is first and foremost a criminal activity perpetrated against its victims.[3] A wide range of non-governmental organisations[4] are working to alert people to the issue and provide support to those who have been trafficked. There are also a growing number of governmental initiatives in the area.[5]

However, professionals coming into contact with children who have been trafficked often fail to recognise the experiences they have been exposed to. There is still a common misconception that trafficking is something that happens abroad, not here, and is exclusively connected with prostitution and sexual exploitation. Unfortunately, there is a growing body of evidence, as yet most of it qualitative, that this is not the case. For example, a significant number of children have gone missing from the care of West Sussex social services.[6] The vast majority were Nigerian girls, now believed to have been trafficked through Gatwick Airport, in transit to being exploited as prostitutes in Italy and elsewhere. More recently it was reported that 150 children from abroad had disappeared from care in Sussex and Kent since 2004.[7]

Other local authorities have discovered young children being kept as domestic slaves in households in London, Glasgow and elsewhere.[8] Sometimes the adults concerned attempt to assert that they have entered into a private fostering arrangement with the children's parents. This is often far from the truth: children have either been abducted as they no longer had an adult protector in their country of origin, or their parents had been led to believe that their children would be educated and given opportunities here. In some cases they had been sold into slavery by their own families.

In other cases, the children had been trafficked here to work in cannabis houses[9] or as beggars.[10] Many have also been brought here for the purposes of benefit fraud, forced marriage or unlawful adoption. When these children are discovered in abusive situations the response from those in authority is often to give undue weight to the fact that they have usually entered the UK illegally or at best overstayed any leave they were initially granted. The issue then becomes one of immigration control and not one of tackling a serious human rights abuse.

Their position is further complicated by the fact that trafficking itself is seen as organised international crime which involves the breaching of immigration controls. There is also a

---

[1] See *Stolen smiles : a summary report on the physical and psychological health consequences of women and adolescents trafficked in Europe* (The London School of Hygiene and Tropical Medicine, 2006).

[2] A joint committee of the Houses of Commons and Lords which scrutinises the human rights implications of a wide range of current issues.

[3] Human Trafficking Twenty-Sixth report of Session, 2005–2006.

[4] These include Anti-Slavery International, ECPAT (UK), UNICEF, Save the Children, BAAF, Amnesty International and the Refugee Council.

[5] Some of these are dealt with below.

[6] Somerset, C *What Professionals Know: the trafficking of children into, and through, the UK for sexual purposes* (ECPAT UK, 2001).

[7] Youngsters 'vanishing' from care, BBC News report, 12 June 2007.

[8] Bhabha, J and Finch, N *Seeking Asylum Alone: Unaccompanied and Separated Children and Refugee Protection in the UK* (November 2006).

[9] Beddoe, C *Missing Out A Study of Child Trafficking in the North-West, North-East and West Midlands* (2007).

[10] These are often Roma children.

tendency to conflate the position of those who are smuggled into the UK and those who are trafficked here. They are in fact very different phenomena.

When a person is smuggled, an agent is paid or undertakes to bring them across an international border but once the border is crossed any relationship with, or obligation to, the agent comes to an end. Where a person is trafficked, the agent brings the person across an international border with the express purpose of exploiting them for gain. The trafficked person is viewed as a commodity and will be exploited until the trafficker can no longer obtain any further profit from their 'investment'. A number of initiatives have been designed to ensure that both central and local government responds more appropriately to the needs of this particular group of exploited and abused children.

LEGISLATIVE REFORM

To date the legislation[11] which has been passed by the UK Parliament has concentrated on creating the necessary offences to ensure that human traffickers can be successfully prosecuted. The UK was also bound by the EU Framework Decision on combating trafficking in human beings; as this decision related to criminal law provisions across the EU the UK had no capacity to opt out of such provisions under the Consolidated Version of the Treaty Establishing the European Community.[12] However, the government exercised its powers to opt out of measures relating to immigration matters and decided not to implement the EU Directive to introduce short-term residence permits to victims of illegal immigration and human trafficking with a view to enhancing measures to combat illegal immigration.

The only purely immigration related measure which has been introduced to date to combat child trafficking has been the introduction of para 46A of the Immigration Rules HC395 which imposes additional requirements on unaccompanied children wishing to visit the UK. It is unclear how effective it will be as it appears that the vast majority of trafficked children are brought into the country by adults, pretending to be a parent, who have added them to their own passports.

COMPLIANCE WITH COUNCIL OF EUROPE[13] MEASURES

The UK Parliament incorporated the European Convention on Human Rights (ECHR) into domestic law when it passed the Human Rights Act 1998, which came into force on 2 October 2000. Article 4 of the ECHR is particularly relevant as it prohibits slavery and forced labour. In the recent case of *Siliadin v France*[14] a minor had been trafficked to France and kept as a domestic slave. The European Court of Justice held that France had breached Article 4 of the ECHR by not putting in place measures to protect people in her position. This was a notable breakthrough on two bases: first, it confirmed that domestic servitude[15] was prohibited by Article 4; secondly, it established that even though France had not been directly responsible for her being kept in domestic servitude it was, as a Member State to the ECHR, vicariously liable on account of not introducing measures to combat this form of modern day slavery.

---

11   Sexual Offences Act 2003, ss 57–59; Criminal Justice (Scotland) Act 2003, s 22; Asylum and Immigration (Treatment of Claimant's etc.) Act 2004, s 4.
12   [2002] OJ C325/33, 24 December 2002.
13   The Council of Europe is not an EU institution but an intergovernmental organisation with 46 members (including members of the EU). Conventions are negotiated between Member States and there is independent monitoring of Member States' compliance.
14   Application No 73316/01.
15   The court did not find that she had been subjected to slavery as she was not deprived of all of her free will.

The UK Government has also signed the Council of Europe Convention on action against Trafficking in Human Beings. It aims to ratify the Convention in 2009 when it has the measures in place to ensure that it can comply with the Convention in its entirety.

COMPLIANCE WITH INTERNATIONAL TREATIES

The UK Government has ratified the United Nations Transnational Organised Crime Convention and its Protocol to Prevent, Suppress and Punish Trafficking in Persons, Especially Women and Children (commonly known as the Palermo Protocol).[16] However, the mandatory obligations of this Protocol are restricted to measures to combat, investigate and prosecute human traffickers. Measures to protect and assist the trafficked persons are discretionary and as yet the UK has not introduced any measures which comply with these provisions in particular.

The UK also entered a reservation to the United Nations Convention on the Rights of the Child which restricts the application of this Convention to children who are subject to immigration control. The Joint Committee on Human Rights has stated that the removal of this reservation is increasingly urgent in response to the growth in child trafficking.[17]

The UK is also bound by a number of International Labour Organisation (ILO) conventions. The most recent one is the ILO Convention 182 concerning the Prohibition and Immediate Action for the Elimination of the Worst Forms of Child Labour.[18]

MODERN DAY SLAVERY

The recognition of human trafficking as a modern day version of human slavery is very recent. In the UK it was in the mid 1990s that social services departments and lawyers first realised that children were being trafficked into the UK from abroad. At first it was thought that most of these children were destined for sexual exploitation. It was only later that it emerged many were also being trafficked for domestic servitude or slavery, benefit fraud and to be used in cannabis factories or as pickpockets.

However, there is still a dearth of comprehensive and quantitative data on these phenomena. One recent piece of research was undertaken by the Child Exploitation and Online Protection Centre (CEOP). Data was collected between September 2006 and 1 March 2007; 330 cases of possible child trafficking were identified from 44 source countries. The largest number of children came from China (70), Nigeria (38), Vietnam (22), Afghanistan (19), Eritrea (14), Romania (14) and Albania (10).

Other very useful research has been undertaken by ECPAT(UK). Its first piece of research reviewed the state of knowledge about child trafficking in 2001.[19] Later research looked at the understanding of child trafficking in London boroughs in 2004[20] and in Manchester, Newcastle-upon-Tyne, Birmingham, Solihull and Coventry in 2007.[21] A wider study undertaken in 2004–2005 into asylum-seeking children also identified the prevalence of child trafficking in a number of different areas in the UK including the ones mentioned above and Glasgow, Sheffield,

---

[16] Adopted by resolution A/RES/55/25 of 15 November 2000, which entered into force in December 2003.

[17] Twenty Sixth Report: Human Trafficking Sessions 2005–2006 Vol 1 Rec 35.

[18] C182 which came into force in November 2000.

[19] Somerset, C *What Professionals Know: The trafficking of children into, and through, the UK for sexual purposes* (ECPAT UK, 2001).

[20] *Cause for Concern*, Somerset C.

[21] Beddoe, C *Missing Out: A study of child trafficking in the North-West, North-East and West Midlands.*

Norfolk and Nottingham.[22] The latter two studies also highlighted a need for the appointment of a legal guardian for every unaccompanied or separated child to ensure that they were offered the domestic and international protection to which they were entitled. This is supported by the Children's Commissioner for England, Professor Sir Albert Aynsley-Green.[23]

THE UK GOVERNMENT'S RESPONSE

The Association of Chief Police Officers persuaded the government to establish a UK Human Trafficking Centre (UKHTC) in Sheffield. It is primarily dedicated to the prevention of human trafficking and the prosecution of the traffickers. However, senior staff are well aware that it is very difficult to mount successful prosecutions if witnesses are not prepared to cooperate and have been advocating for further protection, both domestic and international, for trafficked persons.

There has been considerable concern about children being trafficked to work in cannabis houses then being arrested and prosecuted for drug-related offences. The Crown Prosecution Service has now drawn up a Code of Guidance for its prosecutors advising them to give serious consideration as to whether the coercion connected with trafficking amounts to a defence of duress and whether it is right to be prosecuting these children.

The Centre works closely with the CEOP and a Child Trafficking Desk is planned within the UKHTC which would complement the Child Trafficking Unit within CEOP. CEOP will also publish annual risk assessments in relation to child trafficking.

Of particular interest to childcare practitioners is the fact that CEOP, the NSPCC and ECPAT(UK) in coordination with Comic Relief are setting up a Child Trafficking and Advice Line which will be operational this autumn. It will offer telephone advice to professionals on identifying and safeguarding children who have been trafficked.

The Department for Children, Schools and Families has also drafted a document entitled *Safeguarding Children who may have been trafficked,* which went out for consultation in July 2007. It provides a great deal of very useful information about identifying and safeguarding trafficked children. It is designed to provide supplementary guidance to the April 2006 publication *Working Together to Safeguard Children* which is also being revised. At the same time Local Safeguarding Children Boards are being encouraged to give serious consideration to child trafficking issues and a number of them, including what was previously the London Child Protection Committee, have produced guidance for local authorities in their area in relation to identifying children who have been trafficked.[24]

The Border and Immigration Agency has historically lagged behind other parts of government in relation to the measures it has adopted to protect those who have been trafficked. However, it undertook useful research at Heathrow Airport in 2003[25] in relation to children arriving alone who may have been trafficked. Teams to combat child trafficking have now been established at five major ports of entry. Immigration and police officers have received training on identifying children who may have been trafficked and there are plans to train airline cabin staff and develop a carrier's code of practice. The Agency has historically been reluctant to agree to a new form of leave for those who have been trafficked as it believes that this would act as a pull factor

---

[22] Bhabha, J and Finch, N *Seeking Asylum Alone: Unaccompanied and Separated Children and Refugee Protection in the UK* (November 2006).

[23] Memorandum from the Office to the Children's Commissioner to the Joint Committee on Human Rights on the Treatment of Asylum Seekers, 29 September 2006.

[24] London Procedure for Safeguarding Trafficked and Exploited Children (2006).

[25] Operation Paladin Child.

and encourage 'bogus' applications. There have, as yet, been no concrete proposals to create an immigration status to meet the needs of trafficked children or adults, as is required by the Council of Europe Convention on action against Trafficking in Human Beings.[26] At present if a child has been trafficked it can only obtain sustainable protection by being granted leave to remain here on a permanent basis if it falls within the protection of the United Nations Convention on the Status of Refugees or, that it is entitled to Humanitarian Protection under the Immigration Rules HC395.

However, on a day-to-day basis immigration officers are being encouraged to cooperate more consistently with other agencies. For example, they are being instructed to attend Local Safeguarding Children Boards, where this is appropriate, despite the fact that the Immigration Service is not one of the agencies named in s 13 of the Children Act 2004.

The Agency has also developed guidance on how to identify children in need and instructions and advice on what actions to take. It also plans to extend the present National Register of Unaccompanied Children to all separated children not just asylum-seeking children.

There has been much criticism of the fact that the Border and Immigration Agency was exempted from the duty to have regard to the need to safeguard and promote the welfare of children contained in s 11 of the Children Act 2004. The government is still resisting their inclusion in this statutory duty but it has introduced an amendment to the current UK Borders Bill which would require the Border and Immigration Agency to develop a Code of Practice on how the Agency will help to keep children safe from harm.[27]

UK ACTION PLAN

The government launched a national consultation exercise on its proposed UK Action Plan on 5 August 2006.[28] Following the results of this consultation the government is now developing its Action Plan. To assist it the government has established an NGO Stakeholders Consultative Group on Human Trafficking, which is chaired by Vernon Coaker, the Parliamentary Under-Secretary of State for Policing, Security and Community Safety and Vera Baird, the Solicitor General. It considers current responses to human trafficking in relation to prevention, law enforcement, protection and assistance to victims and international cooperation. It also puts forward potential solutions for consideration by the Inter-Departmental Ministerial Group on Human Trafficking.

There are also other measures being put in place currently which may well be counter-productive in terms of efforts to combat and eradicate child trafficking. One of these is the proposal to disperse child asylum seekers to areas outside London and the South East to certain designated local authorities, as outlined in the recent Home Office Consultation Paper, *Planning Better Outcomes and Support for Unaccompanied Asylum-Seeking Children*. Many non-governmental organisations and lawyers fear that this will make these children more vulnerable as they will be sent to areas with little experience of providing trafficked children with support and will lack the necessary infrastructures to protect them.

There have also been an increasing number of unaccompanied children being age-disputed within the asylum determination process.[29] This mean that professionals do not enquire into whether they are trafficked children and they are liable to be detained in immigration removal

---

26   The Convention requires the provision of reflection periods and also renewable residence permits in some situations.
27   See announcement by Liam Byrne, Minister of State for Nationality, Citizenship and Immigration on the Safety of Children in the Immigration System, 25 June 2007.
28   Tackling Human Trafficking – Consultation on Proposals for a UK Action Plan.
29   Crawley, H *When is a child not a child? Asylum, age disputes and the process of age assessment* (ILPA, May 2007).

centres and placed in fast-track determination procedures. As a result they may well be sent back to the country from which they have been trafficked only to be re-trafficked or be subjected to punishment or retribution.

These are issues which are currently under discussion and it is hoped that a final Action Plan will be published shortly.

The Health and Health Care of Children in the Asylum System

Dr Elspeth Webb

Senior Lecturer, Department of Child Health, Cardiff University

SUMMARY OF PAPER

Dr Webb stated, in her introduction to her paper, that refugees in this country face not only racism in seeking health care but also 'refugeeism'. She also asked that the Conference consider 'childism'. Children are often a marginalised group to whom models of discrimination in respect of race could apply. In this way, refugee children face the multiple jeopardy of discrimination on a number of levels.

Dr Webb asked that we see children not as burdens or nuisances. In particular, she referred to a young person whom she had treated and who had arrived in the UK as an unaccompanied minor. Despite the traumas of his journey to this country and the health difficulties he faced, he is now studying medicine. Dr Webb used this example to stress that many refugee children who arrive in the UK will go on to make very positive contributions to society.

THE PAPER

Introduction

It is estimated that there are about 25 million refugees in the world. Between 2000 and 2003 around 285,000 people applied for asylum in the UK; around one-third were under 18 years of age, including 12,500 unaccompanied or separated children.[1]

Refugee children have unique and broad health needs arising out of their experiences, ranging from the need for treatment as victims and witnesses of human rights abuses to treatment for the prevention of tuberculosis.[2] Their experiences make them extremely vulnerable to poor health. Disadvantageous factors following their arrival include racial violence, homelessness, de-skilling, language difficulties, uncertain residency status, difficulties in adapting to peace, and detention. These are over and above the catastrophic trauma experienced by many refugees, and the loss – of home, family, culture, work, parents, siblings and health – that pervades their lives.

For the purposes of this paper I will use the term refugee as a blanket term to cover both refugees and asylum seekers unless otherwise stated. As trafficking is dealt with in some detail

---

1   UNCRC at www.unhcr.org/statistics/STATISTICS/40f646444.pdf (accessed June 2007).
2   Lynch, M A and Cunninghame, C 'Understanding the needs of young asylum seekers' (2000) 83 *Archives Disease in Childhood* 384–387.

by other contributors to this conference this paper is mainly focused on those children who have arrived here through the asylum process; there is, of course, some overlap between these populations.

RIGHT TO CARE AND SERVICES

Health services: Asylum seekers, during their period of claiming asylum, are entitled to free NHS primary and secondary health care. An HC2 certificate allows for free prescriptions, dental treatment, sight tests and the value of an optical voucher. The situation for unsuccessful asylum seekers, including those on appeal, is unclear, and many NHS Trusts' interpretation of Department of Health (DoH) guidance as a statutory obligation, and the application of guidance intended for adults to child populations may result in children not receiving routine medical care. These children come under the Children Act 1989 as children in need and thus have rights to care. They also have rights under human rights legislation and the United Nations Convention on the Rights of the Child (UNCRC), although the UK persists with its reservation with regard to asylum. Clarification of the law is necessary.

Other services: Dependent children are entitled to schooling. Unaccompanied Minors are supported by the local authority through the looked-after system; if their asylum claim is refused discretionary leave may be granted until their 18th birthday. Children with disabilities are entitled to access services from the local authority as 'children in need' under the 1989 Children Act.

ACCESS TO HEALTH SERVICES

Children in the asylum system are members of minority ethnic communities. These communities, even when well established, do not have equality of access to health services in this country for a variety of reasons, including communication difficulties, discrimination including institutional discrimination, and services that are inaccessible or inappropriate for reasons related to cultural practices and lifestyle patterns.[3] These access difficulties are compounded when families have no knowledge or understanding of how health and welfare systems operate or of their entitlements. They are further compounded by the National Asylum Support Service (NASS) dispersal system; children can be referred to services in one area, have reached the top of a 6-month waiting list, only to be sent to another part of the country and have to start the whole process again.

HEALTH CARE NEEDS

Specific issues need to be considered by those planning or delivering care to these children. These are:

Immunisation: programmes vary from country to country. Children may arrive unvaccinated or with an incomplete or unknown immunisation history. Catch-up immunisation is recommended and advice on how to do this is provided by the Health Protection Agency.[4]

Screening: Health for All[5] provides evidence-based recommendations on child health surveillance. It would seem reasonable to ensure that children arriving from countries without a

---

3   Webb, E 'Health care for ethnic minorities' (2000) 10 *Current Pediatrics* 184–190.

4   See www.hpa.org.uk/infections/topics_az/vaccination/vac_guidelines.htm (accessed June 2007).

5   Hall, D and Elliman, D *Health for All Children: 4th Report* (Oxford University Press, 2003).

comprehensive surveillance programme should have access to a catch-up health review which at least allows screening for common developmental problems and congenital abnormalities and genetic disorders as advised by the Royal College of Paediatrics and Child Health (RCPCH).[6] The inadequate resources put into refugee health services by the Home Office makes it unlikely that this is achieved.

Rarely, children may have been exposed to environmental toxins in their country of origin, or to cultural practices that inadvertently cause harm to children, eg the application of lead-containing kohl.

Refugee children may, depending on their country of origin and their route of travel to the UK, be at risk of specific infections, some of which may also be infectious and thus have wider public health implications. The Department of Health 'Yellow Book' is an invaluable resource with information on disease risks by continent and country.[7] If clinicians have any doubts or queries they should consult the Communicable Disease Surveillance Centre (CDSC) at Colindale. Do not over screen – this is a waste of money.

Dental health: Many asylum seekers arrive with poor dental health, and may need urgent dental treatment. DoH guidance is interpreted in some quarters to mean that these children can only access emergency treatment, with the result that children's dental health problems cannot be addressed until they are in acute pain, an interpretation that should be challenged.

Mental health: It is important to remember that for many children the context of their development has been dominated and influenced by their experience of conflict and/or displacement. Macksoud[8] noted that there were a range of war experiences likely to have a negative effect on children including:

- witnessing parents' fear and panic;

- violent death of a parent;

- witnessing murders, torture or injury of family members;

- separation and forced migration;

- terrorist attacks, bombardments and shelling;

- child-soldier activity, including carrying weapons, taking part in atrocities, and killing;

- war-connected physical injuries and disability; and

- extreme scarcity and famine.

There are many challenges in providing culturally appropriate interventions to migrant children not least the validity in this context of Western medicalised models of psychosocial pathology, focusing predominantly on symptomatology, and Western therapeutic strategies. This is complicated further by the existence of two opposing approaches towards providing

---

6   Levenson, R and Sharma, A *Health of Refugee Children – Guidelines for Paediatricians* (London: RCPCH, 1999).

7   Department of Health *Health information for overseas travel* (The Stationery Office, 2001).

8   Macksoud, M, Dyregrove, A and Raundalen, M 'Traumatic War Experiences and Their Effects on Children' in J P Wilson and B Raphael (eds), *International Handbook of Traumatic Stress Syndromes* (Plenum Press, New York, 1993) 625–633.

appropriate care for refugees: one medically modelled and focused on individual therapy;[9] the other concentrating on community reconstruction, thereby providing a structured, caring and safe environment in which children thrive.[10,11]

A service which responds to the mental health needs of refugee children should include supporting schools to provide a safe environment for refugee children – in effect to become Tier 1 providers, as per the model of Child and Adolescent Mental Health Services (CAMHS) described in 'Together we stand'[12] – and the provision of Tier 3 specialist CAMHS services to intervene with those children who have serious mental health problems.

SAFEGUARDING AND CHILD PROTECTION

The 1989 Children Act introduced the concept of 'significant harm' as the threshold that justifies compulsory intervention. The Act states that harm can be caused by one traumatic event or a compilation of events that interrupt, change, or damage the child's development: for asylum seekers; unplanned and enforced moves after arrival, family separation, and internment will amount to a risk of significant harm. Neglect is defined as 'the persistent failure to meet a child's basic needs, likely to result in the serious impairment of the child's health or development … which may involve … *failing to provide adequate food shelter and clothing, failing to protect a child from physical harm or danger, or the failure to ensure access to appropriate medical care or treatment'* (my italics): the current system, which can result in families with children experiencing serious poverty, living in accommodation unsuitable and unsafe for children, and with great difficulties accessing health services, is ensuring that many asylum children are in effect neglected because they are in situations in which no parent could care for them adequately.

Children may face an increased risk of harm for a number of reasons: poverty and social disintegration; cultural practices that are within their own norms but harmful to children, e g female genital mutilation[13] (FGM); children arriving as unaccompanied minors; children who are trafficked.

There are barriers to the effective protection of children from minority ethnic communities who are at risk of harm.[14] There may be less likelihood that abuse is recognised, acknowledged, or dealt with appropriately, or that effective partnerships with families are established, both to prevent abuse and in rehabilitation. Factors contributing to this include poor practice by professionals compounded by wider societal factors for example: denial of the existence of abuse by some groups; cultural differences in attitudes to childcare; the vulnerability of women in highly patriarchal communities; and a lack of settings in which to provide appropriate alternative care. Some children may not attend school at all, an important safety net for children in danger; this was identified as important in the death of Victoria Climbié. In addition refugees may reject the validity of the statutory child protection process.

9 Hodes, M 'Refugee Children' (1998) 316 *British Medical Journal* 793–794.
10 Timini, S 'Refugee families have many strengths (Letter)' (1998) 317 BMJ 475.
11 Davies, M & Webb, E 'Promoting the psychological well being of refugee children' (2000) 5 (4) *Clinical Child Psychology and Psychiatry* 541–554.
12 Williams, R and Richardson, G *Together we stand: the commissioning, role and management of child and adolescent mental health services* (London: HMSO, 1995).
13 All Wales ACPC Female Genital Mutilation protocol 2006. Available at www.childreninwales.org.uk/5529.file.dld (accessed June 2007).
14 Webb, E, Maddocks, A, Bongilli, J 'Effectively protecting Black and minority ethnic children from harm: overcoming barriers to the child protection process' (2002) 11 (6) *Child Abuse Review* 394–410.

ACCIDENT PREVENTION

The risk from accidents are likely to be related to an interplay of factors that include living in poverty, homelessness, and unfamiliar surroundings.[15] For some adult carers, the mental or emotional trauma through displacement affects their concentration and emotional availability. A child used to low level road traffic faces difficulties trying to negotiate heavy urban UK traffic. This is compounded by a parent's lack of knowledge of safe crossing procedures and inability to read road signs.

Families seeking refuge, especially large families, placed in temporary accommodation are at an increased risk of accidents with over-crowding and lack of space being a particular feature.[16] There is a real possibility of accident to infants who cannot be placed on a floor because of lack of space.[17] Some cultural practices may increase likelihood of accidents, eg a potential cause of serious scalding is very hot black tea.

VULNERABLE GROUPS

Within the asylum seeking population are groups of children who are at even greater risk of poor outcomes unless services take particular care to meet their needs and protect them from harm. These include:

Unaccompanied minors: These are young people under the age of 18 arriving without adult carers. They may have crossed continents alone in difficult physical conditions; they have experienced abuse and exploitation during that period, including from the adults paid to transport them; they may have themselves become involved in the exploitation of others. Once identified these young people become the responsibility of social services, with their health needs met through the looked-after medical service.

Ayotte and Williamson[18] described the difficulties which separated children coming to the UK encounter. These are:

- high levels of racism in the UK;

- detention of young people under the age of 18 when their ages are disputed by the authorities;

- uncertainties associated with the limited form of immigration status which most are awarded ('exceptional leave to remain');

- inadequate care provided by many social services departments to those aged around 15 and above, and the anomalies in government funding for separated children;

- severe dangers experienced by separated children trying to reach the UK who end up in the hands of smugglers and traffickers.

Unborn children: Women asylum seekers, who are often extremely vulnerable to sexual abuse, sexual coercion and sexual exploitation, may become pregnant while seeking asylum; they may

---

[15] Department for Transport *Road accident involvement of children from ethnic minorities (review No.19)* (Dft, London, 2002); also available at www.dft.gov.uk/pgr/roadsafety/research/rsrr/theme1/roadaccidentinvolvementofchi4740 (accessed June 2007).

[16] Levenson, R and Sharma, *A Health of Refugee Children – Guidelines for Paediatricians* (London: RCPCH, 1999).

[17] McLeish, J *Mothers in exile: Maternity experiences of asylum seekers in England* (Maternity Alliance, 2002).

[18] Ayotte, W, Williamson, L *Separated children in the UK: an overview* (Save the Children, London, 2001).

then lose rights to benefits if their application is turned down. Failure of the appeal may mean they are denied antenatal care. All these factors can put the unborn foetus at risk, as a result of poor nutrition, inadequate housing, and the failure of the detection and treatment of inter-current illness and the complications of pregnancy.

Adolescent girls: Girls and women are often victims of sexual exploitation, sexual coercion and rape in conflict zones and refugee camps. Services need to be in place to address the needs of adolescents who may arrive needing antenatal care, termination of pregnancy, access to the genitourinary medicine clinic, contraceptive advice and support, and counselling services to help them come to terms with what has happened to them.

People may not always be who they purport to be, with girls under 16 finding themselves in the care of adults who are not their relatives, with resulting sexual abuse following arrival.

Trafficked and smuggled children: Trafficking is defined within the Palermo Protocol as a means of exploiting vulnerable adults or children through sexual abuse, prostitution or through forced labour, for example as domestic servants.[19] Robust protocols to protect children at risk of trafficking are recommended. Although the terms trafficking and smuggling are distinct, when faced with the child's sudden arrival within a family, the situation is often unclear. Children may have been smuggled for the purposes of, for example:

- reuniting a family fractured by war or political persecution;

- gaining access to health services for a child;

- giving a childless adult parental status within the immigration or asylum systems.

Professionals must make crucial decisions as to whether a child has been trafficked or smuggled and the relative risk to that child remaining with the adult. There may be limited information available and a complex and confusing scenario presented that requires unravelling. A smuggled child may end up living within the extended family, with family acquaintances, or with individuals who have been paid to care for them. However, that same child may be abused – terminology is inconsequential to a child at risk.

The terrible and preventable death of Victoria Climbié highlighted the importance of recognising the true relationships between children and carers. Professionals must be vigilant to the possibility that a child is not part of the family with which they are living. Factors that should raise the suspicion of professionals to this possibility are listed below:

- child appears suddenly within an established family group;

- primary carer unable to answer questions about child's past history;

- history about the child's arrival may change, or be vague and unconvincing;

- child is quiet and subdued;

- child does not play with, or relate to, other children in the family;

- child does not resemble other family members;

---

[19]   United Nations The Palermo Protocol to Prevent, Suppress and Punish trafficking in Persons, especially women and children (UN, Geneva, 2000).

- child appears to belong to a different ethnic group (looks different; speaks a different language);

- neglectful treatment of illness in the child; not visited when in hospital;

- adult appears uncaring, cold or hostile to the child;

- child treated differently to other children or scape-goated within the family, eg used as a household drudge;

- child not attending school on a regular basis.

CHILDREN WITH DISABILITIES OR CHRONIC ILLNESS

Parents may seek to migrate to a country with a developed health service because they have a child whose survival is unlikely without medical support, and some of these will be within the asylum community; rarely, the child's disabled status may have contributed to their predicament in their home country. Families seeking asylum may coincidentally have a dependent child with special needs accompanying them. Occasionally children with disabilities or chronic illness are born in the UK to asylum seekers.

For newly arrived families clinicians must be aware that:

(1) Children may not have had access to therapeutic and rehabilitation services and so have an urgent need for intervention, eg:
  (a) a child with Down's syndrome with untreated congenital heart disease or hypothyroidism;
  (b) a child with epilepsy who requires immediate access to diagnostic and therapeutic services;
  (c) a deaf child who needs access to rehabilitation and audiological services;
  (d) an autistic child whose behaviour the family are unable to contain in a strange environment and without the help of extended family members.

(2) Language and cultural differences may make an accurate assessment of special educational needs difficult.

(3) For those areas accepting a large number of asylum seekers, stretched special educational needs services may not be able to respond quickly to place these children in school.

(4) Families may be unaware that their child has entitlement to care, or that effective interventions are available. Conversely families may have wildly unrealistic expectations of Western medicine, eg arrive in outpatients expecting their child's post-polio paralysis to be cured. These situations are distressing for all, and need sensitive responses.

(5) Families arrive from areas with no neonatal screening, so clinicians need to be mindful of missing diagnoses such as maternal phenylketonurea when investigating developmental delay.

(6) Clinicians must consider infection as a cause of developmental delay, eg delay with diplegia may be HIV encephalopathy; delay with chorioretinitis, hearing loss, heart murmur may follow congenital infection with toxoplasmosis, rubella, or syphilis.

CONCLUSION

Meeting the needs of refugee children requires services that are:

- flexible;

- responsive;

- adequately resourced.

Sadly the experience of many health professionals is that services are not resourced adequately. For example: primary care services are limited to reactive care for emergencies and crises, with no access to health promotion or preventive services; secondary and tertiary care is not commissioned at all; funding does not follow unaccompanied children through the dispersal system, with many local authorities struggling to meet their needs in a context of financially stretched core child and family services. As recommended by Save the Children we need a thorough review of the funding arrangements for services to these children and young people.[20]

Apart from being stressful for professionals seeking to provide equitable care for refugee children, these system failures serve to further increase the disadvantages faced by them, sometimes even contributing to continuing trauma. Furthermore, by creating what is in effect a sub-class of the black and minority ethnic population, with reduced rights, unequal and poorer-quality care, and worse health, we risk threatening the whole equality agenda at a time when this has assumed even greater importance than before.

I do not wish to end this paper with an image of these children and young people as merely victims. Many will live out their lives in this country as UK citizens, and contribute, in small and great ways, to the social and economic well-being of our society. Failing them is not just bad for them, but bad for all of us.

---

[20] Hewett, T, Smalley, N, Dunkerley, D, Scourfield, J *Uncertain futures: Children seeking asylum in Wales* (Save the Children Wales, Cardiff, 2005); also available at www.savethechildren.org.uk/en/docs/wales_uncertain_futures_full.pdf (accessed June 2007).

The Meaning of Safety, Belonging and Success for Unaccompanied Asylum-Seeking Children

Dr Ravi Kohli

Head of Applied Social Studies, University of Bedfordshire

SUMMARY OF THE PAPER

Dr Ravi Kohli explained that his aim, in introducing his paper, was to make sense of forced migration in terms of the evolutions of cultures from a position of 'us' and 'them' to a position of 'we'. Dr Kohli's paper considers three important and interdependent themes for asylum-seeking and unaccompanied minors: safety, belonging and success. He emphasised, that in giving meaning to these three elements it is important to consider the loss and recovery of ordinary life for these children.

The importance of safety, belonging and succeeding is resonant for all vulnerable children but these elements are particularly poignant to unaccompanied minors. This is echoed strongly in the research in this area. Unaccompanied children want education, training and a rhythm to their lives. They also want companionable people, to do good and to make good. They are keen to exercise their own capacities to use their talents in terms of making valuable contributions.

The current statistics show that around 30% of unaccompanied minors are returned, 65% are enabled to remain in the UK temporarily and only 5% get long-term leave to remain. This means that only a small minority achieve resettlement. The research maps out relatively clearly what the terms safety, belonging and success mean for those who are able to remain in the UK. There is next to no understanding, however, as to how to generate these three elements for those children who are returned. The research base is very weak and urgently needs to catch up with the policy inclinations of the UK and other countries so that we have some grasp of what happens to the children when they return.

Dr Kohli concluded the introduction to his paper with an old adage in refugee studies that 'we make the journey, and the journey makes us', reflecting the transformational nature of forced migration for those entering new territories, as well as their hosts.

THE PAPER

Introduction

When children seek asylum, they look for safety in a practical and psychological sense. They have many borders to cross, some that exist between the homeland and other countries, some that are procedural within the country of asylum, and some that they carry in their minds (Bash, 2005; Newman, 2006). Not all borders are bad in the sense that they offer ways of containing the ebb and flow of resettlement. However, only some of them are in the control of unaccompanied children themselves. Mostly they are erected and maintained by powerful adults, who shape their lives and trajectories. This paper is addressed to those of us who are border guards of one sort or another, whether we seek, through maintaining the border, to make children into citizens in our own country, or to return them to their countries of origin in safe ways.

Whichever ways safety is established, other border crossings appear at different times during journeys of asylum. For children who may have moved away from family, friends, locations and a sense of entitlement to a home, the need to belong to someone, to somewhere, becomes a conscious goal, and the refurbishment of ordinary life takes on a precedence that is at times vivid and urgent. So this paper reviews the research evidence that illuminates the movements towards connection that the children make, or hope to make, as they wait to see where they can safely relocate themselves.

As unaccompanied children make a journey from the edge to the centre in these ways, they also attempt journeys that will take them to success – from the bottom to the top, so to speak. Aspects of their lives where they can feel in charge, and find their way to locations where their talents and abilities can yield rewards beyond survival, are beginning to be understood in research terms, as researchers begin to move from examining how lives become compromised through forced migration, to the ways in which children become the guardians of their own success through using their strengths. So the final part of this paper explores this aspect of their capability and fortitude as responses to instability.

Taken together, safety, belonging and success are three dimensions that act as the foundations of a stable life for all vulnerable children. Finding them as repeating kaleidoscopic patterns over time in the lives of unaccompanied children is being better understood through research. Wade et al (2005), in an extensive study within the UK of social services provided to unaccompanied minors suggest that asylum-seeking children settle if they have:

- a safe and supportive place to live;

- continuities with past relationships, customs and cultures, and opportunities to create new ones;

- access to purposeful education and training; and

- opportunities to move forward from troubling experiences, re-centre their lives and find new purpose in everyday routines and activities.

To a degree, it can be argued that to settle within these terms is possible both within a reception country, as well as in the country of origin if returned. However, in the main, researchers have tended to focus on the lives of unaccompanied children in Western industrialised nations, and it is these studies that this paper primarily draws upon in considering safety, belonging and success.

SAFETY

To have what many of us have – the legal right to regard ourselves as citizens within a stable and successful country – is for many unaccompanied children, a dramatic desire. Children who come to industrialised nations as asylum seekers often cite this as a primary goal (Ayotte, 2000) as do their adult counterparts (Robinson and Segrott, 2002). The foundation of feeling safe comes through legally winning the right to remain in the country of asylum indefinitely. Very few children win this right in the UK but the majority are given temporary admission, and wait on edge through their childhood years, hoping to remain (Crawley, 2006). This pattern is confirmed in other parts of Europe (Silove and Ekblad, 2002; Smith, 2003). There is a broad sense that life in waiting is contingent, hedged with hope and worry, and that this sense of an occluded future echoes uncertainty about the past – other family members about whom there is no news, with whom there is little or no contact. Worries mount up. Silence becomes a way of communicating (Kohli, 2007). In the meantime stories of leaving and arrival are told purposefully – Goodman (2004: 1181) refers to them having *'a common plot'* – to those who might let the children remain within their territories. If the children's claims for indefinite leave to remain are rejected, then they face return. As yet there is very little research evidence to confirm what a 'safe return' may be, and how this may vary across countries, circumstances and cultures. In particular, the research base in relation to safe return of unaccompanied children to countries of origin is very weak (Sutton, 2004; van Wijk, 2005) in comparison to a broader understanding of assisted returns for refugees more generally (ECRE, 2005; Bradley, 2006). So despite policy developments that are focused in part on returning children into the safe hands of responsible adults within home countries (Home Office, 2007), there is continued concern that the parameters and thresholds of safety are as yet insufficiently understood.

While in the country of asylum, there is evidence to show that beyond the basics of leave to remain, a good school, prompt medical care, and finding trustworthy, reliable and companionable people increases a sense of safety, and creates stability in changing circumstances (Stanley, 2001). People who are kind, honest and make the effort and time to understand the worlds that unaccompanied minors can safely show, and understand that there are some of their worlds that no one has permission to enter while they wait for the asylum decision, are known to be comforting (Williamson,1998; Kohli, 2006). A safe life takes time to grow back, and children make efforts to help it grow. By design, and sometimes by chance, companions spring up from the formal and informal networks that the children grow around themselves, as they regenerate belonging.

BELONGING

To have parents who may have said to you that they love you enough to give you up to the care of strangers, is not a new phenomenon. Vivid accounts of ambivalent partings in dangerous circumstances exist in relation to wars and natural disasters in other times, particularly for *Kindertransport* children sent from other parts of Europe to the UK during the Second World War (Ressler et al, 1988; Bell, 1996; Harris and Oppenheimer, 2001). But the evidence is that it is no easier now for children to make peace with this heartfelt paradox than it was a generation ago, not least because the parents, as then, are now dead, or disappeared, or hidden from view. There is evidence that some children struggle to look back at their ordinary lives before departure in such circumstances (Minority Rights Group, 1998), because the loss of trusted relationships and familiar routines is hard to bear, particularly when compounded by harsh lives following forced migration. As with Hoffman's (1998: 151) experience of migration to a bewildering new country, they carry the risk that they too might 'fall out of the net of meaning into the weightlessness of chaos'.

However, a steady voice has now emerged in the research literature that presents refugee and asylum seekers as actors in their new territories in terms of the ways they cope with the challenges they face, and the manner in which hope changes from a diffuse element of their lives to something more solid and purposeful (Ahern, 2000; Goodman, 2004). While there are many psycho-social components to this transformation, it is worth examining it in relation to two key elements in the lives of unaccompanied minors. First, the ways they use their own talents and capacities to grow webs of belonging that hold them in place, and, secondly, their use of their own faith of origin.

Boyden and de Berry (2004; xvii), through examining a number of ethnographic studies, note that children in armed conflict have a certain elasticity that lets them give meaning and shape to their experiences. Their premise is that 'war does not destroy all it touches ... while [it] causes many to become extremely vulnerable, vulnerability does not in itself preclude ability'.

Importantly, the suggestion through much of the research literature is that refugee children exist within multiple worlds, where fracture and a dogged will to get better co-exist, and children endure vicissitudes and get through them if allowed to do so. As time passes, the capacity to regroup practically and psychologically is based on holding on to a broad sense of solidarity that extends to political and religious loyalties and affiliations from the past, to trustworthy people in the present, and the wish for ordinary family life, if not now, then in the future.

In terms of the re-growth of networks of solidarity and hope, Rousseau et al's (1998: 633) study of unaccompanied minors in Canada suggests that it is important to 'shift the focus of our reflections on resilience away from the person who displays it and more towards the social space within which it is woven', so that the layers of sustaining interaction that these children engage in within their new environments become the focus of study rather than the narrower focus on individual characteristics, for good or ill. Similarly, Miller et al's (in press) study of refugee young people in the United States, confirm that in part they discover equilibrium and the rhythm of day-to-day life through joining with others. This joining also appears within formal networks. For example, Kia-Keating and Ellis (2007) tentatively confirm that having a safe, confirming position within school, where young refugees can form attachments, make commitments and carry out small reciprocally valuable acts, allows a buffer against some of the complexity and uncertainty they have to endure.

These findings, related to Somali adolescents in the United States, fit well with UK findings delineated by Blackwell and Melzak (2000). Their clinical work establishes that distressing experiences can be mitigated by a sense of having at least one reliable adult companion in their lives among a protective network of people, having opportunities within respectful relationships to think about what happened to them and give it meaning, a sense of their own 'agency', so they know that they can make choices to counter-balance helplessness, and continuity of habits and rituals from their past. Williamson's (1998) study of asylum-seeking children in London also confirms the importance of mundane living, of eating 'home food', with asylum-seeking children wanting to engage with people and activities to distract and occupy them, bringing a little light relief from larger preoccupations. Particularly relevant to the notion of activities that bring comfort, is the newly recognised notion (within contexts of secular humanitarianism at least) that children who keep their faith of origin, and are given opportunities to practice their religion, appear to fare well in hostile contexts. Religion activates and sustains a sense of belonging with a visible, present and powerful sense of God being in charge in a rudderless world (Goodman, 2004). It helps them cope, and provides a framework for solace and continuity (Whittaker et al, 2005; Ni Raghallaigh, 2006). This appears to be true of unaccompanied children who are Muslim or Christian, and while religion appears as an unremarkable artefact in some studies (eg Stanley, 2001), its embedded nature and its bold importance in the revival of ordinary lives needs to be better understood than it is at present (Children's Society, 2006).

SUCCESS

Apart from the longed for permission to remain in the country of asylum, unaccompanied children and young people are known to want to succeed educationally and materially (Kohli and Mather, 2003). To some extent, having had a great deal of investment from families that have funded the journey, the child may be an expression of the family's wish not only to survive in some from, but for the survivor to thrive even if it is itself destroyed. Wade et al (2005: 110) refer to unaccompanied children's will to do well and their commitment and motivation, illuminated in one instance by Kamuran, a young man from Kurdistan saying, 'I thought if I could get to school and if I could learn English, I could be something. I could be something in the future. I did work hard for myself', reflecting a general observation within the research literature that emphasises the ways in which unaccompanied minors develop strategies to succeed as they navigate towards resources and people who will help them to achieve. Jackson et al (2005: xiii), in a study of children in care moving on to university education, similarly noted the high proportion of asylum-seeking young people in their sample, and observed that they 'tended to be more focused on their studies and in many cases worked much harder than UK-born students with a care background, putting in on average twice as many hours of private study'. The protectiveness offered by becoming accomplished, in addition to the comfort of learning in a stable school environment, has traditionally propelled migrants and well as refugees from positions of receiving, to positions of achieving within host societies (Aciman, 1997). It also fits well within the established paradigms of research on resilience in young people where educational success is one factor in framing a life built on endurance, capability, and a sense of being in charge of one's circumstances (Newman and Blackburn, 2002).

Having said this, it is also important to note that the research base that informs best practice in relation to sustained success for refugee children is at a relatively modest level of maturity, both nationally and internationally (Wilkinson, 2002). We do not yet have a very clear and systematic understanding of the trajectories of success for unaccompanied minors whether they remain in the asylum country and resettle, or return to their countries of origin. At this stage, all we can assert is that if they are offered resettlement then they appear to do well. In circumstances of prolonged uncertainty, when they do not know where they will end up, feeling successful is difficult no matter how strong the will. In that respect, safety, belonging and success are inter-dependent factors, only some elements of which they control. But they appear to do the best that they can with what they can govern, reaching out to others to advise, assist and befriend them at times and in places that are both fearful and hopeful, waiting for entitlement to an ordinary life within borders that can protect them.

REFERENCES

Aciman, A (ed) *Letters of Transit. Reflections on Exile, Identity, Language and Loss* (New York: The New Press, 1997)

Ahern, F L (ed) *Psychosocial wellness of refugees. Issues of qualitative and quantitative research* (New York: Berghahn Books, 2000)

Ayotte, W *Separated Children Coming To Western Europe. Why they travel and how they arrive* (London: Save the Children, 2000)

Bash, L 'Identity, boundary and schooling: perspectives on the experiences and perceptions of refugee children' (2005) 16 (4) Intercultural Education 351–366

Bell, A *Only for Three Months: The Basque Children in Exile* (Norwich: Mousehold Press, 1996)

Blackwell, D and Melzak, S *Far From the Battle but Still At War. Troubled Refugee Children In School* (London. The Child Psychotherapy Trust, 2000)

Bradley, M 'Return of Forced Migrants' (FMO Research Guide, 2006), available at Forced Migration online, www.forcedmigration.org/guides/fmo042/ (accessed 9 July 2007)

Boyden, J and de Berry, J *Children and Youth on the Front Line. Ethnography, Armed Conflict and Displacement* (New York: Berghahn Books, 2004)

Children's Society Making a new life in Newham: a study investigating the factors that facilitate and prevent young refugee resettlement in Newham (2006)

Crawley, H *Child first, migrant second: Ensuring that every child matters* (London: Immigration Law Practitioners' Association, 2006)

ECRE *The Return of Asylum Seekers whose Applications have been Rejected in Europe* (European Council on Refugees and Exiles, 2005)

Goodman, J H 'Coping with Trauma and Hardship among Unaccompanied Refugee Youths from Sudan' (2004) 14 (9) Qualitative Health Research 1177–1196

Harris M J and Oppenheimer D *Into the Arms of Strangers. Stories of the Kindertransport* (London: Bloomsbury, 2001)

Home Office *Planning Better Outcomes and Support for Unaccompanied Asylum Seeking Children: Consultation Paper* (2007), available at www.ind.homeoffice.gov.uk/6353/6356/17715/uasc.pdf (accessed 24 April 2007)

Hoffman, E *Lost in Translation* (London, Vintage, 1998)

Jackson, J, Ajayi, A and Quigley, M *Going to University from Care* (Institute of Education, University of London, 2005)

Kia-Keating, M and Ellis, B H 'Belonging and Connection to School in Resettlement: Young Refugees, School Belonging and Psychosocial Adjustment' (2007) 12(1) Clinical Child Psychology and Psychiatry 29–43

Kohli, R and Mather, R 'Promoting psychosocial well-being in unaccompanied asylum seeking people in the United Kingdom' (2003) 8(3) Child & Family Social Work 201–212

Kohli, R 'The sound of silence: listening to what unaccompanied children say and do not say' (2006) 36 British Journal of Social Work 707–721

Kohli, R *Social work with unaccompanied asylum seeking children* (Palgrave Macmillan: Basingstoke, 2007)

Miller, K, Kushner, H, McCall, J, Martell, Z, Kulkarni, M and Laurel, D 'Growing up in exile: psychosocial challenges facing refugee youth in the United States' in J Hart (ed), *Years of Conflict, Adolescence, Political Violence and Displacement* (New York: Berghahn Books, 2007)

Minority Rights Group International (eds) *Forging New Identities. Young Refugee and Minority Students Tell their Stories* (London: Minority Rights Group, 1998)

Newman, D 'The lines that continue to separate us: borders in our "borderless" world' (2006) 30(2) Progress in Human Geography 143–161

Newman, T and Blackburn, S *Transitions in the Lives of Children and Young People: Resilience Factors* (Scottish Executive Education Department, Edinburgh, 2002)

Ni Raghallaigh, M *Negotiating changed contexts and challenging circumstances: the experience of unaccompanied minors living in Ireland* (University of Dublin, Trinity College, PhD thesis, unpublished, 2006)

Robinson, V and Segrott, J *Understanding the decision making of asylum seekers* (Finding 172, Research, Development and Statistics Directorate, Home Office, London, 2002)

Ressler, E M, Boothby, N and Steinbock D *Unaccompanied Children. Care and Protection in Wars, Natural Disasters, and Refugee Movements* (Oxford: Oxford University Press, 1988)

Rousseau, C, Said, T, Gagné, M J and Bibeau, G 'Resilience in Unaccompanied Minors from the North of Somalia' (1998) 85 Psychoanalytic Review 615–637

Silove, D and Ekblad, S 'How well do refugees adapt after resettlement in Western countries?' (2002) 106 (6) Acta Psychiatrica Scandinavica 401–402

Smith, T *Separated Children in Europe: Policies and Practices in European Union Member States: A Comparative Analysis* (SCEP, Geneva, 2003)

Stanley, K *Cold comfort. Young separated refugees in England* (London: Save the Children, 2001)

Sutton, D *Save the Children and the Separated Children in Europe Programme Position Paper on Returns and Separated Children* (SCEP, Geneva, 2004)

Van Wijk, J 'Dutch "safe zone" in Angola' (2005) Forced Migration Review (May 2005) 32

Wade, J; Mitchell, F and Baylis, G *Unaccompanied asylum seeking children. The response of social work services* (British Association for Adoption and Fostering (BAAF), London, 2005)

Whittaker, S, Hardy, G, Lewis, K, Buchan, L 'An exploration of psychological well-being with young Somali refugee and asylum-seeker women' (2005) 10(2) Clinical Child Psychology and Psychiatry 177–196

Wilkinson, L 'Factors influencing the academic success of refugee youth in Canada' (2002) 5(2) Journal of Youth Studies 173–193

Williamson, L 'Unaccompanied – but not Unsupported' in J Rutter and C C Jones (eds), *Refugee Education. Mapping the Field* (Wiltshire: Trentham Books, 1998)

PLENARY 3

CHANGING FACE OF FAMILIES

LESBIAN AND GAY PARENTING

Current Issues in Relation to Gay and Non-biological Parenting

Dr Claire Sturge

Consultant Child Psychiatrist, Alexandra Health Centre

SUMMARY

Dr Sturge explained that the theme of her paper is: are there any limits to diversity in the different sorts of family structures and in the ways of creating babies?

She noted that there is very little research on whether there is benefit to children knowing their fathers. One can extrapolate from other research that it may be of advantage to have some knowledge of male progenitors and this fact is likely to have an impact on decisions on contact. Dr Sturge expressed her view that 'progenitor' is not a wholly satisfactory term in this context but that there are problems with using the word 'father' as it implies a parenting role. It is difficult to find a word that does not have a role implied in it. This difficulty reflects the confusion experienced by male sperm donors.

When known sperm donors are used they are often chosen from the same community as the lesbian woman seeking to become pregnant and the sperm donors are, therefore, often themselves homosexual. Children created in these situations theoretically then have a double genetic loading for unusual sexual orientations. Dr Sturge looks forward to what the research in this area will reveal. It might be expected that there will be a slight increase in children in such families going on to choose homosexual partners purely as a result of genetics.

Dr Sturge highlighted the diagrams in her paper as illustrations of particular sorts of diversity:

- The first example illustrates the facts of a case which was subject to a decision by Mr Justice Black. It involved two biological half sisters who had the same mother who was in a lesbian relationship. The children had three fathers between them.

- The second example covers the scenario where both lesbian partners have biological children of their own. This is an unusual pattern. The children are completely biologically unrelated.

- The third example involved a woman who considered herself too old to have a child and so it fell to the younger woman in the relationship to conceive and carry the child. The sperm of the older woman's brother was used. In terms of genetics, the child shared one quarter of the genes of the non-biological mother. This mechanism created a biological link for both women.

- The fourth example (gay family structure) illustrates the only structure in which a homosexual father has a genetic child.

- The fifth example illustrates a scenario in which children may not know their parentage because of a mother's unfaithfulness or the use of IVF. Such secrets can be maintained forever. However, the Parliamentary Committee has made a sensational suggestion under which this information may be put on birth certificates.

THE PAPER

Introduction

The wishes of gay couples, the structure of the law and attitudes in society are at odds and full of contradictions.

This paper is by way of an introduction to the talk by Professor Golombok who is a pioneer in the research in this area and whose paper outlines what can be learnt from the research.

This paper is based on limited professional experience but a great deal of reading and seeking of information from gay and lesbian contacts and organisations. It is an attempt to draw together themes and thoughts in this fascinating area.

My medical background may give the paper a particular slant. I hope to set a context for what Professor Golombok has to share.

TERMS

I am using the term 'gay' to mean a male homosexual, the term 'lesbian' to mean a female homosexual and the term 'co-parent' to mean the gay or lesbian partner committed to jointly bringing up a child with their partner but who is not the genetic mother or father of that child.

The terms mother and father can be seen as problematic as each carries a role meaning within it. But the more neutral 'male' and 'female progenitor' are clumsy.

ISSUES

The issues are fundamental ones and the problem is one for all of us – what are the limits in new approaches to the creation of new life (conception), gestation (human and animal surrogacy) and structures of the environment in which children are reared?

I am focusing in this paper on lesbian mothers and co-parents. This is because they form by far the largest group and it is on them that most research has focused. Unlike gay men wishing to reproduce, lesbian women can do so without 'borrowing' a womb. With a few exceptions of men who have managed to find a surrogate woman to gestate the baby, homosexual men bringing up children are those separated from the mother of the child, foster carers and adopters.

And what are the limits? Already we have fertilised embryos being used up to the eight cell division stage being used in research and discarded; fertilisation is possible in vitro and has become so successful that the 'hit' rate is comparable to that achieved through sexual intercourse. A real possibility is that technology will be developed to use nuclear material for conception. Two women or two men could have a form of nuclear fusion to create an embryo – the two women (or two men) would then be the genetic parents of the child. Women would only be able to create girls – men could create both. And cloning is waiting in the wings.

The gay and lesbian community is pushing forward the frontiers of anomalous conception at dizzying speed. And recent Court cases appear to be opening the door a little wider with each case to accepting the concept of a homonuclear family (see legal issues below). It is only 50 years since homosexuality was classified as a disease and 40 years since the Sexual Offences Act (the decriminalisation of homosexual acts in private). But real equality and acceptance has been much slower in coming. Terms such as 'gay' and 'lessie' remain the currency of taunts in the school playground. Children growing up within a gay or lesbian household will have to face such prejudicial attitudes.

ANOMALOUS CONCEPTION

Deciding to have a child (as opposed to unplanned pregnancies) has never been a child-centred decision but rather one that appears to be driven by what could be seen as the strong instinct to reproduce or reproduce one's genetic endowment. Motivated by our 'selfish genes'.

Within anomalous conception, for all, the issue is one of infertility – in heterosexual or homosexual couples.

Gays and lesbians choosing to have children, by known person insemination, anonymous but later to be revealed insemination, surrogacy or adoption, wish to be viewed as complete families by society and in law: not as families where the non-resident, biological parent is viewed as having rights comparable with theirs. They want the co-parent (when there is one) to be viewed as a legitimate parent, not a lesser parent because of the absence of a biological tie.

A Court can confer 'parental responsibility' (PR) to the co-parent, and now the biological parent and the co-parent can adopt.

The courts seem to have difficulty grasping that PR has no meaning or direct relevance for the child. The child may not ever be aware whether or not the 'other' genetic parent had or has PR.

NATURE VERSUS NURTURE

From the child's perspective the nurture is overwhelmingly more important for their healthy development than nature (all research would broadly support this). The child's healthy development depends on the quality of relationships – with anyone who is committed to them. Psychologically it is the nurturing parent or co-parent who is all important in meeting their emotional needs. In contrast, the Courts give a lot of weight to the biological connections.

There is the further nature–nurture debate regarding the sexual orientation of the children. To what extent might the increase, if any, in homosexual or bisexual orientation be seen as nature (genetic) or nurture (the largely homosexual environment in which the child grows up)?

Professor Golombok refers to the research in this area.

PATTERNS OF GAY AND LESBIAN PARENTING

The biggest group, at least to date, is the group of children who live with a parent or parents and where the child's mother comes to realise or comes out as 'lesbian', leaves her male partner and brings up the child as a single, albeit lesbian, parent. Children may have the experience of a father realising he is or coming out as gay.

Wedlock (and now birth certificate registration) confers special responsibilities (exercised as rights) to parents. But the Law, in effect, upholds anomalous situations, analogous to those for the gay and lesbian parents, within 'heterosexual' society: children born in wedlock but conceived through an extra-marital affair (see family trees below) and children for whom the father entry on their birth certificate is a lie have two 'parents' with PR. This deception may be lifelong.

Conception is arranged in all sorts of different ways in gay and lesbian families. The higher success rates with fresh sperm mean that lesbian couples, even when they had favoured an 'unknown' donor, seek out a known donor particularly if there have been many previous attempts with bank sperm. Both the women may have both tried unsuccessfully to conceive. Some favour known donors as being in the child's interests.

Others seek genetic links by choosing within family sperm donors.

The focus on the mechanics of conception seems to blind the participants to the strong emotions that underlie reproduction. It is these strong emotions that are driving the cases that get to Court.

Below are some illustrations of the complexities of these family structures.

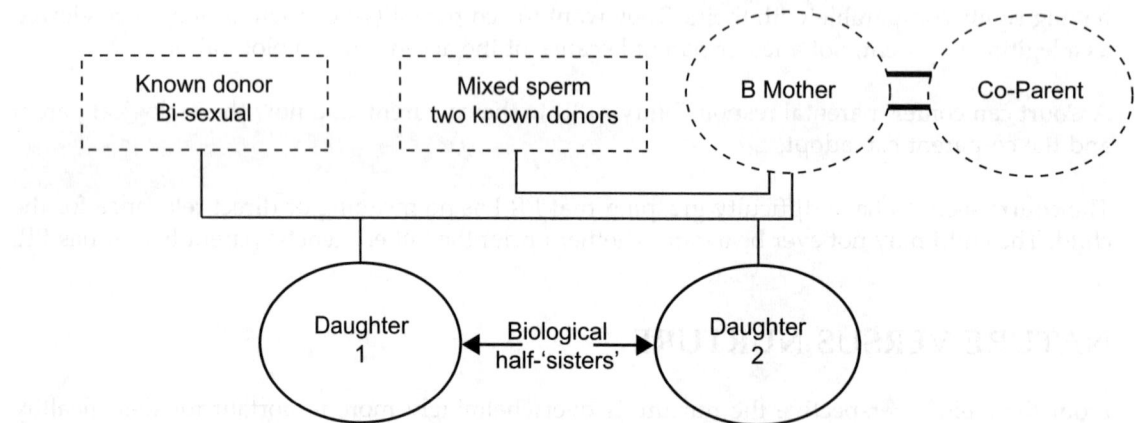

Legend

- - - - - Indicates homosexual orientation

———— Indicates heterosexual (or undetermined) orientation

B Mother - Biological Mother

Lesbian/Co-parenting family trees: Example 1

Prevalence

Unknown. There is a little information from gay and lesbian groups and fertility clinics. Extrapolations from one survey suggest there are 600,000 families headed by a gay parent in the UK. The situation is changing rapidly. From a position only 2 or 3 years ago where the majority of families headed by a lesbian woman contained children conceived in former heterosexual relationships, now many lesbian couples want to have their 'own' children.

Magazine surveys indicate that approximately half of lesbian couples want to have a child: no sex preference is expressed. In 2006, the D'Arcy Lainey Foundation (which incorporates Gay Dads UK and Pink Parents) had over 2,000 calls relating to women wanting donor insemination.

The choices are, put somewhat crudely:

1.   donor sperm from an unknown man (identity can be revealed when the child is 18);

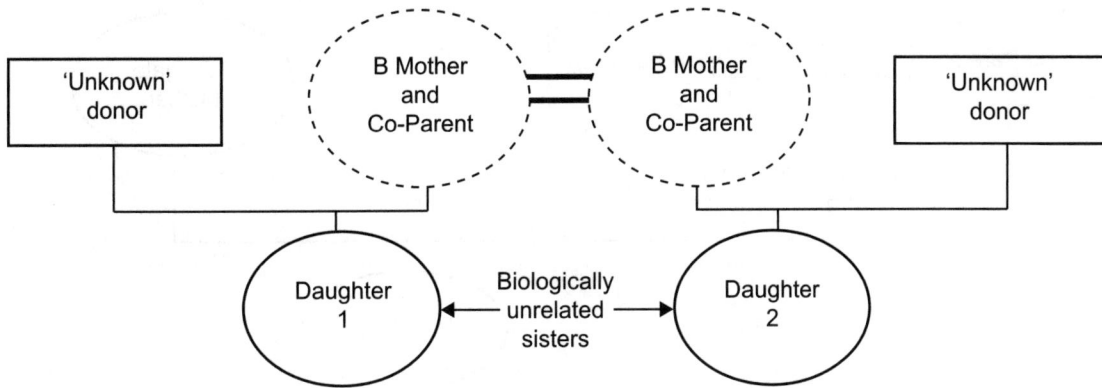

Legend

- - - - -   Indicates homosexual orientation

————   Indicates heterosexual (or undetermined) orientation

B Mother - Biological Mother

Lesbian/Co-parenting family trees: Example 2

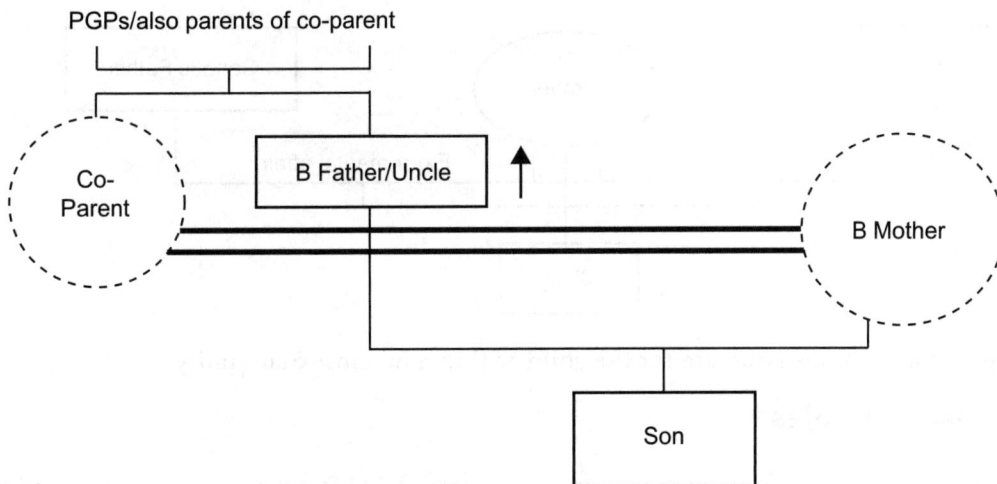

Legend

- - - - -   Indicates homosexual orientation

————   Indicates heterosexual (or undetermined) orientation

B Mother - Biological Mother

B Father - Biological Father

Lesbian/Co-parenting family trees: Example 3

2.   donor sperm from a known man;

3.   'mixed' donor sperm from known men, in which the sperm of several men is combined so the actual genetic father is not identified;

4.   'one night stands'.

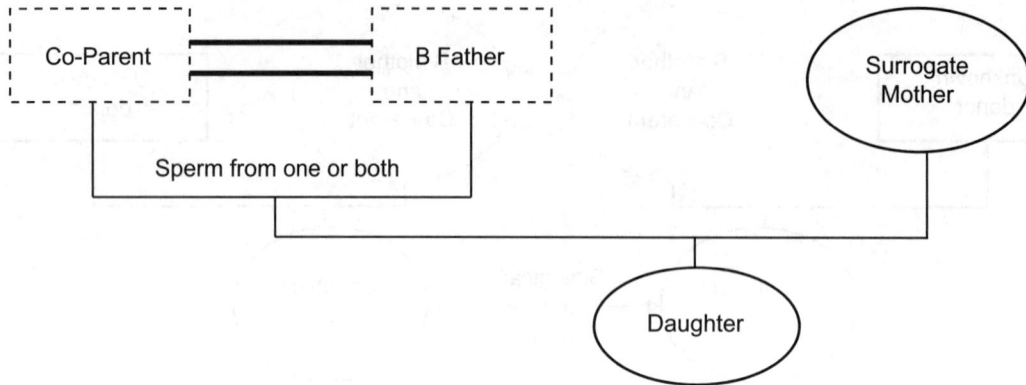

Co-Parent —— B Father

Surrogate Mother

Sperm from one or both

Daughter

Legend

- - - - -   Indicates homosexual orientation

————   Indicates heterosexual (or undetermined) orientation

B Father - Biological Father

Surrogate mother: gives of an egg, lender of a womb

Example of a gay family structure

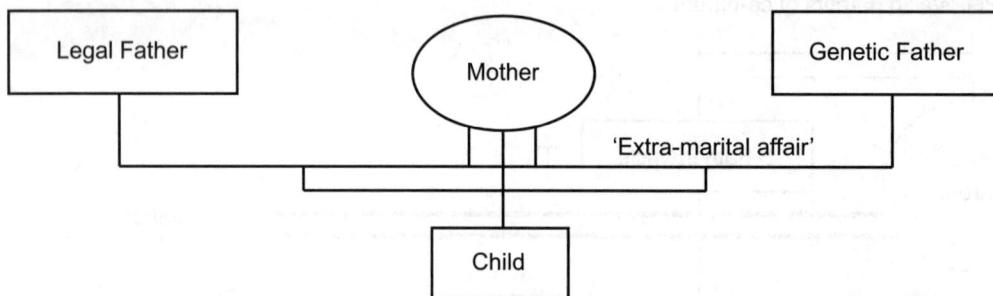

Legal Father

Mother

Genetic Father

'Extra-marital affair'

Child

Example of anomalous structure for the child within a heterosexual family

Two case examples

1. *Julie* was 4 and was frighteningly bright and composed with a well integrated sense of who she was and of her secure position in her family. From Julie's perspective, she had two mothers and one father, she had a sister who had two mothers and two fathers, she considered herself lucky, telling me most children only had two parents, some only one and then there were orphans who had none. Of her two mothers, the one gave her milk from her breasts when she was a baby and the other is the one who always gives her milk at breakfast. She was securely attached to both of them. She had no 'special' relationship with or attachment to her father but enjoyed the time when he visited.

    Julie's mother and co-mother could not be faulted in their approach to parenting and their sensitivity to and openness with Julie.

    From my perspective (and, in my view, the child's), the case was complicated by three things:

    (i)   the genetic father was as desperate to be a father as the lesbian couple were to be mothers;

    (ii) the father had interfered in health issues in a detrimental way; and

    (iii) there was a younger sibling conceived differently from her sister and for whom there were two 'fathers' seeking PR.

I gave my opinion that the PR was of little or no direct relevance to the little girl. The co-parents were offering excellent parenting. I posited that the issue was really one of how society or, in this case the court, considered the lesbian family structure as representing a 'complete' family.

2.   *Jake* is only 18 months old. He is the child in the family tree example 3 above, ie his biological father is also his uncle and his co-mother is also his aunt. The biological father wants a meaningful role in Jake's life. The two co-parents (both have PR) and the biological father give completely opposing accounts of what agreement was reached about what, if any, involvement the biological father was to have. A particular issue for me was the genealogical confusions for Jake. The central issues were similar in both cases.

Outcomes: see below.

WHAT HAVE I LEARNT?

The central lesson that I have learnt to date is that it is passions and feelings that drive the players.

1.   Procreational feelings:
      Neither the men (where they 'knowingly' donate sperm) nor the women have taken account of the feelings that will overwhelm them once conception and pregnancy is achieved and, even more, feelings once the child is born.
      Misunderstandings, lies and conflict follow.
      This is what is tearing at the hearts of the players in these cases. The resulting conflict is a potential source of harm to the child far greater than that of their anomalous situation.

2.   Feelings of discrimination:
      I have been taken by surprise by the almost paranoid feelings of the lesbian 'mothers' I have met and talked to. It is as if they assume that the world – heterosexuals and the society at large – is against them, that everything for them will be a fight and a battle.
      It is not so surprising. They very much feel a minority group, those deciding on having children being in an even smaller minority. There is disapprobation by much of society.
      I have learnt how easy it is to offend – for example, just by the loose use of a word. To imply that the co-parent is not a 'full' mother causes great offence.
      The Law allows 'known' donors to seek involvement with the child and this is experienced as a threat to the integrity and security of the lesbian household (the 'homonuclear' family). Until now, rules for Fertility Clinics discriminated against gay and lesbian people seeking help.

3.   Secrecy:
      There are an unusual number of secrets in these families and plans to keep certain secrets from the child (permanently or for a number of years). This cloak of secrecy is worrying from the child's perspective. It is not as in, for example, a case where there has been artificial insemination by donor where the couple concerned can maintain the secret. In the instance of gay and lesbian families, that there is a mystery or secret is all too obvious – other children will ask even if adults are too polite to do so.
      Energy invested in keeping secrets and uncomfortable tensions obvious to the child arise. Worst of all, there can be a destructive undermining of trust if the child learns the truth from outsiders.

RECENT LEGAL CASES AND PROPOSED CHANGES IN THE LAW

1. *Bi dad sues gay mum over tot: Re D (contact and Parental Responsibility: Lesbian Mothers and Known Father)* (2006). See case example 1 above. The main issue was around parental responsibility although there were also contact issues.
    Outcome: The father was given PR, but he was not to be involved in health or educational issues, and defined and increased contact.

2. *Re G (children 2006): Lesbian parents separate – dispute over residence.* In this case the genetic mother, following the separation, behaved in a way that clearly undermined the child's relationship with the co-parent. Residence was given to the co-parent but reversed on appeal and that reversal was upheld in the Lords with a clearly stated opinion about the importance of the blood tie and its outweighing other factors.

3. *Re BA* (2007) EWHC 1952 (Fam). See case example 2 above. In his judgment Mr Justice Hedley refers to the proposed change of removing 'including the need of a father' from the child welfare assessment by Infertility Clinics. He went further than in (1) above, denying the biological father PR but granting defined contact.
    He comments on the absence of satisfactory nomenclature and how approaches have varied from ignoring a male contribution altogether, focusing simply on the biological role of the male to insisting on a true (if limited) species of fatherhood. In granting contact he says this is not to give the male progenitor parental status in BA's eyes but to identify him as someone significant with whom he can later, if he so wishes, explore implications.

4. *Case in Canada: AA v BB and CC:* Ontario Court of Appeal: 2 January 2007. The mother and co-parent did not seek an adoption so as not to exclude the genetic father. The Court found there was a gap in their legislature. The High Court judge made a 'declaration of parentage' using its *'parens patriae'* jurisdiction to bridge a legislative gap. The co-parent is now a second mother so the child now has two mothers and a father.

5. There are several cases, e g *Re CH (contact: parentage)* 1996, *Re H and A (paternity: blood tests)* 2002, that have dealt with issues of disputed paternity within marriage when couples separate. The Courts held that it was important for the truth to come out.

PROPOSED CHANGES TO THE LAW

The review of the Human Fertilisation and Embryo Act (HFE Act)

I here pick out themes relevant to my topic.

The revised proposals include the following:

Section 13.5: licences for fertility treatment

It is proposed to remove the phrase 'including the need of that child for a father' from the consideration of the welfare of the child.

The proposals seek to extend the information exchange so that donor conceived young people can access not only the identity of the gamete donor but whether they have donor-conceived siblings. The gamete donor would be able to get limited information about whether his or her offspring has requested their identifying details.

The anomaly persists whereby Parental Orders in 'favour of the commissioning couple' continues to apply only to surrogacy. There is a suggestion (para 2.69) that it may be further extended the status and legal parenthood provisions of the HFE Act will be revised to enable a greater range of persons to be recognised as parents following assisted reproduction'.

The Parliamentary Committee considering the proposals has made an exciting new proposal – that children conceived through donated eggs or sperm should have that information on their birth certificates which would enable them to trace their 'genetic parent'.

DISCUSSION

There is resistance to embracing what research seems to overwhelmingly indicate: the factors determining good outcomes for children are the nature and quality of the care they receive, not the structure of their families or the presence (partial or with full involvement) or absence of a parent with biological ties. This applies both to the child's living situation and to the issue of the benefits or otherwise of contact.

Why do we feel so challenged by these issues? One factor is the sheer speed with which gay and lesbian people are challenging traditional views and seeking to redraw the nature of families. I can only presume that the other is our deep-seated beliefs about what is 'natural' and what is ordained by our biological potential: the centrality of reproduction to the human race. We are anxious about the potential for chaos if biology ceases to be a determining factor in the constitution of families.

From the child's perspective, I have a serious concern about how the decisions of the Courts about giving biological fathers PR, or significant contact, is likely to deter lesbians from using known donors. From my knowledge of the literature, of research (none of it directly related to this topic) and my experience of children in terms of those who do and do not know and have contact with fathers, I consider it in children's interests for there to be a known male progenitor to satisfy their genealogical curiosity and give them knowledge of their genetic roots. In 2002, a Belgian study of 10-year-old children conceived through donor insemination showed that 46% of these children would like to know more about the donor (but not necessarily his identity).

Do we need an adjustment to the Law so that a biological father (or a mother in the parallel situation) can be officially recognised but without this meaning he gets PR? From the child's perspective, it is such recognition that might be important symbolically, not the legal jargon and rules that go with PR.

I favour a change in the law to achieve this.

QUESTIONS

1.   What is the research question that most needs answering?

2.   Is there a limit for what children can cope with in terms of structural/biological anomalies?

3.   Does every child have a right to *accurate* information in relation to their origins? If so, do we countenance all children and adults having DNA analyses?

4.   If the genetic loading together with an environmental one predisposes to homosexuality is this a cause for concern or for celebration?

5. Is political correctness limiting necessary open debate?

6. Should the completeness of a homosexual family be upheld in law?

7. What are the implications of recent and proposed changes in the law for women (whether single or married, heterosexual or homosexual) accessing artificial insemination? And for the children thus conceived?

REFERENCES

Anderssen, N, Amlie, C and Ytteroy, E A 'Outcomes for children with lesbian or gay parents. A review of studies from 1978 to 2000' (2002) 43 (4) Scand J Psychol 335-351

Baetens, P and Brewaeys, A 'Lesbian couples requesting donor insemination: an update of the knowledge with regard to lesbian mother families' (2001) 7 (5) Hum Reprod Update 512-519

Bos, H M, Van Balen, F and Van Den Boom, D C 'Planned lesbian families: their desire and motivation to have children' (2003) 18 (10) Hum Reprod 2216-2224

Bos, H M, Van Balen, F and Van Den Boom, D C 'Experience of parenthood, couple relationship, social support, and child-rearing goals in planned lesbian mother families' (2004) 45 (4) J Child Psychol Psychiatry 755-764

Brewaeys, A, et al 'Anonymous or identity-registered sperm donors? A study of Dutch recipient's choices' (2005) 20 (3) Hum Reprod 820-824

Brewaeys, A, et al 'Donor insemination: child development and family functioning in lesbian mother families' (1997) 12 (6) Hum Reprod 1349-1359

Cameron, P and Cameron, K 'Children of homosexual parents report childhood difficulties (Comment in (2002) 91 (1) Psychol Rep 331-332) (2002) 90 (1) Psychol Rep 71-82

Chan, R W, Raboy, B and Patterson, C J 'Psychosocial adjustment among children conceived via donor insemination by lesbian and heterosexual mothers' (1998) 69 (2) *Child Development* 443-457

Ciano-Boyce, C and Shelley-Sireci, L 'Who is mommy tonight? Lesbian parenting issues' (2002) 43 (2) J Homosex 1-13

Clarke, V, Kitzinger, C and Potter, J '"Kids are just cruel anyway": lesbian and gay parents' talk about homophobic bullying' (2004) 43 (4) Br J Soc Psychol 531-550

Connolly, C *The description of gay and lesbian families in second-parent adoption cases* (1996)

Coolidge, F L, and Young, S E 'The heritability of gender identity disorder in a child and adolescent twin sample' (2002) 32 (4) Behav Genet 251-257

Dundas, S and Kaufman, M 'The Toronto Lesbian Family Study' (2000) 40 (2) J Homosex 65-79

Fuscaldo, G 'Fatherless families: how important is genetic relatedness?' (2002) 21 (3) Monash Bioeth Rev 18-29

Gartrell, N, et al 'The national lesbian family study: 1. Interviews with prospective mothers' (1996) 66 (2) Am J Orthopsychiatry 272-281

Gartrell, N, et al 'The National Lesbian Family Study: 2. Interviews with mothers of toddlers' (1999) 69 (3) Am J Orthopsychiatry 362–369

Gartrell, N, et al 'The National Lesbian Family Study: 3. Interviews with mothers of five-year-olds' (2000) 70 (4) Am J Orthopsychiatry 542–548

Gold, M A, et al 'Children of gay or lesbian parents' (1994) 15 (9) Pediatr Rev 354–358

Golombok, S, Spencer, A. and Rutter, M 'Children in lesbian and single parent households: Psychosexual and Psychiatric Appraisal' (1983) 24 (4) L Child Psychol Psychiat 551–572

Golombok, S, Tasker, F and Murray, C 'Children raised in fatherless families from infancy: family relationships and the socioemotional development of children of lesbian and single heterosexual mothers' (1997) 37 (7) J Child Psychol Psychiatry 783–791

Golombok, S and Tasker, F 'Do parents influence the sexual orientation of their children? Findings from a longitudinal study of lesbian families' (1996) 32 (1) *Developmental Psychology* 3–11

Green, R J '"Lesbians, gay men, and their parents": a critique of LaSala and the prevailing clinical "wisdom"' (2000) 39 (2) Fam Process 257–266

King, B R and Black, K N 'College students' perceptual stigmatization of the children of lesbian mothers' (1999) 69 (2) Am J Orthopsychiatry 220–227

King, B R 'Ranking of stigmatization toward lesbians and their children and the influence of perceptions of controllability of homosexuality' (2001) 41 (2) J Homosex 77–97

Leiblum, S R, Palmer, M G and Spector, I P 'Non-traditional mothers: single heterosexual/ lesbian women and lesbian couples electing motherhood via donor insemination' (1995) 16 (1) J Psychosom Obstet Gynaecol 11–20

Lynch, J M 'Integrating identities' (2004) 48 (2) J Homosex 45–60

Maccallum, F and Golombok, S 'Children raised in fatherless families from infancy: a follow-up of children of lesbian and single heterosexual mothers at early adolescence' (2004) 45 (8) J Child Psychol Psychiatry 1407–1419

Perrin, E C 'Technical report: Coparent or second-parent adoption by same-sex parents', 2002

Scheib, J E, Riordan, M and Rubin, S 'Adolescents with open-identity sperm donors: reports from 12–17 year olds' (2005) 20 (1) Hum Reprod 239–252

Scheib, J E, Riordan, M and Rubin, S 'Choosing identity-release sperm donors: the parents' perspective 13–18 years later' (2003) 18 (5) Hum Reprod 1115–1127

Schumm, W R 'Response to Kirkpatrick (2004): differential risk theory and lesbian parenthood' (2004) 95 (3) Pt 2 Psychol Rep 1203–1206

Schumm, W R 'What was really learned from Tasker and Golombok's (1995) study of lesbian and single parent mothers?' Comment in (2004) 94 (3) Pt 2 Psychol Rep 1185–1186) (2004) 94 (2) Psychol Rep 422–424

Tasker, F and Golombok, S 'Adults raised as children in lesbian families' (1995) 65 (2) Am J Orthopsychiatry 203–215

Tasker, F 'Lesbian mothers, gay fathers, and their children: a review' (2005) 3 J Dev Behav Pediatr 224–240

Vanfraussen, K, Ponjaert-Kristoffersen, I and Brewaeys, A 'Family functioning in lesbian families created by donor insemination' (2003) 73 (1) Am J Orthopsychiatry 78–90

Wendland, C L, Burn, F and Hill, C 'Donor insemination: a comparison of lesbian couples, heterosexual couples and single women' (1996) 64 (4) Fertil Steril 764–770

What Really Matters for the Psychological Wellbeing of Children?

Professor Susan Golombok

Centre for Family Research, University of Cambridge

SUMMARY OF THE PAPER

Professor Susan Golombok introduced her paper as a whistle-stop tour through the research on children growing up in same-sex families. She noted that public awareness and perception of such families has changed markedly since the 1970s when she first began work in this area. Professor Golombok has conducted a number of studies in this field. The research arose from the need to assess whether there was substance in the opinions, like that of Rhodes Boyson MP quoted in the paper, widely held in the 1970s in relation to lesbian mothers.

The findings of the research in this area are strikingly consistent: there is no evidence that being brought up by a lesbian mother causes children to experience greater levels of identity confusion. Later studies, undertaken to address the criticisms made of the earlier research, showed that the existence of a lesbian mother makes no difference to the quality of a child's relationship with either parent; many children maintained relationships with their fathers and this was often encouraged by their mothers. Further, it was found that young people in lesbian families grew up enjoying far better relationships with step-parents than children in heterosexual step-families. This was likely to be the result of the lesbian step-parent being perceived by the child as an additional parent, rather than as a replacement parent.

The later research also addressed the concern that children brought up in lesbian families would suffer bullying from their peers. The research suggests that these children are no more likely, at primary school level, to experience bullying although there were differences for teenagers. Teenagers, although no more likely to be teased in general, were more likely to be teased about sexuality, whether their own or their mother's. The extent to which this caused problems for teenagers with lesbian mothers was dependent upon the environment in which they lived, particularly in terms of social background and geography.

The research established that being brought up by a lesbian mother made no difference to psychological wellbeing in adulthood. Further, in spite of the assumptions, the large majority of those surveyed were heterosexual indicating that having a lesbian mother makes little difference to sexual orientation of the children.

More recent research has been able to survey a more representative sample of families with lesbian mothers but the same conclusions were reached compared with the previous studies.

Professor Golombok noted that much less is known about gay fathers. There is currently no research available about children living with gay fathers although a study is about to begin in the USA on this topic. The empirical research conducted in relation to lesbian mothers has contributed to many changes in legal and social policy. These changes have also been spurred on by pressure groups and developing social attitudes. Professor Golombok concluded with a 'plug' for empirical research to enable us to find out, in a clear and objective way, what happens in different family types so that the evidence can be fed to those making decisions in policy as it affects family life.

THE PAPER

Adapted from Golombok (2007) research on lesbian and gay parenting: A historical perspective across 30 years. Foreword for special edition on gay and lesbian parenting for the Journal of GLBT Family Studies.

> 'This evil must stop for the sake of the potential children and society, which both have enough problems without the extension of this horrific practice. Children have a right to be born into a natural family with a father and a mother. Anything less will cause lifelong deprivation of the most acute kind for the child' (Rhodes Boyson (1978))

This was the view expressed by a prominent member of the British Parliament following a controversial article in a London evening newspaper entitled 'Ban these babies' that called for the prohibition of donor insemination to lesbian women. At that time, public awareness of lesbian families was minimal and the article produced an outcry, not only about children being conceived by lesbian women through donor insemination but also about the fact that lesbian women were raising children at all. Although this may seem strange today, the prevailing view in the mid-1970s was that a woman could be *either* a lesbian *or* a mother. The idea that a lesbian woman could *also* be a mother had not occurred to the majority of the population, most of whom had never previously thought about this issue. One change that has certainly occurred over the past 30 years is that most people in the Western world now know that lesbian mothers do exist.

Although a great deal of fuss was made in the 1970s about lesbian women conceiving children through donor insemination, the majority of lesbian mother families at that time were formed by women who had had their children while married or cohabiting with a male partner. Due to the growth of both the women's movement and the gay liberation movement, an increasing number of lesbian women began to seek custody of their children when they separated or divorced. Almost without exception, they lost custody to the father on the grounds that growing up in a lesbian family would not be in the best interests of the child. It was argued in Courts of Law that the children would be teased and bullied by their peers which would result in psychological problems, and that they would show atypical gender development such that the boys would be less masculine in their identity and behaviour, and girls less feminine, than their counterparts from heterosexual homes. Often expert witnesses would be called, with the expert giving evidence on behalf of the mother suggesting that it was the quality of family relationships that mattered most for children's healthy psychological development whereas the expert brought in on behalf of the father argued that a two-parent heterosexual family was essential for children's social and emotional adjustment as well as for the acquisition of sex-typed behaviour. In the absence of empirical studies of what actually happened to children in lesbian mother families, judges opted for the more traditional family environment and awarded custody to heterosexual fathers in preference to lesbian mothers. This outcome was in stark contrast to that of custody cases involving heterosexual mothers where custody was almost always awarded to the mother and not the father.

It was these custody cases that prompted the first systematic studies of children growing up in lesbian families. In the United States, two investigations were initiated in the 1970s, one on the west coast (Kirkpatrick et al, 1981) and the other on the east coast (Green et al, 1986). An investigation was also begun in the UK (Golombok et al, 1983). The early studies of lesbian mother families adopted a similar approach in that they compared children in lesbian mother families with children raised in families headed by a single heterosexual mother, and focused on the children's socio-emotional development and gender development, ie the two main areas of concern in custody cases involving a lesbian mother. The reason for the choice of single heterosexual mothers as a comparison group was that the two types of family were alike in that the children were being raised by women without the presence of a father, but differed in the sexual orientation of the mother. This allowed the influence of the mothers' sexual orientation on children's development to be examined without the confounding effect of the presence of a father in the family home. Although the measures used differed from study to study, data were generally obtained using standardised interviews and questionnaires administered to mothers and children, and information on the children's psychological adjustment was rated by a child psychiatrist who was 'blind' to the children's family type in order to minimise bias.

So what did we learn? Regardless of the geographical or demographic characteristics of the samples studied, the findings of these early investigations were strikingly consistent. First, children from lesbian mother families did not show a higher incidence of psychological disorder, or of difficulties in peer relationships, than their counterparts from heterosexual homes – and for measures for which norms were available, they were found to be functioning within the normal range. With respect to gender development, a distinction is usually made between gender identity (a person's concept of him or herself as male or female) and gender role behaviour (the behaviours and attitudes considered typical of males and females in a particular culture). There was no evidence of gender identity confusion for any of the children studied; all of the boys identified as boys and all of the girls identified as girls. In terms of gender role behaviour, no differences were found between children in lesbian and heterosexual families for either boys or girls. Daughters of lesbian mothers were no less feminine, and the sons no less masculine, than the daughters and sons of heterosexual mothers – this was in spite of the lesbian mothers' preference for less sex-typed toys and activities for their daughters and sons! It was concluded from these initial studies that children in lesbian families did not differ from other children as a result of their non-traditional family environment. These findings were replicated by other researchers over the years, culminating in a seminal review by Charlotte Patterson in the journal *Child Development* (Patterson, 1992).

But that wasn't the end of the story. A number of criticisms were made about this body of research. First, only school-age children had been studied. It was argued that 'sleeper effects' may exist such that children raised in lesbian households may experience emotional problems, and difficulties with intimate relationships, when they grow up. It was also assumed that the children would themselves identify as lesbian or gay in adulthood, an outcome that was generally considered to be undesirable by Courts of Law.

In order to address these issues, the children from the British study were followed up in 1991–1992, 14 years after they had first been seen, when their average age was 23 years old (Tasker and Golombok, 1995 and 1997; Golombok and Tasker, 1996). It was found that young adults from lesbian backgrounds did not differ from their counterparts from heterosexual homes in terms of the quality of their current relationship with either their mother or their father. But, interestingly, young adults who had been brought up in a lesbian household described their relationship with their mother's partner more positively than those who had been raised by a heterosexual mother and her new male partner. This seemed to be because she was more likely to be seen as an additional parent than as a replacement parent. The findings relating to psychological well-being showed that children raised by lesbian mothers continued to function well in adulthood and did not experience long-term detrimental effects arising from their early upbringing. In addition, young adults from lesbian families were no more likely to report having been teased or bullied during adolescence than those from heterosexual single parent homes although there was a tendency for those from lesbian families to be more likely to remember having been teased specifically about being gay or lesbian themselves, possibly because they were more likely to recall such incidents. Those who were negative about their experiences of growing up in a lesbian family tended to come from poorer backgrounds and to live in social environments that were generally hostile towards homosexuality. It seems, therefore, that the social context of the lesbian mother family is an important factor in the experiences of the child. How the mother handled the situation also made a difference. It was important to the children that their mother was sensitive to their need for discretion, and that they themselves controlled who, and who not, to tell. In terms of sexual attraction, similar proportions of young adults from lesbian families and single heterosexual mother families reported experiencing sexual attraction to someone of the same sex, although those from lesbian families were more likely to have had a same-sex relationship. Regarding sexual identity, the large majority of children who grew up in lesbian families identified as heterosexual in adulthood so the commonly held assumption that lesbian mothers would have lesbian daughters and gay sons was not supported by the findings of the study.

Another criticism of research on lesbian mother families was that most of the children studied had spent their first years in a heterosexual home before making the transition to a lesbian family. To the extent that early experience influences later development, knowledge about these children cannot not be generalised to children raised by a lesbian mother from birth. In recent years, however, studies of lesbian families with children conceived by donor insemination have begun to be reported; three from the United States (Flaks et al, 1995; Chan et al, 1998; Gartrell et al, 1999, 2000 and 2005), one from Belgium (Brewaeys et al, 1997), one from the Netherlands (Bos, 2004) and one from the UK (Golombok et al, 1997; MacCallum et al, 2004). Unlike lesbian women who had their children while married, these couples planned their family together after coming out as lesbian and so the children were being raised in lesbian families with no father present right from the start. The evidence so far suggests that they do not differ from their peers in two-parent heterosexual families in terms of either psychological well-being or gender development. In fact, the only clear difference to emerge from these studies was that co-mothers in lesbian families were more involved with their children than were fathers in heterosexual homes.

A further limitation of the body of research on lesbian mother families was that only volunteer or convenience samples had been studied. Lesbian mothers whose children were experiencing problems may have been unlikely to volunteer for research thus producing an over-positive picture of the well-being of children in these families. In order to address this issue, two studies of general population samples of children raised by lesbian mothers have recently been carried out. The first, conducted in the United States, became possible through collaboration with the National Longitudinal Study of Youth, and was based on a national sample of adolescents (Wainright et al, 2004). No differences were found in psychological adjustment, school outcomes, family relationships, romantic relationships or sexual behaviour. The second study focused on a general population sample of 7 year olds from the Avon Longitudinal Study of Parents and Children, an epidemiological study of mothers and their children conducted in the west of England (Golombok et al, 2003). No differences were found in the quality of mother-child relationships between lesbian and heterosexual families, or in children's psychological adjustment, self-esteem, quality of peer relationships or gender development. Thus, the findings of these two investigations are in line with those of the earlier studies that showed positive mother-child relationships and well-adjusted children. Even with general population samples, children raised by lesbian mothers appear to be functioning well.

Much less research has been conducted on children with gay fathers than on children with lesbian mothers, largely because the majority of children with gay fathers are raised by their mothers. With the odds stacked against them because of their gender as well as their sexual orientation, most gay fathers do not even attempt to gain custody of their children following divorce. Although some gay men adopt children and others father children with lesbian women or become parents through a surrogacy arrangement, the number of gay men who have children living with them remains very small. To date, no study has focused directly on the psychological well-being of children with gay fathers. However, there are no indications, either from fathers' reports, or from the limited number of interviews with the children themselves, that children who remain in contact with their gay father experience marked emotional or behavioural problems (Miller, 1979; Harris and Turner, 1986; Bozett, 1987; Barrett and Tasker, 2001). As yet, no investigations have been carried out of children raised in gay father families from birth.

So what has been the impact of 30 years of research? From a theoretical point of view, the findings have challenged deeply rooted beliefs in child psychology about the processes through which parents influence the development of their children. With respect to gender development, it seems that the presence of a father, or of heterosexual role models, is not essential for children's development of a secure gender identity or sex-typed behaviour. And in terms of children's socio-emotional development, what seems to matter for children's psychological well-being is not whether the mother is lesbian or heterosexual. What really matters appears to be the same for all families – it is the quality of family life.

And what about social policy and legislation? Has 30 years of research produced any change? In many ways, the answer is yes, although it is important to point out that geographical differences exist. In relation to child custody cases, a lesbian sexual orientation is no longer considered by many Courts of Law to be a sufficient reason to deny a mother the custody of her children. Whereas in the mid-1970s, lesbian women almost without exception lost custody of their children, most cases these days do not even go to Court. In addition, lesbian women and gay men may adopt and foster children, and in some places may adopt children jointly. Regarding assisted reproduction, lesbian women have access to assisted reproduction procedures such as donor insemination, and gay men have become fathers through surrogacy. Furthermore, same-sex marriage, or legal recognition of same-sex relationships, has become possible in some countries and in some parts of the United States. So there have been marked changes in policy and legislation regarding same-sex parenting since the early days of research in this field. This has come about largely through the efforts of the women's movement and the gay liberation movement beginning in the 1970s. However, research has also had a part to play. There will always be those who believe that it is morally wrong for lesbian or gay parents to raise children whatever the outcome for the child – and we have seen a concerted attempt to undermine the research findings in this area as a strategy to bolster this position. However, for others, whose objection was based on the belief that children would be psychologically harmed by such an upbringing, the empirical evidence to the contrary has brought about a change of mind.

Historically, research on families led by same-sex parents has tended to compare these families with families headed by heterosexual parents. This was because of the need to obtain empirical data that addressed the questions raised by lawyers and by social policy makers who were making decisions about whether or not non-heterosexual couples or individuals could parent children. In recent years, however, the focus has changed. A growing number of studies are looking at diversity in families with same-sex parents and at the processes through which different approaches to parenting influence child outcomes. And commentators such as Judith Stacey and Timothy Biblarz have urged researchers to highlight rather than downplay differences between families with same-sex and opposite-sex parents (Stacey and Biblarz, 2001). The question originally posed in the 1970s, 'Are children who grow up in lesbian families more at risk for psychological problems than other children?', has been answered; having a lesbian mother does not, in itself, affect children's psychological adjustment. Nevertheless, different family experiences have different implications for children's lives. It is new questions such as 'What are the consequences of different routes to same-sex parenthood?' and 'How do the perceptions of members of the wider community impact on gay and lesbian family life?' that the new wave of research in this area is setting out to explore.

REFERENCES

Barrett, H and Tasker, F 'Growing up with a gay parent: Views of 101 gay fathers and their sons' and daughters' experiences' (2001) 18 Educational and Child Psychology 62–77

Bos, H *Parenting in planned lesbian families* (Amsterdam: Vossiuspers UvA, 2004)

Bozett, F 'Children of gay fathers' in F W Bozett (ed), *Gay and lesbian parents* (New York: Praeger, 1987)

Brewaeys, A, Ponjaert, I, Van Hall, E and Golombok, S 'Donor Insemination: Child development and family functioning in lesbian-mother families with 4–8 year old children' (1997) 12(6) Human Reproduction 1349–1359

Chan, R W, Raboy, B and Patterson, C 'Psychosocial adjustment among children conceived via donor insemination by lesbian and heterosexual mothers' (1998) 69 (2) Child Development 443–457

Flaks, D K, Ficher, I, Masterpasqua, F and Joseph, G 'Lesbians choosing motherhood: A comparative study of lesbian and heterosexual parents and their children' (1995) 31(1) Developmental Psychology 105–114

Gartrell, N, Banks, A, Reed, N, Hamilton, J, Rodas, C and Deck, A 'The national lesbian family study: 2. Interviews with mothers of toddlers' (1999) 69 American Journal of Orthopsychiatry 362–369

Gartrell, N, Banks, A, Reed, N, Hamilton, J, Rodas, C and Deck, A 'The national lesbian family study: 3. Interviews with mothers of five year olds' (2000) 70 American Journal of Orthopsychiatry 542–548

Gartrell, N, Deck, A, Rodas, C, Peyser, H and Banks, A 'The national lesbian family study: 4. Interviews with the 10-year-old year children' (2005) 75 American Journal of Orthopsychiatry 518–524

Golombok, S, Spencer, A and Rutter, M 'Children in lesbian and single-parent households: Psychosexual and psychiatric appraisal' (1983) 24 Journal of Child Psychology and Psychiatry 551–572

Golombok, S and Tasker, F 'Do parents influence the sexual orientation of their children? Findings from a longitudinal study of lesbian families' (1996) 32(1) Developmental Psychology 3–11

Golombok, S, Tasker, F and Murray, C 'Children raised in fatherless families from infancy: Family relationships and the socioemotional development of children of lesbian and single heterosexual mothers' (1997) 38(7) Journal of Child Psychology and Psychiatry 783–792

Golombok, S, Perry, B, Burston, A, Murray, C, Mooney-Somers, J, Stevens, M, Golding, J and the ALSPAC Team 'Children with lesbian parents: A community study' (2003) 39 Developmental Psychology 20–33

Green, R, Mandel, J B, Hotvedt, M E, Gray, J and Smith, L 'Lesbian mothers and their children: A comparison with solo parent heterosexual mothers and their children' (1986) 15 (2) Archives of Sexual Behavior 167–184

Harris, M and Turner, P 'Gay and lesbian parents' (1986) 12 Journal of Homosexuality 101–113

Kirkpatrick, M , MacCallum, F and Golombok, S 'Children raised in fatherless families from infancy: a follow-up of children of lesbian and single heterosexual mothers' (2004) 45 Journal of Child Psychology and Psychiatry 1407–1419

Miller, B 'Gay fathers and their children' (1979) 28 Family Coordinator 544–552

Patterson, C J 'Children of lesbian and gay parents' (1992) 63 Child Development 1025–1042

Stacey, J and Biblarz, T '(How) does the sexual orientation of parents matter?' (2001) 66 American Sociological Review 159–183

Tasker, F, and Golombok, S 'Adults raised as children in lesbian families' (1995) 65 (2) American Journal of Orthopsychiatry 203–215

Tasker, F and Golombok, S *Growing up in a Lesbian Family* (New York: Guildford Press, 1997)

Wainright, J, Russell, S and Patterson, C 'Psychosocial adjustment, school outcomes and romantic relationships of adolescents with same-sex parents' (2004) 75 Child Development 1886–1898

MEETING THE NEEDS OF MIXED HERITAGE CHILDREN

A Focus on the Specific Needs of Black Children of Dual Heritage

Julia Isikwe Hughes

Independent Social Worker, Trainer and Children's Guardian

SUMMARY OF PAPER

Julia Isikwe Hughes introduced her paper by emphasising that racism affects different minority groups in different ways. Her paper considers the experience of black children of dual heritage. The aim of the paper was to ensure a greater understanding and awareness of these children's needs by considering their experiences of living in Britain and society's often hostile perception of them.

The paper covers four specific areas:

- *The Children Looked After Statistics*

- *Terminology*

- *Group Belonging – White, Black or Other?*

- *Identity Issues*

In relation to the topic of terminology, there is wide-ranging debate on the appropriate terms to be used to describe black children of dual heritage. Julia Isikwe Hughes sought to provide examples of these terms and argued why 'Black of dual heritage' was the most appropriate term. In relation to the issue of 'group belonging', Julia Isikwe Hughes argued that the widely used term 'mixed' has neither cultural, geographic, linguistic nor political meaning and therefore could not be relevant to this group of children. She sought to explore this issue further by considering definitions of the terms used by reference to the following definitions of the term 'black':

> *'Black is more a state of mind than an expression of origin.' (Biko, South African Civil Rights Activist, 1984)*

> *'Black is a political definition which is open and inclusive and takes into account the common experiences of slavery, colonisation and contemporary European racism of the large and heterogenous Black population which has lived in Britain over 400 years and was recently supplemented by the post war economic migrants from the Caribbean, Africa and parts of the Indian Subcontinent. At the same time it recognises differences of language, religion, ethnicity and culture within this black population.' (Paul Gilroy, Black British sociologist, 1993)*

Julia Isikwe Hughes argued that to deny these children the definition of 'black' would deny their real and painful experiences of racism about which they have no choice. The factors that these children have in common include:

- *they are the direct offspring of a black/white relationship;*

- *they share the experience of racism on the basis of their skin colour;*

- *they share the experience of hostility towards their parentage.*

In most of these respects their experiences are likely to be separate and distinct from other minority groups.

What black children of dual heritage do not generally have in common are:

- *the languages they speak;*

- *ethnicities;*

- *religions; and*

- *their distinct cultures.*

These aspects of communality are likely to be diverse and are more likely to be shared with groups other than within the 'mixed' group.

Julia Isikwe Hughes considered that the use of the term 'mixed' to describe these children ignores the distinction between race and ethnicity. She referred to the following definition of 'ethnicity':

> *'A term which may be confused with "race", but which **refers to a shared cultural identity that has a range of distinctive behavioural and possibly linguistic features, passed on through socialisation from generation to another**. There are never clear boundaries, cultural or geographic that mark the limits of ethnic groups even though many regard ethnicity as though it were naturally determined.' (Crystal Reference Encyclopaedia (**emphasis added**))*

Having considered these definitions, Julia Isikwe Hughes posed the rhetorical question: how can the term 'mixed' be a definition of an ethnicity? Also, since the term 'black' is an open and inclusive concept, black children of dual heritage fit well within this and should therefore be defined as such because of their experiences of racism.

Julia Isikwe Hughes highlighted the important components necessary for development of identity which are explored in more depth in her paper. These components are political, cultural and personal identity. The dual heritage child needs to develop the skills to defend and protect him or herself from psychological racist insults; to develop a healthy sense of belonging and social exchange.

She concluded by referring to the poem from 'Spider Woman' by Nadra Quideer which appears at the beginning of her paper. This poem reflects upon the difficulties that society appears to have in accepting and defining black children of dual heritage.

THE PAPER

I am the mystery that nobody touches

mimicking the colours of the spider;

Brown, white blends

One leg on land the other dangling ...

I am the fascination in the cage ...

(Nadra Quideer 'Spider Woman' in Camper (ed) (1994))

Racism affects different individual minority ethnic groups in Britain in different ways (Gilroy, 1993: 55). It is important to recognise that each group has very separate and distinct needs, since this ensures a greater understanding of each group and of each group's needs and experiences. This paper aims to raise awareness and understanding of black children of dual heritage and sets out to consider society's perception of black children of dual heritage and their experience of living in Britain. The debate will focus on four specific areas: the terminology used to describe this group of children; the issue of group belonging, the identity debate relating to black children of dual heritage; and the specific ingredients that black children of dual heritage require for the development of a healthy identity.

Most findings confirm that black children are disproportionately over represented in care. The most recent figures demonstrate that children of 'mixed, Asian and Black British ethnicity' make up 19% of children looked after; 8% of which are children of 'mixed ethnicity' (DfES National Statistics, 2006). The total ethnic minority population in Britain is 7.9% of which 1.2% are from 'mixed' backgrounds (National Statistics, 2001). The rate of admission among 'mixed parentage' children is therefore particularly alarming (see Table 1 below). Other research has shown that children of mixed race are eight times more likely to be received into care than any other children and that their age at entry into care is younger (Batta and Mawby, 1981).

Table 1 'children looked after by local authorities'

Black Children in Care

Ethnicity	In Care (%)	In Population (%)
White	81	92.1
Mixed	6	1.2
Asian	2	4
Black	6	2
Other	5	0.7

Source: National population statistics census 2001 (DfES, 2006)

Poverty and institutional racism are to some extent likely to account for the over representation of these children in the care system as it does for all black children in care, however it is also suggested that the high representation of black children of dual heritage in care may be as a result of a lack of family and community support for 'mixed families'. This is supported by Katz who found that single white mothers of 'mixed race sons in the face of experiencing serious parenting difficulties are more likely than other groups to turn to social work agencies for support' (1996). Barn found that the majority of black children in care were from 'single mother headed families' (1993) and that the majority of black children of dual heritage in care were from one particular type of liaison: they had an African-Caribbean father and a white indigenous mother.

The terminology used to define people who have one white and one black parent is variable and wide ranging, from overtly racist to the most 'politically correct' and includes terms such as 'half caste', 'half breed', 'mulatto', 'mixed race', 'mixed parentage', 'mixed origin', 'mixed ethnicity', 'dual heritage' and 'dual descent'. Some of these terms are applied without any understanding of their meaning or offensiveness. Each is a description of the offspring of a black/white parental relationship and none give any indication as to the specific culture or ethnicity of the individual. It is important to recognise the negative connotations of each of these terms and the effect they can have on societal perceptions of this group of children, as well as on the child's individual self perception. The difficulty in defining this group of children reflects the ambiguous position of such families in our society.

The term, 'black of dual heritage' is preferred to describe blacks who are direct offspring of a black/white relationship – this being one of the more positive and least derogatory terms for this social category.

A debate rages among academics and within society about whether children of dual heritage can legitimately define themselves as 'black'; the argument against defining them as 'black' considers that they are not always accepted as such by the black community, and by defining themselves as 'black' (Goodyer, in Okitikpi (ed) 2005: 86) they are ignoring the 'white' aspects of their heritage. It is therefore concluded that to use the term 'black' to define this group of children is likely to cause alienation and identity confusion. Alternative terms such as 'mixed' is suggested and a proposal is made in favour of 'the development of a mixed race culture that is separate from both black and white and has its own identity. If this happens, mixed race will be positively identified as "mixed" and may eventually become a recognisable group' (Katz and Treacher in Okitikpi (ed) 2005: 58). Goodyer (in Okitikpi, 2005: 86) supports this argument and suggests that these children are capable of adopting identities other than a black identity and that they are capable of having 'flexible identities which can adjust to varying social contexts'. Owusu-Bempah (in Okitikpi, 2005: 38) similarly suggests that they have a 'legitimate claim to both groups' and is critical of attempts to 'impose upon them the culture or membership of the group which we perceive to be inferior'. Further, it is suggested that these children are able choose their group membership and opt in and out of groups.

These arguments assume that the 'black community' in Britain is homogenous and a single cohesive group, when it in fact encompasses a variety of cultures, nations, religions, histories, languages, traditions and nationalities which has lived in Britain for over 400 years and has recently been supplemented by the post-war economic migrants from the Caribbean, Africa and parts of the Indian subcontinent.

The suggestion is made that an alternative identity of 'mixed' (a term, which has neither cultural, geographic, linguistic nor political meaning) might be more applicable to these children than the term 'black'. This suggestion demonstrates confusion between the terms 'ethnicity' and 'race'. 'Race' and 'ethnicity' are not interchangeable terms although are often used interchangeably. By suggesting that the term 'black' is not applicable to black children of dual heritage the arguments ignore the fact that the term 'black' is a political definition which is open and inclusive and essentially reflects a person's experience of racism. As Kirton (2000: 72) argues, not only are these children 'seen as "black" in terms of their social identification, but they are just as likely to be victims of racism as other black children'. Banks reminds us that most African-Americans and black people who have a common history of being taken from Africa as slaves will have the undeniable historical fact of having enforced mixing as part of their heritage (1992a). To deny these children the political definition of 'black' would deny their real and painful experiences of racism about which they have no choice.

The suggestion that children of dual heritage have flexible and changeable identities demonstrates a limited understanding of the components required in the formation of a healthy identity.

Black children of dual heritage directly challenge one of the tenets of racism, which is the maintenance of the superiority and purity of the 'white race' since such children are born of unions between black and white people and they are therefore often met with hostility and disapproval and are considered to be a threat to the rigidly imposed categories of an untenable classification – that of race (Banks, 1992a: 37).

The impact of such attitudes towards black children of dual heritage has in the past resulted in enforced sterilisation programmes (in 1939 in Germany) of black children of dual heritage, who were considered to have been conceived either by force or whose mothers were deemed to be prostitutes. Research was undertaken at the time to attempt to establish that these children suffered from early psychosis and were labelled as 'biologically inferior' and 'socially maladjusted' (Opitz, 1992).

Okitikpi points out that 'pathological assumptions' are deduced as to the adults' motivation for entering into such relationships, which appear to be specific to this specific liaison and 'include sexual curiosity and self hatred as well as a shortage of same race partners' (2005: 3).

Benson (1981:72) found frequent hostility and rejection from relatives of black/white relationships. Banks (1992b) considered that this hostility often leads to involuntary isolation and particularly impacts on single parents.

The attitude of the white carer towards the child is significant. Banks found that where the black parent is absent, it is likely to create significantly more confusion and trauma than for a child who has at least one black parent. Banks also talks of the damage that a white parent can involuntarily cause to their child through their anger and resentment and can result in an 'unrecognised and unconsidered form of child abuse – that of "in house" or "familial racism"' (1992b). In my experience the single white mother of a black child of dual heritage is also more likely than a black mother to lack an understanding of racism and how this impacts upon her child's sense of self and is less likely to understand her child's need to develop a positive black identity. She is more likely to fear that in positively promoting the child's black identity that the child might become emotionally alienated from her.

A frequently made assumption – which appears to be a development of the confusion between race and culture (detailed above) – is that by dint of their backgrounds black children of dual heritage are likely to automatically experience confusion and difficulties about their sense of identity since they do not have a clear idea of whether they are 'black' or 'white' and that they are therefore incapable of developing a self concept and identity that is integrative. Such gross generalisations are in my experience very commonly held both by social work professionals and academics (Okitikpi, 2005: 73; Wilson, 1987: 1; Tizzard and Phoenix, 1993: 1).

Banks asserts that there is not enough evidence to suggest that being of dual heritage is a distinct psychological disadvantage compared to black children who are not directly mixed (1992a). Where a child's very existence is viewed with such hostility on a personal and societal level it is likely to have a significant negative impact on the individual's sense of self. Particularly when one considers Jung's definition of identity or 'persona' which forms from early childhood out of 'a need to conform to the wishes and expectations of parents, peers and teachers, children quickly learn that certain attitudes and behaviours are acceptable and may be rewarded with approval while others are unacceptable and may result in punishment or the withdrawal of love. The tendency is to build acceptable traits to the persona and to keep unacceptable traits hidden or repressed' (Stevens, 1994: 63). The psychological consequences of direct, indirect or institutional racism and oppression are likely to affect the self esteem of all individuals who are subjected to these negative stereotypes. Hooks supports this view: 'For black people, the pain of learning that we can not control our images, how we see ourselves (if our vision is not decolonised) or how we are seen is so intense that it rends us. It rips and tears at the seams of our efforts to construct self and identify' (1992: 3).

Banks suggests that some children in some groups may have a greater need for additional help to counter the negative images that they might encounter (Dwivedi, 2002: 157). It is essential that any direct work is also undertaken by workers who have a sound understanding of the impact of racism on the individual. It is also important that work is also undertaken with single white parents of black children who come into contact with social services to enable them to cope with the pressures and stresses of the impact of racism and to enable them to gain a better understanding of their children's emotional needs.

The development of a positive identity is a complex process for all children. Each child's process is likely to be complicated depending on the child's developmental experience, sexuality, ethnicity and class and the need to belong resides at the heart of the very existence of all human beings. The development of a healthy identity for a black child of dual heritage is a particularly complex process, which is ongoing throughout the child's lifespan. Because of the child's dual heritage its task is to integrate several complex dynamics into its identity; which include languages, religions, race, sexuality, culture and ethnicity. The child needs to develop the skills to defend and protect itself from psychological racist insults; to develop a healthy sense of belonging and social exchange; to develop an understanding of its diverse ethnicities which should include aspects of music, art, literature, political and cultural value systems; as well as a knowledge and understanding of its languages and religions. This will enable the child to develop an integrated identity based on three specific aspects: a *political* understanding of its identity (ie blackness), which should include an understanding of how racism operates and how it impacts upon their sense of self; a *cultural identity* which should be dynamic and fluid where the child can embrace or reject aspects of each of its cultures depending on the child's own values, interests and beliefs, and a *personal identity* – an individual and real sense of self with which the child is confident and content. A solid foundation encompassing all these aspects will enable the child to function effectively and confidently in society.

The over representation of black children of dual heritage in care indicates that they are among the most disadvantaged children in society today; what they have in common as a group is the fact that they are the direct offspring of a black/white relationships, their shared experience of racism on the basis of their skin colour and their shared experience of hostility towards their parentage. In most of these respects their experiences are likely to be separate and distinct from other minority groups. However, the languages spoken within this group, their ethnicities, religions and cultures are likely to be very diverse and they are more likely to share these aspects of communality with groups other than their own, be they minority or indigenous.

In understanding the needs of black children of dual heritage it is important to question the widely held and damaging assumptions made about them and the often meaningless categorisations that they are often placed into. In particular it is essential not to remove this group's experiences from the common experience of black people living in a racist society; since to do so would deny them an integral part of their identity and would ignore their very real experience.

BIBLIOGRAPHY

Batta, I and Mawby, R 'Children in Local Authority Care: A monitoring of racial difference in Bradford' (1991) 9 (2) *Police and Politics* 137–149

Banks, N 'Some considerations of "racial" identification and self esteem when working with mixed ethnicity children and their mothers as social services clients' (1992a) 3 *Social Services Research*

Banks, N 'Mixed up Kid' (1992b) 24 *Social work today*, 10 September

Barn, R *Black Children in the Public Care System* (Batsford, London, 1993)

Camper, C (ed) *Miscegenation Blues, Voices of Mixed Race Women* (Sister vision, Toronto, 1994)

DfEs, 'Children Looked after By Local Authorities' (National statistics, 2006)

Dwivedi, K N (ed) *Meeting the needs of Ethnic Minority Children, A Handbook for Professionals* (Jessica Kingsley, London, 2002)

Gilroy, P *Small Acts, thoughts on the politics of black cultures* (Serpents Tail, London, 1993)

Hooks, B *Black looks, race and representation* (London, Turnaround, 1992)

Katz, I *The Construction of Racial Identity of Children of Mixed Parentage* (Jessica Kingsley, London, 1996)

Kirton, D *'Race', Ethnicity and Adoption* (Open University Press, Buckingham, 2000)

Office for National Statistics, Census April 2001

Okitikpi, T (ed) *Working with Children of Mixed Parentage* (Russell House Publishing, Dorset, 2005)

Opitz, M, Ogutoye, K, Schoulz D *Showing our colours/ Afro German women speak out* (London, Open Letters, 1992)

Tizzard, B & Phoenix, A *Black, White or Mixed Race* (London, Routledge, 1993)

Wilson, A *Mixed Race Children: A study of identity* (London, Allen and Unwin, 1987)

Post Colonial Attitudes and their Damaging Legacy for Children of Dual Heritage in the United Kingdom

Lennox K Thomas

Consultant Psychotherapist, Refugee Therapy Centre

SUMMARY

Lennox Thomas introduced his paper by explaining that although 'damage' appears in the title of the paper, damage is not part of the legacy of mixed heritage.

Most people from the Caribbean and Latin America are 'mixed'. Many people from those parts of the world see being 'mixed' as desirable and not a source of shame. People from former colonies are accustomed to being 'mixed'. However, there is real contrast in attitudes when dealing with issues of prejudice and shame.

From the 1940s onwards the idea of being 'mixed' was a new concept and since that time we have been catching up; in the colonies they have been used to this concept for around 300 years.

Lennox Thomas noted that there remains confusion among professionals about purity and black and white thinking. Professionals often worry when faced with the task of meeting the best interests of children with mixed backgrounds. He recalled the story of two blond girls of mixed generation heritage. The black professionals said that the girls needed to be in a black or mixed placement as this would give them important interpersonal skills in terms of their background. However, these were white children who had been with foster carers for 9 months and to whom they were attached. It was agreed, in that case, that what was most important was a good attached relationship as the children did not know that they had black ancestry. They, therefore, remained where they were. It was important, however, that the children learned about their history.

Lennox Thomas was of the view that one issue needs particular emphasis: family development of the dual heritage of children. This issue is often dealt with in the context of issues relating to residence or contact where parents become so entrenched that it is difficult to comprehend how they saw each other for who they were at the initial stages of their relationship. Backgrounds and ethnicity often provide the scope for increased tension in such cases. It was emphasised, however, that mixed relationships also work. Such relationships can frequently be unproblematic. We have to stop thinking about children of mixed heritage as problematic. The problem is with us in society and with racism.

With the knowledge that mixed relationships do work and that the children of these relationships can experience healthy development, we cannot always blame difference in skin colour when they do not work. Two individuals will possess different pathologies and social values and lack of support for mixed relationships makes it more difficult to fare and prosper.

It appeared to Lennox Thomas that the Conference was about giving thought to diversity and the degree to which old attitudes affect professional judgement. What must be taken from the Conference is that nothing will change until we confront the issues. In this respect, Lennox Thomas was thinking about racism and its after-effects in terms of inherited attitudes and values about mixed heritage children.

Attitudes, in this context, come down on the heads of children. Attitudes like 'black and whites should not mix' and 'mixed relationships do not work' are confounded by the experience over centuries in the colonies. Most of the black people in the audience would be mixed. Attitudes such as 'the white gene pool must be protected' and 'children will suffer and be confused' are not borne out. Intrinsically, being of mixed heritage does not produce confusion; the attitudes around us cause confusion.

Lennox Thomas concluded his introduction to his paper by considering the issues raised by Julia Isikwe Hughes in her paper. He noted that there was diversity of thinking on these issues between himself and Julia Hughes and that, generally, conformity between people will not be found when discussing these issues. Lennox Thomas considered that children of mixed parentage are black but they are, first, children of mixed heritage. He queried why such children cannot choose to be white. Is the 'white club' so exclusive that it cannot be adulterated by anything that is not white?

THE PAPER

We have names, codes and categories for each other in society and the names keep changing depending on the political climate. Unpleasant as it is to remember, the names have been half-breed, half-caste and Mulatto, Europeans being the horse part and Africans the donkey. So, using that as a standard, we have come a very long way with the names, but what about the attitudes?

Many battles are fought around the ideology values and politics of 'race', a pseudo-biological concept. Some of this has its history in the fact of the enslavement and colonisation of one half of the heritage. Being mixed in the UK is viewed very differently as compared with the Caribbean and South America. Crossing the so-called boundary has always been the illicit privilege of white men and slave owners, with African Caribbean women as their property, so the product of such a union was not regarded as noble. In more recent years since the abandonment of the plantations, the creolised children that they left behind have taken on the leadership roles left by the Whites and tend not to be referred to as mixed parentage or dual heritage. These titles have currency in the UK but not in the Caribbean. While celebrating the European part of their ancestry they see themselves as people of the Caribbean region. People of mixed backgrounds in the Caribbean have come to realise that what is not White in Europe is seen as Black.

In her short stories Jean Rhys (1934), the Caribbean born writer, talks of her shock of being regarded as inferior while a student at RADA on arriving from the Caribbean in the early 1920s. She was born of a Welsh physician father and a Creole mother on the island of Dominica. In 1966, she published *Wide Sargasso Sea* a novel about the Creole wife of Mr Rochester in Charlotte Bronte's novel Jane Eyre. Antoinette Cosway-Rochester had a complex childhood in Jamaica, shunned by the Whites for not being white enough, and despised by the Blacks for not being White enough to be respected as a *real* White. Europeaness and Englishness is so privileged that 'adulteration' of Englishness and whiteness is jealously guarded and disdain is reserved for transgressors. In the 1950s nothing was more to the fore than the marriage of Seretse Khama, a Southern African nobleman, and Ruth, an upper middle class Englishwoman. Defilement and purity was a preoccupation in the UK with the question at the time, 'Would you let your daughter marry one?' (a Black man). In more recent years it has not been uncommon for parents of adult children contemplating a mixed marriage to be told to think carefully, if not for yourselves, for your children. Not understanding or not wanting to be part of a mixed extended family, an appeal is made for children of the union as if they would suffer because of the mix.

There is still confusion around purity, and Black and White thinking. Warring professionals consulted me 10 years ago over two little blond sisters who were placed with white foster parents 9 months earlier. On discovering that the children had one Black grandparent the placement was being reconsidered. One faction held the view that the girls needed to have a placement that would be able to help them with their mixed ethnic background making their white rural foster parents unsuitable, the other holding to the view that they were now settled after some 9 months and that their growing attachment was more important for their healthy development at this stage.

FAMILY AND SOCIAL DEVELOPMENT OF THE DUAL HERITAGE CHILD

Given that the state of being born of two or more ethnic or 'racial' heritage is unproblematic in a stable loving family and extended network, it is clear that problems become apparent in some homes when the love relationship begins to fall apart. Some couples who had previously adopted the colour-blind approach, or the 'love will conquer all' view of the world, can disintegrate into ugly war which serve to undermine the confidence of their young children. This is of course true of many couples regardless of ethnicity but in the case of mixed couples the break-up of the relationship or marriage can be shot through with racial slurs or implied racial hatred sometimes understood by the child as the White parent now hating the part of them that is Black and the Black parent hating the part of them that is White. These issues loom large when the issue of residence and contact are being discussed. Frantz Fanon, a French Caribbean Psychiatrist in his (1952) book *Black Skin White Mask*, is pessimistic about Black White mixed relationships. He sees these relationships as doomed to failure because it becomes a theatre for the working out of racial war, sexual mystique, the negotiation of position in the relationship or atonement. Whilst individuals might have these difficulties that are worked out in mixed relationships Fanon's view has to be seen against the background of post-war colonial struggles for independence from France.

Mixed relationships work and their children achieve healthy development. As professionals we tend to witness the horror of the ones that do not work and where finding remedies in law are complex. When such relationships do not work out, the failure cannot be blamed on the fact that the couple were from different ethnicities or had different skin colour, their personal pathology would have played a large part. Often what happens in families has to be set against the backdrop of societal racism and prejudice. Statistics from 10 years ago showed that 40% of Black men and 30% of Black women married out of their ethnic group. Given that Black, White, Asian and other children attend nursery, school and university together it should be of no surprise to anyone that some would develop romantic attachments. Successful family life is the best preparation for good development particularly for children of mixed parentage. Because these families are not positively reflected in society parents might need to pay attention to the strengths of having two or more cultures, folklore, literature, etc. Living in a dominant European culture can sometimes render the 'non-European' culture as secondary and not an equal part of the child's development. Similarly, children need to learn not to disregard the Black or dark skin parent thereby enacting what takes place all around them in society at large. Like Black children those of mixed parentage need to know about valuing people not by skin tone or shade. Not understanding this can lead to problems of self worth seeing their darker skin as a mark of their inferiority in relation to others with light skin shades and European features. There will be increasing numbers of children of mixed heritage in the UK and hopefully their existence will not be seen as problematic. In a race-sensitive society racial skirmishes are played out around children of mixed parentage.

Even when the parental relationships are good, children and young people are able to pick up the prejudices in society at large. While there has been a marked decrease in societal prejudice in recent years racism is still alive and kicking. This can be absorbed subliminally as well as the full impact of direct racist acts. Being of mixed heritage is no protection from prejudice, which comes from Black people as well as Whites. The history of Black prejudice has its roots on the plantation where the master's children were spared the brutal reality of slavery even in families where this child has siblings born of Black fathers. The Black children did not have these favours, and to make matters worse these mixed children were used as spies to inform of disquiet plots or rebellion. This was a divide and rule tactic advocated by Willy Lynch in his 17th-Century paper 'How to create a Slave'. Historically, the Blacks learnt to mistrust those of mixed parentage even when their cause was helped by mixed people and other Blacks like themselves had from time to time also betrayed them. The envy of a lighter skin shade and the privileges that this has historically afforded has always been a source of tension between Black people and those of mixed parentage. Proving one's loyalty and presenting credentials has always been the burden of the mixed person before being able to join the Black group. I have often wondered what happens to gain entry to the White group, is there more subtlety? Does the person of dual heritage enter into a tacit agreement with the White group that they are not 'quite the ticket', thereby accepting a reduced position in relation to whiteness?

THERAPEUTIC WORK WITH YOUNG PEOPLE OF MIXED HERITAGE

In the mid 1990s myself and a White female colleague decided to run a one-year group in response to the referrals and self referrals we received in our organisation of people who wanted to explore the issues that being of mixed parentage had presented for them. The organisation provided a specialist service to people from Black and minority ethnic groups. Therapy was available in 20 languages excluding English and British Sign Language. Most of the group members were in their early to mid 20s and were on the whole successful in their choice of career. Of the eight, one was unemployed, three were students in higher education, two were office workers, one a teacher and one on long-term sick from a good civil service job. There were three men and five women. Most of them had experienced depression or anxiety and one was diagnosed with bi-polar disorder. The teacher was born of a West African mother, the others having White mothers. All group members were raised by both, or one parent, other people referred who were raised in care or by foster or adopted parents were referred to individual therapists. We felt that their issues might be beyond the scope of a one-year, once a week group.

Apart from work by Tizard and Phoenix (1993) and Barn (1993) and Nick Banks, there is not a great deal written about people of mixed parentage. Due to the complex relationships that exist in society, counselling and therapy could present some pitfalls. There is often a risk of wrong footedness on the part of the Black or White counsellor or therapist. Apart from the presentation of a specific problem, eg depression, loss, relationship break-up, the therapist might not fully understand the particular issues and concerns that the client might bring from their history and their perspective of being raised in a mixed family. Most therapies tend to play it safe and adopt a colour-blind approach in order to cause or give little offence. In doing so, playing safe, a valuable opportunity for the individual to appraise their life experiences might be at best limited or worse lost. Many of the group members were happy to be in a group with each other and felt that they would be able to have some good discussions, having more in common with each other than with any other group they had been in before. One member was highly suspicious that the therapists were a White woman and a Black man and thought that there might be some 'grand Freudian theory behind it'. After a few weeks the group settled down and were able to share stories of their childhood. Many talked about being out shopping with their mothers and being stared at, their mother being insulted, or being told how wonderful she was for adopting a 'little darkie'.

These recollections evoked laughter, anger and tears; later opening the floodgates of childhood despair of families that appeared to have been standing against a rejecting world and a barrage of insults and censure. The teacher said that his White father holding his hand in the streets would attract inquisitive looks from those unsure that the White man could be his dad. Black husbands and fathers were more visible with White partners and mixed parentage children. For this they parried many threats and insults during a time in our society when right-wing fascist groups were on the rise. Many of the young people felt that their parent's marriages were under unfair pressure from the start having few, or no, Black relatives and many White families who broke off contact after the marriage or their parents living together. A couple of members admitted to feeling resentful at having a Black father feeling that life would be so much easier if their fathers had been white. Opposite views were expressed by some people who felt a particular closeness with their fathers feeling that he had a tough time of it most of the time.

The group was valued as a safe space to talk about difficult issues. They said that most of all it was good to meet other people of mixed heritage. One of the young women said that during her childhood she was glued to the television when the singer Shirley Bassey was on because she was so *real*, because the client always felt so invisible.

To conclude, social attitudes have had a detrimental effect on the lives of a couple of generations of children and young people of dual heritage. We need to ask ourselves if we as a society are different now and what precisely that difference is. Might we, for example, talk about White children of dual heritage? Or are they always first of all Black?

REFERENCES

Barn, R *Black Children in the Public Care System* (Batsford, London 1993)

Fanon, F *Black Skin White Mask* (Grove Press, New York, 1952)

Lynch, W 'How to Create a Slave' (Internet article)

Rhys, J (1934) *Voyage in the Dark* (W W Norton, 1982)

Rhys, J *Wide Sargasso Sea* (Andre Deutshe, 1966)

Thomas, L K 'The Psycho-historical relationship between people of mixed heritage and Diaspora Africans' in B Hawkes (ed), *Attachment perspectives on mixed parentage* (Separation and Reunion Forum/ London Metropolitan University, 2005)

Tizard, B & Phoenix, A *Black White or Mixed Race* (Routledge, London, 1993)

TRANS-GENERATIONAL AND CULTURAL CLASHES

Consideration of Race, Culture and Religion in Family Proceedings

Nadira Huda

Child Protection Coordinator, London Borough of Tower Hamlets

I work as a Child Protection Co-ordinator for the London Borough of Tower Hamlets. I have also provided expert advice for courts on cultural and religious matters impacting upon Muslim families.

The following is an account of some of the issues which affect Muslim families as they become involved in the court process through Care Proceedings based on my experiences. It also includes a recommendation on the way forward for courts.

Tower Hamlets has the highest concentration of Bangladeshis (33.4%, Census 2001) and Muslims (36.4%, Census 2001) in the UK. I will draw upon my experiences of working with this community to highlight some of the general issues which impact upon Muslim families who are drawn into court proceedings.

Tower Hamlets is in the East End of London and has historically been host to a number of immigrant communities, the most recent being the Bangladeshis, who are, in the main, Muslims from the district of Sylhet in the north east of Bangladesh.

Levels of deprivation in Tower Hamlets are among the highest in the Country.

- Unemployment is high – 31% among the Bangladeshi community.

- In 2001, 33.8% of households within the Borough had one or more persons with a limiting long-term illness. The national medium is 32.65%.

- During the first 6 months of 2006–07, 2,600 incidents of domestic violence were recorded in the Borough by the main reporting agencies. It is estimated that approximately half of the domestic violence service users have children living with them.

- Tower Hamlets has over 1,000 problematic drug users and over 1,000 children affected by parental substance misuse.

- There are at any one time, at least 465 children living in Tower Hamlets in families where there is 'severe and enduring' parental mental illness.

- Within Children's Social Care there are 1,580 children in need, including 351 children in public care. In July 2007 there were 219 children on the child protection register – 28% of parents of children on the child protection register had a history of domestic violence.

It is against this background that Bangladeshi families are raising their children. On the whole many families are succeeding; in fact until recently Tower Hamlets had one of the lowest numbers of children on the child protection register in London which seems incredible given the levels of deprivation in the Borough.

The first generation of Bangladeshis who came to the UK did so to work, save money and then return permanently back to their own country. They did not see a future in this country, so did not plan for their long-term futures in the UK, in terms of learning the language or becoming more integrated into British Society. However, this idea of returning to the homeland was termed the 'myth of return' (Muhammed Anwar, 1979) as most of the men settled down to life in the UK and started to bring their families over in the late 1970s and early 1980s.

I have worked in Tower Hamlets since the 1980s, initially as a community worker and then as a social worker. I have observed that over the years Bangladeshi families are increasingly coming to the attention of children's social care and some are inevitably entering into the court arena because care proceedings have been initiated by the local authority.

Some reasons for this could be that:

- in Tower Hamlets the majority of school-age children are Bangladeshi so statistically this will be reflected in the referrals; 52% of all school age children in Tower Hamlets are Bangladeshi;

- the pressures of living in overcrowded conditions, experiencing high unemployment and lack of opportunities lead to family breakdowns. The majority of domestic violence referrals to Children's Services concern Bangladeshi families. In addition the physical loss of the extended family has lead to more reliance on help from 'outsiders';

- younger Bangladeshis – the 'third generation' are more aware of the society around them, less likely to respect time-honoured concepts such as family honour and therefore more likely to break the code of conduct of 'keeping it in the family' by disclosing abuse. In a discussion with a group of young women, they informed me that their parents' generation focused too much on cultural issues some of which contradicted their Islamic faith and they would not be adhering to these cultural ideas.

So what are the experiences of Muslim families entering the court system?

It has to be said that the idea that the State can intervene in family life is an extremely difficult concept for many families to understand. Many are from countries including Bangladesh where there are no laws or institutions to regulate how a family raises its children. The family in its extended form and the community regulates behaviour and issues sanctions if someone has overstepped the boundaries of acceptable behaviour. Courts are for criminals not for parents who have exercised, for example, *their right* to discipline *their* child. I have worked with parents who have found it almost impossible to come to terms with the fact that the court has the right to remove their children from their care and years after the event cling on to the hope that there will be a reversal in the judgment. So, right from the beginning, the idea that they are perceived as 'criminals' may colour the cooperation of parents during proceedings and put them at a disadvantage.

Attendance at court is linked to the loss of family honour and bringing shame upon the whole family.

Add to this the lack of fluency in the English language and the court process becomes an even more bewildering experience for Bangladeshi families than for their English counterparts. While the legal process has to take its course, I feel that there could be a lot more work carried out by solicitors and the courts in explaining the procedures to the parents, rather than taking it for granted that they will know.

Most Bangladeshi Muslim families have cultural practices and beliefs which are often directly opposed to or alien to that of the host society. Often the Islamic faith is used to justify actions that parents have taken, often mistakenly, for example arguing that Islam sanctions forced marriages when it clearly does not. There are cultural practices such as 'Jadhu' (evil eye) which are brought into the equation when parents are justifying behaviours or actions that they have taken which have been detrimental to the child's welfare.

Ideas such as izzat (honour), and how it can be destroyed by the actions of family members, particularly women are complex and difficult for those outside the communities to grasp fully. Most social workers are obliged to include information on cultural issues in their statements but most only touch on these on a superficial level as there is not the depth of understanding of these issues to make sense of what they mean to the families and the children.

At times there is a reluctance to fully engage in attempting to understand the issues due to the conflicts and demands of timescales that are placed upon local authorities.

A recent case example is of a Local Authority wishing to disclose information about a birth of a child outside marriage, which the mother had managed to conceal from her family, to that very family. The Local Authority wanted to start the process of permanency planning for the child but in doing so would have jeopardised the mother's life and the futures of her female siblings. The issue of 'honour killing' of the mother due to the transgression from cultural and religious taboos had not entered into the equation for the social workers.

Work with families from minority ethnic backgrounds does take longer if one is making a genuine attempt to consider and assess all the religious and cultural options available. This unfortunately does not always sit well with timescales that have been set for Local Authorities and for Courts working under the principle of no delay. However, assessments such as these could be considered under the principle of 'purposeful delay'.

While culture cannot be used as an excuse to abuse a child, what does need to be understood is the cultural context of the child's and the parents' environment. Concepts such as parenting assessments are alien to many parents and they often fail to see how crucial these are in deciding the future of their children. I would argue that many of these assessments are undertaken by professionals who are not 'culturally competent' to do this work and who arrive at conclusions which are not remotely accurate. For example, I came across a case where the mother was judged to be emotionally abusive to her child because she had asked her to call the fire brigade as she, the mother, could not speak English properly. This argument was accepted by the court in granting the ICO without questioning whether the time it took for the mother to explain and be understood by the operator would have caused a major delay and burnt the family home down, thus endangering the lives of all the children.

Courts are regarded as places where people can receive a fair hearing and in giving due consideration to culture and religion, as stated in the Children Act 1989, courts have to take Local Authorities to task and insist on them demonstrating how they have done this when working with minority ethnic families. The use of interpreters is not enough because their role is to interpret what is being said, not to provide explanations, analysis and meanings to what is being observed. There are many cultural nuances that get lost in translation. There are experts in the communities that can be consulted with by those involved in proceedings to assist in the decision-making process. As an example, I am aware that the Imam from the East London Mosque in Tower Hamlets has been asked to provide expert evidence in care proceedings. The point I am making is that expertise does not always lie with psychiatrist and psychologists. Often their reports on minority ethnic parents are woefully lacking in cultural and religious perspectives.

In *Significant harm: child protection litigation in a multi cultural setting*, Dr Julia Brophy, Dr Jagbir Jhutti-Johal and Charles Owen, 2003, examined whether the legal criteria engaged to assess harm and risks to children are sufficiently receptive to different styles and cultural contexts to parenting. They found that:

> '... written information on diversity remains the primary mechanism for conveying these issues to the Court. If issues are not documented and analysed in reports/statements, it will generally be assumed by the Court that they have no relevance.'

In the research conducted by the authors they found that:

> '... there was some reticence at all levels to judges, magistrates and legal advisers raising issues independently of the work of parties. Courts tended to assume that diverse cultural/religious contexts would be addressed if parties or experts thought they were relevant. Thus, the onus is on the author of the report to include or exclude this type of information.'

My view is that the onus must be on the Courts to make inclusion of this information routine practice and where parties feel unable to comment on cultural practices that they do not understand they must seek advice from those that do and incorporate these in their reports.

The authors of the above report suggest that to improve the focus and understanding of cultural diversity in family proceedings and achieving national consistency a directive to address these issues:

> '... would give national coherence to the development of family law policy in this field placing a clear obligation on all parties and courts.'

The authors recommend that an amendment to the welfare checklist under s 1(3)(d) of the Children Act 1989 could achieve this; it could be amended slightly to read:

> 'his age, sex, background, particularly his *racial, religious, cultural and linguistic background* and any other characteristic of his, which the court considers relevant.'

The above research was published in 2003 and 4 years on this recommendation has not been implemented. Certainly this conference could revisit this research and take this recommendation forward. Consideration of diversity issues will then not be for individual parties to consider but an obligation on all parties and the court. Having a good understanding of cultural diversity and applying the analysis of this in assessments is essential if families are to be given a fair hearing in Court.

PLENARY 4

PARENTAL DISABILITIES AND THEIR IMPACT ON CHILDREN

Assessing Parents with Learning Disabilities for Child Care Proceedings

Dr Sally Hodges

Clinical Psychologist, The Tavistock Centre

SUMMARY OF THE PAPER

Dr Sally Hodges introduced her paper by emphasising its focus upon a question which she is frequently asked in care proceedings: whether a parent has a learning disability. The idea, however, of those with learning disabilities being a group which has the same characteristics is problematic.

There are some aspects which are shared between people with learning disabilities, for example their experience of 'special' education or being singled out in mainstream education, a sense of being different and the associated prejudice of having a negative attribute. It can be much easier to think in terms of 'them and us' whereas, in fact, there is a continuum and we all have areas of functioning that are weaker or stronger. Individuals with learning disabilities are also likely to share experience of professional input in that it is common to have had physical health problems. They also often have anxiety and depression as common mental health problems.

Dr Hodges emphasised the importance, in this context, of considering cognitive ability on a continuum. She noted that IQ is problematic as a measure of cognitive ability because ability is not fixed and many factors can have an impact upon it on a daily basis. In particular, amount of sleep, being in pain and mental health issues can affect results. More worryingly, there is a period after giving birth when all mothers' IQ levels or performance on tests is affected as hormones and sleep can affect capacity to function. Dr Hodges cautioned that careful thought must be given to testing after the birth of a child for this reason.

It is important to bear in mind parental and cognitive ability are not mutually dependent; a person can be cognitively able but emotionally detached. The reverse is also true. Cognitive difficulties, depending on where these originated from, are not the same for all parents. These difficulties can impact memory, executive function and learning styles – for example, there may be need for visual or auditory methods. This is a consideration that can be missed out when supporting parents.

Dr Hodges considered the importance of having regard to the origin of the disability. A disability which is primarily organic in origin is more straightforward to assess. However, life-experience related disability requires an account of mental health and personality functioning. The main point is that it is very rare that the focus needs to be on simply a learning disability. There must also be consideration of capacity to use mental health resources.

Dr Hodges concluded by providing some case examples. The first case involved a couple who both had questions surrounding their learning ability. The relevant features of the case were:

- *the mother had an IQ of 60;*

- *she also had mental health issues but these had been addressed;*

- *the father had missed a lot of schooling as he had acted as a carer to his own mother who had health needs;*

- *the wider families supported the couple;*

- *the father had mild depression following his mother's death;*

- *he had an IQ of 78.*

The couple was placed in a post-birth assessment which focused on child protection when the couple had no history of difficulties in this respect. They were provided with no skills training. The guardian in that case expressed concern about the assessment and the parents felt persecuted. They needed an environment for assessment which focused on parents with learning difficulties.

In the second case, the reverse was true. That case involved a single mother with a significant history of severe abuse. She had, herself, been placed in care since the age of 4 years. She was also identified as having a learning disability and because of this was pre-birth assessed with a focus on parenting, not on emotional functioning. At that time she had significant personality and mental health difficulties. Dr Hodges was concerned by the lack of focus on mental health in a case such as this.

THE PAPER

Introduction

As part of my work for the Tavistock clinic in childcare proceedings, I am often asked to undertake assessments to establish whether or not a parent has a learning disability. This is normally linked to a request to comment on the parents' capacity to provide 'good enough' parenting given any learning disabilities they may have. Inevitably, when the assessment starts, I am confronted with a far more complex profile of functioning than simply the presence or absence of a 'learning disability'.

There has been much written about parents with learning disabilities capacity to parent, and there is evidence that a disproportionate number of children of parents with learning disabilities are received into care (Glaun and Brown, 1999). However, this literature tends to make the assumption that having a learning disability is a valid way of categorising parents, and that the presence of a learning disability is the defining factor in parenting difficulties. Obviously there will be many experiences that parents with learning disabilities will have in common as a result of the disability, such as the likelihood of the experience of 'special' education, the experience of health and educational professionals having an input to their lives, the experience of having society push the 'them and us' categorisation, which makes the experience of 'difference' feel less uncomfortable. However, while people diagnosed as having a learning disability will normally have an IQ as less than 69 in common, and some shared experiences as a result, this grouping is in many ways unhelpful. People with learning disabilities may also have had very different experiences, come from a wide range of backgrounds and have very different difficulties, such as physical, emotional and different kinds of cognitive difficulties. The literature on disabilities tends to make the assumption that this is a homogonous grouping, but I would argue that there is a wide spectrum of ability, emotional functioning, and personality functioning within the range of 'learning disability'.

Having a learning disability does not automatically lead to poor parenting abilities, and over the course of the 17 years I have been working in the field of learning disabilities I have worked with many families where either one or both parents have a learning disability but who provide exemplary care to their children, often working against the prejudices and values of others in their system. Having a learning disability is not, in itself, necessarily a precursor to exhibiting difficulties in parenting. However, evidence suggests that, in the absence of adequate support, parents with IQs less than 60 are more likely to have difficulties in parenting (Tymchuck, 1992), and armed with this knowledge, it is appropriate that support mechanisms are mobilised, such as described in the recent DOH paper 'Good practice guidance on working with parents with a learning disability' (2007).

Many families come to my attention through the court system, where one or both parents have a learning disability and there is concern about their capacity to provide 'good enough' parenting. Several authors have written about the bias in the care and court systems against people with learning disabilities, and it continues to be apparent that joined up thinking about people with learning disabilities as parents is not adequate. For example, Green and Vetere (2002) note often within social services departments, child protection specialists work in a different team to long-term needs specialists, with little cross-team thinking. This leads to the 'support' and intervention provided to families in need being inappropriate to their learning styles or needs. The court system is additionally biased against people with disabilities as much of the communication, reports, case conference minutes are written, placing parents with a learning disability at a marked disadvantage. This may create additional stress and anxiety which can feed into poor relationships with professionals.

PSYCHOLOGICAL ASSESSMENT OF LEARNING DISABILITIES

When asked to undertake an assessment of parents in care proceedings, I normally use a standardised cognitive assessment. For this I usually complete a Wechsler Adult Intelligence Scale (WAIS III uk) which has UK norms for comparison. However, in common with most assessment tools that assess a 'normal' distribution, the sensitivity is greatly reduced at the more extreme ends of the scale, both the lower and higher ends. This is of concern for parents with learning disabilities as the difference of two or three points can make the difference between a diagnosis of learning disability or not. Thus, when I make an assessment, I always complete a wider range of psychological assessments, including those that explore personality functioning as well as interviewing the parent about their life experiences and understanding of their situation and their children's needs. I tend to use projective assessments to get another perspective on their personality functioning. Projective assessments consist of ambiguous stimuli, such as pictures, which can stimulate people to project aspects of their current situation, their anxieties and preoccupations, as well as their typical coping strategies and defences. While the projective assessments used are well researched, such as the On-Going Reliability Test (ORT) and the Draw a Person test, and there is clear guidance on interpretation, it is always important to remember that this kind of assessment is not a 'test' as such and its results are a guide which need to be taken into account alongside all the other 'evidence' such as social work assessments, contact observations, results on cognitive assessment and information and clinical impression from the clinical interview. Where possible assessments are completed at the person's home or somewhere local where they feel comfortable, in order to reduce the impact of anxiety on their performance. I also find it helpful to observe contacts as part of my overall assessment.

WHAT ARE THE COMMON THEMES IN COGNITIVE ASSESSMENT REQUESTS FOR COURT?

By the time a psychological assessment is requested, parents have usually had considerable input in relation to the concerns about their parenting. This is a real disadvantage to the parents being assessed. Full psychological assessments may provide essential information for workers, such as the identification of specific memory difficulties, visual processing difficulties, executive functioning difficulties or specific learning styles. Not having this information at the start of supportive work and wider parenting assessments, can mean that input is ineffective and at worst, inappropriate.

Assessments requested normally fall into two main categories. First, there are the requests for an assessment where there is no doubt that the parent has some degree of learning disability, but there is a question about the parent's capacity to learn new skills and how best to help them. Secondly (and far more commonly), whether indeed they have a learning disability at all (and if they do have a disability to what extent has this contributed towards their difficulties).

I find it helpful to consider at the outset whether the learning disability itself is at the root of any difficulties, or whether there is the presence of complicating mental health or personality difficulties, normally associated with extreme and traumatic life events and upbringing.

PRIMARILY ORGANIC DISABILITY

This group includes people who primarily have an organic disability, for example as a result of chromosomal abnormalities, or known physical trauma such as birth difficulties. People with a clear organic difficulty can come from all socio-economic groups and backgrounds. Assessments of parents who fall into this subgroup are normally more straightforward, as there are helpful and well researched and standardised assessment protocols for assessing the parenting capacity of parents with learning disabilities (see McGraw and Newman, 2005 and the Parent Assessment Manual, McGraw et al, 1999). It is relatively straightforward to assess a parents' ability on a range of parenting tasks, and then to think with them about parenting scenarios to assess their capacity to think ahead/change. Ensuring they receive appropriate input is less straightforward. The Department of Health has recently produced a helpful guide to working with parents with a learning disability that includes information on safeguarding children (DOH, 2007).

James (2004) reviewed the literature on parenting with learning disabilities and highlighted the most likely areas of potential difficulty; that of antenatal risk (not getting appropriate support and acting on advice), and the risk of developmental delay of children through increased genetic and environmental risk. Evidence suggests that the vulnerable children are those who are either more able than their parents, or who have increased dependency needs. James also notes that while parents with learning disabilities are at increased risk of neglecting their children, any physical or sexual abuse their children suffer tends to be perpetrated by other people in the system, such as partners. The evidence reviewed highlights the importance of protective factors, such as having good family and social support, professional support that is acceptable to them and having had good emotional experiences in their own upbringings. It is this last key point which is reduced in the subgroup of parents with learning disabilities, whom I meet in my court work practice.

LIFE EXPERIENCE RELATED DISABILITY

However, the majority of the parents I meet through care proceedings where learning disabilities have been identified, on assessment, prove to present with a far more complex picture. While there are frequently the hardships associated with learning disabilities (such as social isolation, financial and housing hardship and often lack of family support) the impact of these difficulties is frequently secondary to the impact of the negative life events that parents have suffered in childhood themselves and the consequent personality and psychological difficulties they have developed. They can range from physical trauma such as physical and sexual abuse, non-organic failure to thrive, severe neglect and perhaps most frequently, emotional abuse.

I think that the processes by which these personality and emotional difficulties develop are complex. One of the fundamental issues in work with families where one parent has a disability is the origin of the disability itself. Over the last few decades there has been a much greater understanding of the impact of trauma on early development. For example, Shore (2003) has demonstrated that extreme experiences of trauma, neglect or abuse can have an impact on brain development. He describes how the human brain is 'experience dependent', that is the brain develops according to the experiences received. This is especially so during the first year to 2 years of life. Negative life experiences can have an impact on not only emotional development, but also cognitive development, in some cases it is likely that some cognitive impairment is linked to early life experiences. As pointed out by Music (2006) severe neglect can lead to atrophy in parts of the brain leading to developmental delay, deficits in the ability to empathise, to regulate emotions and to manage more ordinary social interaction. It is important to note that this process is not a given with negative early experiences, there are protective factors and risk factors that can minimise or accentuate the possibility of more longstanding difficulties, such as the presence of positive experiences elsewhere in the network, the innate resilience or vulnerability of the child as well as the extent and timing of any negative experiences.

Families that come into child protection services frequently have histories of difficult and neglectful life experiences, often over the course of several generations. These families often present with borderline learning disabilities in both parents and children, and often there is no obvious genetic or organic 'cause' for the difficulties. The helpful work of Schore, Perry and others (Schore, 2003; Perry et al, 2003) have contributed greatly to the process of understanding how these types of difficulties can be 'transmitted' through families.

Valerie Sinason, has described the high incidence of trauma in the early lives of the patients with learning disabilities whom she worked with. It has long since been recognised that people with a learning disability are more vulnerable to abuse (Corbett, 1996), and that developmental delay can result from ineffective parenting (Music, 2006), however, it is only relatively recently that the more profound effects of abusive experiences on early development have been properly understood. Sinason hypothesised that the impact of early abuse and trauma could contribute to the development of learning disabilities (Sinason, 1992, Hodges, 2004).

In my child protection work, I have found a marked association between negative traumatic life experiences and the presence of learning difficulties, as well as with mental health and personality difficulties. This tends to be more so in the 'borderline' disabilities range. My assessment is then more concerned with which aspects of their functioning are to do with a disability, which are to do with emotional difficulties or personality difficulties.

For parents who have mental health difficulties as well as a learning disability the assessment of their capacity to parent will be secondary to an assessment of their emotional and personality functioning. Therefore a fundamental part of the assessment will be an assessment of their capacity to make use of treatment for their mental health difficulties. The literature that focuses on 'treatability' highlights the factors that are most associated with the capacity to learn from others, and to change the more concerning aspects of their behaviour. The key factors that are linked to change are (Fitzpatrick, 1995):

(i)   an ability to form a positive treatment alliance;

(ii)   an acceptance of the difficulties and an ability to own one's contribution to these;

(iii) the absence/reduction of the psychological conflict that results in being cut off from or denying one's feelings.

While parents with a very low IQ (less than 60) may have more of a conceptual difficulty in understanding their contribution to any difficulties, cognitive and emotional understanding are not dependent on each other, it is possible to be emotionally able, but cognitively disabled (and vice versa).

TREATMENT FACTORS

As part of a 'treatability' assessment, it is important to take into account all the well-established risk and protective factors. These include previous experience of difficulties, poverty, children with significant needs and social isolation (risk factors) social support, a supportive partnership where each others strengths and weaknesses are not in the same areas, a small number of children, and the absence of financial hardship (protective factors).

If the assessment identifies a parent's mental health difficulties as the primary area of concern, then their capacity to use therapeutic work will be paramount. Obviously their capacity to engage in work will be important, as well as establishing the kind of treatment, such as individual work, family work, psychoanalytic psychotherapy, cognitive therapy or any other relevant psychological treatment. Treatment type will need to be considered on an individual basis. However, if the difficulties are longstanding then the treatment is also likely to be long term. If a parent(s) engages in therapeutic work, it may also be possible to undertake any necessary parent training work concurrently, as often, the age of the children makes the need for prompt change paramount. Sadly the families I see where one or both parents have enduring mental health difficulties, tragic histories, as well as a learning disability tend to have deeply entrenched difficulties and change is inevitably slow.

The need to keep to a word count does not allow me to give examples of families that have, with appropriate support, successfully parented their children following court proceedings and families where the challenge has been insurmountable, but I am happy to provide these during the discussion of the paper.

REFERENCES

Corbett, A *Witnessing, nurturing, protesting; Therapeutic responses to sexual abuse of people with learning disabilities* (London: Fulton, 1996)

Department of Health *Good Practice Guidance on Working with Parents with a Learning Disability* (DOH, 2007)

Glaun, D E and Brown, P F 'Motherhood Intellectual Disability and Child Protection: Characteristics of a court sample' (1999) 24(1) Journal of Intellectual and Developmental Disability 95–105

Green, G and Vetere, A 'Parenting, learning disabilities and inequality: can systemic thinking help?' (2002) 14 Clinical Psychology Forum 9–12

Fitzpatrick, G 'Assessing treatability' in P Reder and C Lucey (eds), *Assessment of Parenting; Psychiatric and Psychological contributions* (Hove and New York Brunner Routledge, 1995)

Hodges, S R *Counselling Adults with Learning Disabilities* (London: Palgrave Macmillan, 2005)

James, H 'Promoting Effective Working with Parents with Learning Disabilities' (2004) 13 Child Abuse Review 31–41

McGaw, S, Beckley, K Connolly, N Ball, K *Parent Assessment Manual* (Truro: Trecare NHS Trust, 1999)

McGaw, S and Sturmey, P 'Assessing parents with Learning Disabilities: The parental Skills Model' (1994) 3 Child Abuse Review 36–51

McGraw, S and Newman, T *What works for parents with learning disabilities* (London: Barnardos, 2005)

Music, G 'The Uses of a Neuroscientific Perspective' in J Kendrick, C Lindsey and L Tollemache (eds), *Creating New Families* (London: The Tavistock Clinic Series, 2006)

Perry, B D, Pollard, R A, Bleakeley, T L, Baker, W L and Vigilante, D 'Childhood Trauma, the neurobiology of adaptation and "use dependent" development of the brain' (1995) 16 Infant Mental Health Journal 271–291

Schore, A N *Affect Regulation and the repair of the self* (New York: Norton, 2003)

Sinason, V *Mental Handicap and the Human Condition* (London: Free Association Press, 1995)

Tymchuck, A J 'Predicting Adequacy of Parenting by People with Mental Retardation' (1992) 16 Child Abuse and Neglect 165–178

Identifying High Risk vs Low Risk Parents with Learning Disabilities

Dr Sue McGaw

Consultant Clinical Psychologist, Director, Special Parenting Service, Cornwall Partnership Trust

SUMMARY OF PAPER

Dr Sue McGaw highlighted that the removal rate of children from parents with learning disabilities has always been controversial. The levels of removal are reported to be as high as 60% on occasions, although this appears to be averaging about 50% currently. There is evidence that parents with learning disabilities are at a disadvantage when they are involved in court proceedings. Research by Tarleton, Ward and Howarth (2006) highlights that parents often feel disempowered within the court systems and poor use is made of tools and methodologies which have been designed to facilitate parents' with learning disabilities understanding of the court process. Also, there has been discrimination evidenced within child protection proceedings resulting from a poor understanding of those involved in the court process as to whether the presence of a learning disability is a risk factor in itself. In some instances, outcomes have been based on IQ scores alone. Also, there is poor understanding in some courts regarding the learning capacity of parents with learning disabilities. As a result, the erroneous assumption has sometimes been made that as greater time and effort is needed to raise the parental competency of parents with learning disabilities, this relieves the authorities of the duty to provide any intervention at all.

Dr McGaw runs a Special Parenting Service in Cornwall which assists parents with IQ scores below 85. She gave a brief outline of a retrospective study which she conducted over a 5-year period. This study sampled the perception of need across parents, professionals and the Special Parenting Service regarding family support. The results indicate that in terms of perception of need, the professionals and referrers were generally quite accurate. Whilst parents tended to identify their child's disruptive behaviours as an issue for them in their parenting, they were poor in acknowledging the lack of routines in their parenting and inadequate hygiene or safety concerns within the home.

The research reveals that if parents with learning disabilities find the right partner the issues that arise in relation to their parenting ability reduce. Further, there was no difference when examining couples and singles and the length of the relationship did not alter the result. However, for mothers who have partners with an IQ over 85 the risk to the child is over eight times greater than for partners with an IQ less than 70. Also, for mothers with partners with an IQ of 70–84 the risk to the child is three times greater than for partners with an IQ less than 70. Dr McGaw highlighted that other research, such as that of Booth et al (2005), partially supports the findings. In particular, Booth's research revealed a percentage rate of 60% for removal of children from families where just the mother had learning disabilities compared with 11% where the father alone had such a disability.

Dr McGaw noted that there is now more work being done to follow up the study undertaken in 2005 by Booth et al. In particular, research into families with one or more parent with a learning disability is indicating a different referral pattern in that professionals are more likely to refer parents with learning disabilities who have children under 5 years old.

The difficulties faced by these parents are compounded by poor housing and poor health. They rarely ask for help for themselves and often there is a lack of specialist tools available when help is sought. The difficulties experienced by these families are heightened by poor collaboration and a lack of inter-agency protocols and care pathways across child and family and learning disability teams. In addition, lack of joint commissioning results in poor planning, development and continuity of service provision for these vulnerable families. Dr McGaw made the point that the Service she runs in Cornwall provides support to 80–100 families each year and only costs £160,000 whereas the removal of each child into care costs around £250,000. A proactive approach to supporting parents with learning disabilities is a cost-effective option that needs to be considered by authorities, in preference to a reactive response which can be traumatic for families.

Dr McGaw made reference to the Good Practice Guidance on Working with Parents with a Learning Disability issued by the Department of Health in 2007. The Guidance recommends joint commissioning with specialised responses from social care services and clear and coordinated care.

Dr McGaw also noted that the Disability Discrimination Act 2000 was amended in 2005 to include a duty to promote disability equality. The Disability Rights Commission has issued a code of practice which includes consideration, at page 76, Chapter 76, of the extent to which services and functions take account of the needs of disabled people. It is provided that:

> *'A local authority's information-gathering indicates that parents with learning disability are more likely to have their children taken into care than parents who do not have a learning disability. To tackle this, the authority, in conjunction with the primary care trust, establishes a parenting service which aims to work positively with parents with learning disabilities. The service develops a parenting assessment tool which focuses on parents' capacity and what support and training would assist them in parenting effectively. It offers both home-based and group-based programmes as well as running courses for parents with learning disabilities.'*

Dr McGaw concluded the introduction to her paper by raising a question for discussion: how might the 'Disability Equality Duty' impact care proceedings involving parents with learning disabilities when the issue of parenting capacity does not appear to have been assessed or exercised by the public sector services?

THE PAPER

Historically, the numbers of parents with intellectual disabilities who have experienced the termination of their parental rights has always been in excess of those parents without intellectual disabilities, despite improvements in removal rates over the past decade. According to the latest research, between 50–60% of children of parents with learning disabilities are subjected to care proceedings and are currently being placed with alternate families for the remainder of their childhood (Booth, Booth and McConnell, 2005; McConnell, Llewellyn and Ferronato, 2000). It is therefore, a matter of concern that in some quarters discriminatory attitudes and current policies still exist towards parents with intellectual disabilities (Emerson, Malam, Davies and Spencer, 2005) and that these may be contributory factors in the parenting breakdown of these families (Goodinge, 2000). Erroneous presumptions of parenting incompetence among professionals are often rooted more in behavioural mythology than scientific findings, despite the availability of empirical research to provide clarification.

Contrary to popular belief low IQ is not a dominant factor determining the parenting competency of parents with learning disabilities, until IQ falls below 60 (McGaw, Scully and Pritchard 2007; Tymchuk, 1992). Risk levels associating with single mothers with learning disabilities have not been found to be significantly different from those mothers with learning disabilities in relationships. Also, the majority of risks associating with partners without learning disabilities tends to be related to child protection outcomes, histories of sex offending, domestic violence, substance misuse and poor parenting (Booth et al, 2005; McGaw et al, 2007; Mickleson, 1949). In addition, recent evidence indicates that children of parents with learning disabilities are more likely to be placed on the child protection register or be the subject of care proceedings if their parents (predominantly mothers) have a history of childhood trauma, a 'physical disability' or they have a child with 'special needs' (McGaw, et al, 2007).

Other evidence suggests that many of the discriminatory practices and inequalities which many parents with learning difficulties face, also result from shortcomings in the provision of support services available to them (Booth and Booth, 1996; Jewell, 1997). It is reported that parents with intellectual disabilities are infrequently empowered by their service providers, with very few specialist services being made available to them, despite recommendations from national surveys that this is what they need most (McConnell, Llewellyn and Bye, 1997; McGaw et al, 2005). In response to this and other related situations, a number of initiatives have been developed over the past 2 years, which are attempting to address the inequality in service provision for parents with learning disabilities across the UK.

FINDING THE RIGHT SUPPORT (TARLETON, WARD AND HOWARTH, 2006)

Norah Fry Research Centre conducted a mapping study in 2006, the aim of which was to review the issues and positive practice in supporting parents with learning disabilities and their children. Data was collected using a web-questionnaire, telephone interviews with professionals and case study visits across six areas of the UK, in England, Scotland and Wales. The key findings confirmed that many barriers existed that obstructed the provision of support services, including negative or stereotypical attitudes projected towards parents by some staff. The most effective support services offered a diverse range of interventions that focused on early identification of family's needs, specialist family assessments, engagement issues and multi-agency working. The provision of easy to understand information on all aspects of parenting and advocacy, especially when this involved child protection and judicial proceedings were a basic requirement underpinning this support. Also, professional training on all aspects of family life involving parents with learning disabilities including child protection, multi-agency working across children's services, adult's services, learning disability services and generic services was identified. Lastly, national and local strategic planning of service provision for parents with learning disabilities was a recommendation of the survey. Clearer clarification and simplification of eligibility criteria across services was another recommendation.

GOOD PRACTICE GUIDANCE ON WORKING WITH PARENTS WITH A LEARNING DISABILITY (2007)

The Department of Health (DH) and Department for Education and Skills (DfES) issued the *Good Practice Guidance on Working with Parents with a Learning Disability* (2007) with the intention of improving practice across children and adult services. It identified that there was a need for these departments to work together when supporting parents with a learning disability, so that the children of parents with a learning disability can live in a positive and supportive environment that meets their needs and reduces the risk of removal from their birth families. The guidance recognised that a specialised response was required for all adult and children's services, the commissioners of education and social care services as well as Primary Care Trusts, when working with these families.

Also, the *Good Practice* guidance emphasises that it is particularly important to avoid the situation where poor standards of parental care, which do not meet the threshold of significant harm to a child, subsequently deteriorate because of a lack of support provided to a parent with learning disabilities. It points out that there is a need to provide any necessary support when a child is no longer the subject of a child protection plan, in order to prevent a subsequent deterioration in parental care. Ultimately, a failure to provide support in this type of situation can undermine a child's right to remain with their family. The document points out that the policy, legislation and guidance framework for supporting parents with learning disabilities and their children is already established across several government Green and White Papers including: *Improving Life Chances of Disabled People* (Prime Minister's Strategy Unit, 2005), *Valuing People: A national strategy for learning disability in the 21st century* (Department of Health, 2001) and *Every Child Matters, Change for Children* (2003). In particular, these papers are emphasising the following.

- Children have the right to be protected from harm and their interests are paramount. Also, that their needs are usually best met by supporting the parents who are trying to look after them.

To this effect, The Good Practice Guidance recommends that if this situation involves a parent with learning disabilities, that the identification of needs should start when a pregnancy is confirmed. Pregnant women with learning disabilities are entitled to universal services, which should make reasonable adjustments to make their services accessible to them. Early assessments of the support needed by a parent with learning disabilities to look after a new baby will help to prevent avoidable difficulties arising in the future.

- Local Authorities and all other agencies who have contact with children have a responsibility to safeguard and promote children's welfare.

The Good Practice Guidance recommends that children should be monitored on a regular basis or intermittent basis, according to the level of family support provided. Many children of parents with learning disabilities are known to be at increased vulnerability to developmental delays, attachment issues and removal from their parent's care than for other children of parents with mental health problems, or who are victims of domestic violence.

- Parents with learning disabilities are entitled to equal access to services, including parenting support and information services.

The Good Practice Guidance recommends that children should be provided with support in their own right. Their health or developmental needs may suffer while their parent is learning to better meet these needs and/or parent support services are being put in place. Also, older children may be at risk of taking on inappropriate caring roles within the family, or their welfare may be threatened by inadequate parental supervision. In such situations, children will meet the 'child in need' criteria and adult and children's services should work together to address children's needs, while at the same time work is done with parents to increase their capacity to meet their children's needs. Neither intervention is a substitute for the other but should be provided in tandem.

THE DUTY TO PROMOTE DISABILITY EQUALITY: STATUTORY CODE OF PRACTICE (2006)

Bearing in mind the lack of specialist service provision for parents with learning disability, it is of relevance that since 2006 the Disability Rights Commission (DRC) are ensuring that any public body who has no regard for the principles of equality or for ensuring their services are geared towards the needs of their disabled customers may find themselves held to account for their shortcomings. They recently issued compliance notices on nine public bodies for failure to provide evidence of a disability equality scheme in contravention of *The Duty to Promote Disability Equality: Statutory Code of Practice* (2006). This document now places a duty on all public authorities, when carrying out their function, to have due regard to the need to:

- promote equality of opportunity between disabled persons and other persons;

- eliminate discrimination that is unlawful under the Act;

- eliminate harassment of disabled persons that is related to their disabilities;

- promote positive attitudes towards disabled persons;

- encourage participation by disabled persons in public life; and

- take steps to take account of disabled persons' disabilities, even where that involves treating disabled persons more favourably than other persons.

Rather than providing restitution when a disabled person has been the subject of discriminatory treatment, the duty provides a framework for public authorities to carry out their functions more effectively and to tackle discrimination and its causes in a proactive way. Essentially, the general duty:

(a) requires public authorities to adopt a proactive approach mainstreaming disability equality into all decisions and activities. This is framed as a requirement on authorities to have due regard to disability equality in its various dimensions;

(b) requires authorities not only to have due regard to disability equality when making decisions about the future. They will also need to take action to tackle the consequences of decisions in the past which failed to give due regard to disability equality. This is best approached by working towards closing the gaps in service or employment outcomes, so that, for example, disabled and non-disabled people express the same level of satisfaction with their social housing, or achieve a more equal pattern of educational achievement;

(c) ensures equality for disabled people which may mean treating them 'more favourably'. The Act states that the duty requires public authorities to have due regard to the need to take steps to take account of disabled persons' disabilities, even where that involves treating disabled persons more favourably than other persons. This underlines the fact that equality of opportunity cannot be achieved simply by treating disabled and non-disabled people alike.

Example: A local authority's information-gathering indicates that parents with a learning disability are more likely to have their children taken into care than parents who do not have a learning disability. To tackle this, the authority, in conjunction with the local primary care trust, establishes a parenting service that aims to work positively with parents with learning disabilities. The service develops a parental assessment tool that focuses on parents' capacity and what support and training would assist them in parenting effectively. It offers both home-based and group-based programmes as well as running courses for parents with learning disabilities.

In summary, authorities will need to consider the full range of services that they provide and those functions they perform for vulnerable people, including disability-specific services. This means that if an authority is providing support for parents with learning disabilities, the authority will need to consider to what extent there are deficits in support services and whether the authority adequately takes account of the specific needs of these families. If it does not, the authority will need to consider whether due regard is being paid to disability equality in its budget allocation. Hopefully, *The Duty to Promote Disability Equality: Statutory Code of Practice* (2006), together with the findings of the *Finding the Right Support* (2006) and *Good Practice Guidance on Working with Parents with a Learning Disability* (2006) will safeguard against pejorative attitudes, previously shown towards parents with disabilities. Also, if they are provided with the specialist help that they require, these parents will be given the best chance possible to succeed in their parenting. Long term it remains uncertain as to whether this will ensure that their parenting will be 'good enough' for all of the children in their care.

REFERENCES

Booth, T, Booth, W and McConnell, D 'Care proceedings and parents with learning difficulties: comparative prevalence and outcomes in an English and Australian court sample' (2005) 10 *Child and Family Social Work* 353–360

Department of Health and Department for Education and Skills *Good Practice Guidance on Working with Parents with a Learning Disability* (2007), available at www.valuingpeople.org.uk

Department of Health *Valuing People: a national strategy for learning disability in the 21st century* (London: The Stationery Office, 2001)

Department for Education and Skills *Every Child Matters. Change for Children* (2003), available at www.everychildmatters.gov.uk

Disability Rights Commission *The Duty to Promote Disability Equality: Statutory Code of Practice* (2006), available at www.drc.org.uk

Emerson, E, Malam, S M, Davids, I and Spencer, K *Adults with Learning Difficulties in England 2003/4* (2005), available at www.ic.nhs.uk/pubs/leandiff2004

Goodinge, S *A Jigsaw of Services: Inspection of services to support disabled adults in their parenting role* (Department of Health, 2000)

McConnell, D, Llewellyn, G and Ferronato, L *Parents with a Disability and The NSW Children's Court* (University of Sydney, 2000)

McGaw, S, Scully, T and Pritchard, C 'Identifying High Risk versus Low Risk Parents with Intellectual Disabilities' *Child Abuse and Neglect* (Submitted)

Mickelson, P 'Can mentally deficient parents be helped to give their children better care?' (1949) 3 *American Journal of Mental Deficiency* (January)

Prime Minister's Strategy Unity *Improving the Life Chances of Disabled People* (London: Cabinet Office, 2005), available at www.strategy.gov.uk

Tarleton, B, Ward, L and Howard, J *Finding the Right Support: A review of issues and positive practice in supporting parents with learning difficulties and their children* (Bristol: University of Bristol, 2006), available at www.baringfoundation.org.uk/FRSupportSummary.pdf

Tymchuk, A 'Predicting adequacy of parenting by people with mental retardation' (1992) 16 *Child Abuse and Neglect* 165–178

PLENARY 5

CHILD PROTECTION AND CULTURE

Child Discipline and Ethnicity: Contextualising Parental Practices

Professor Ravinder Barn

Royal Holloway, University of London

SUMMARY OF THE PAPER

Professor Ravinder Barn introduced her paper by emphasising that much of our real understanding of this topic comes from social interactions whether in the context of different professions or backgrounds. She referred to a study funded by the Joseph Rowntree Foundation (Barn, 2006). The key point is that parenting has a high profile in public political debates and we need to be mindful of the debates on multiculturalism and Britishness in this context. Professor Barn noted the comment of Trevor Phillips, the head of what was formerly known as the Commission for Racial Equality, that multiculturalism could cause Britain to sleep walk into segregation.

Professor Barn noted that we live in increasingly diverse societies. As a result, there is a need to recognise that while cultural generalisations may be important, they can be dangerous in the context of professional judgements that we might be required to make.

Over the last 20 years there has been steady growth in child protection literature. The most notable issues and concerns arising from this literature relate to the prevalence of ethnic minority cases that are referred to social services. Professor Barn considered that the reason child discipline and ethnicity cause concern is that we live in a racial and cultural heterogeneous society. She questioned, in this respect, the extent to which local authorities made reference to s 22(5)(c) of the Children Act 1989 which requires consideration of 'the child's religious persuasion, racial origin and cultural and linguistic background' when complying with the duty in relation to looked after children.

Professor Barn referred to the Department for Education and Skills statistics on child protection which give a glimpse of the ethnic picture of children in care. There is clear over-representation of black children and under-representation of Asian children. These statistics, however, reveal very little about the lives of ordinary families. She referred, in this respect, to the study considered in her paper which sought to examine the attitudes of members of different ethnic groups to discipline whose families were not necessarily involved in the care system.

Professor Barn noted that the key findings of the study shatter the popular myths and stereotypes that some ethnic groups mete out harsher punishment. In particular, there was found to be no significant differences between ethnic groups with regard to physical punishment. The majority of the parents in the study told the researchers that physical punishment was very much a last resort. Parents also widely reported experiencing physical punishment as a primary method of discipline during their own childhoods. Importantly, these common aspects of the research were present across the different groups surveyed.

A number of the parents in the study mentioned breaking the cycle. They described their own upbringing as very strict and expressed desire to break away from that cycle. There was a strong belief that smacking is ineffective and did little to change behaviour. Professor Barn also highlighted that minority parents, in particular, expressed dissatisfaction with over-intervention and prohibition of physical punishments. However, this view also existed within white families.

The study highlighted the relevance of the context and neighbourhood in which children are being brought up as a key aspect of discipline. Black and Asian parents emphasised their fears about the urban environment and racism which was also said to be felt by the children. Strict rules were said to be adopted to ensure the safety of the children.

Professor Barn concluded that it is crucial to examine cultural pathology and cultural relativity models as they represent significant difficulty in policy and practice terms. We need to be mindful of the prevalence of commonalities across ethnic groups as well as recognising the differences among these groups. In particular, we need to deconstruct the mythological norm which separates them and us in the context of power and inequality.

THE PAPER

Introduction

Child discipline in minority ethnic families remains an important concern in contemporary Western multi-cultural societies. By focusing upon physical punishment, this paper explores the extant literature into child protection and ethnicity and presents findings from a new empirical study to argue that it is important that we broaden our understanding of parenting by looking at 'ordinary' minority ethnic families. Moreover, it is argued that in an attempt to understand parenting practices, it is crucial that the context in which parenting takes place is taken into account to make sense of diversity and difference while being mindful of the prevalence of commonalities in parenting practices across differing ethnic groups – both majority and minority.

BACKGROUND

Over the last 50 years or so, there has been a significant shift in the social and cultural terrain of the British landscape. A number of factors including colonialism, slavery, global inequality, wars and conflict and modern day imperialism have created the push and pull factors to assist the process of migration resulting in the arrival of people from former British colonies and elsewhere to Britain. Such an unprecedented arrival and settlement of non-European people has challenged traditional social service policy and service delivery to seek to ensure that the diversity of need is addressed adequately and appropriately.

As British society becomes increasingly diverse, the concept of cross-cultural understanding and mutual respect is widely recognised. However, there are some areas of life that generate difficulties and dilemmas and test the boundaries of cultural relativity and acceptability. Child discipline, or more specifically physical punishment of children, is one such area.

There has been a steady growth in the British literature on child protection and ethnicity over the last two decades (Phillips and Dutt, 1989, Channer and Parton, 1990, Gibbons et al, 1995, Barn et al, 1997, Humphreys et al, 1999, Brophy and Jhutti-Johal, 2003, Chand, 2000, 2005, Parton, 2004, Bernard and Gupta, 2006). The most notable issues and concerns raised include the nature and prevalence of cases involving minority ethnic child abuse cases referred to and dealt with by child protection services (Gibbons et al, 1995, Barn et al, 1997, Barn 2006). For example, in a study of eight local authorities in the UK, Gibbons et al (1995) found that among referrals involving physical injury minority ethnic families were over-represented compared with White families. Moreover, the nature of the punishment was also said to be harsher in that minority ethnic families were reportedly more likely to make use of an implement to inflict physical injury than white families – 43% African, 40% of Asian, and 30% African-Caribbean families were said to have used an implement to cause injury to a child compared to 16% of White families. In a later study of three local authorities, Barn et al (1997) warned that proportionately more minority ethnic children were subject to child abuse investigations than White children.

There have been long-standing concerns about the disproportionate number of minority ethnic families involved with child protection services. Government's latest available statistics reveal that in 2005, of the 25,900 children on child protection registers, 81% were of a white background, 7% of a mixed background, 5% Black or Black British, 4% Asian or Asian British and 1% were unborn on 31 March 2005 (DfES, 2006). The remainder were of other ethnic origins. Compared to the general child population, these figures suggest an over-representation of African/Caribbean and mixed-parentage children, and an under-representation of Asians. They also confirm previous research studies that have documented ethnic differences (Gibbons et al, 1995, Barn et al, 1997), and that have identified some key factors associated with working with minority ethnic families (Dutt and Phillips, 2000; Humphreys et al, 1999; Chand 2000), namely cultural relativity, the role of the social worker as advocate in multi-disciplinary working, and an understanding of overt and covert racism, and culture and language issues when engaging with families.

An increasing diversity has required social services agencies to re-evaluate their policies and practices in the light of prevalent thinking that ethnicity (cultural values and beliefs) impacts individual and group behaviour (Strauss, 1992; Modood et al, 1997; Korbin, 2002). The impact of ethnicity upon family life and parenting is also an important concern. Research literature from the US stresses that although there are commonalities between ethnic groups in terms of parenting practices, there are also important cultural differences in terms of parental goals, values, and practices (LeVine, 1980). Other research has gone beyond culture to discuss the impact of race and racism upon child abuse investigations. For example, Barn et al (1997) found that in general, White practitioners and managers emphasised culture as the key concern, while minority ethnic professionals de-emphasised culture and placed greater stress on issues of race, racism and Euro-centric thinking.

Much of the research is focused upon clinical samples, and there is a dearth of knowledge and understanding about the ways in which 'ordinary' minority ethnic families living in Britain employ discipline strategies in child behaviour management. By drawing upon the findings of author's own empirical study, this paper documents white and minority ethnic parental practices on physical discipline and the messages parents aim to transmit to their offspring through discipline (Barn, 2006). Parents' own experiences of childhood are discussed within the context of change and continuity.

THE STUDY

This study was conducted within the context of an almost total paucity of literature on parenting and child discipline within 'ordinary' minority ethnic families. A quantitative and qualitative approach was adopted to attempt to obtain data relating to a diverse group of parents. The quantitative sample included 156 Asian and 106 Black, and 123 White parents from four geographical locations in London and Berkshire (n=385). Access to parents was obtained via primary schools, and parenting practices in relation to children between the ages of 7 and 11 became the subject of study. Qualitative interviews were carried out with a cross-representation of a sub-sample of mothers and fathers to further understand their situation (n=61).

RESULTS

While the popular myth and stereotype is that some cultural groups mete out harsher punishment, our study documents that there are no significant differences between ethnic groups with regard to physical punishment of children. Less than two-fifths of the parents in our study reported that they had used physical punishment (mostly occasionally) in disciplining their children. While this figure may seem high, it is relatively low compared to other studies (Thompson and Pearce, 2001; Wissow, 2001).

The strategy of physical punishment of children was often the last resort for parents. It was evident that parenting strategies were determined by a range of factors including the age of the child and were in a constant state of flux (Day et al, 1998). Many parents reported hitting their child when the child was younger, however it was believed that as children were growing older it was no longer an effective or desirable way to discipline them. Also, some parents used physical punishment after other strategies had been tried but failed. At times, the threat of being smacked or hit was said to be effective by some parents.

> 'When she was about six, she really made me cross and I gave her a smacking. Nothing excessive, but it was enough for me to say, this isn't the way I want to go with this, this isn't the attitude I want to portray, and from that day onwards I tried not to use spanking in any way and tried to use other ways of doing it.' (White father)

Parents reported that during their childhood, their 'own parents' had invariably employed physical punishment as the primary strategy but believed that they themselves only resorted to smacking/slapping when all other attempts had failed.

> 'My mum would slap us straight away, she'd stop it there and then … I just let things go on and on and then, at the very end, then I slap, when I can't take anymore which I don't like to. It hurts me more than it hurts her.' (White mother of Caribbean/white mixed-parentage child)

> 'It [hitting] would be for me a last resort, I would have done other things, it isn't the first thing I seek, so as a last resort it would be very effective, a short sharp shock, in fact I'm just visualising his shock, it wasn't the hurt, it was that I'd actually done it and I remember thinking that's going to stop now, that's taken care of that, and we can move on to something else.' (Indian mother)

Some parents who described their own upbringing as very strict which included 'shouting' and 'smacking' expressed a desire to 'break the cycle'. It was expressed that children do, at times, behave badly, but that parental anger needed to be curtailed. There was a strong belief that smacking was ineffective and did little to change the child's behaviour.

> 'I can certainly remember at the age of 14 my mother giving me one heck of a hiding with a stick, and I don't want that for my daughter, not at all.' (White father)

> 'To me you have to break that cycle. I cannot do to my children what … I'd seen with my older siblings, no I just can't do it, they are my children. I didn't bring them into this world to abuse them, it's not my way.' (Caribbean mother)

Our study suggested that while most parents emphasised the value and importance of a culture of respect, minority ethnic parents tended to focus on this within the context of discipline. It was evident that certain types of misbehaviour were considered intolerable in the wider sense; and parents highlighted the impact of such behaviour within the family and community network. An example of this is given below by an African father whose 7-year-old son demonstrated disrespect by swearing at his visiting grandmother.

> 'I expect every child to misbehave from time to time, but Paul … sometimes I find difficult to handle. My mother visited some time ago and he was insulting to her, said a lot of nasty things to her… in my

country you couldn't imagine a child using such words. She likes her grandchildren but this was bad ... my mother was ready to pack up and return to Ghana ... I whipped him ... I wanted to bring him down, down to the level that he would accept and know that this is wrong, and he should be able to go back to this woman and kneel and say, Gran, I'm sorry, I won't do that again.' (African father)

Adopting a particular tone of voice was a preferred way of disciplining children for some parents. This was considered to be more effective than shouting, or hitting. For some minority ethnic parents, reverting to their own ethnic language to express their annoyance with the child was also an effective discipline strategy.

'Yeah give them a little slap you know. But as they get older you talk to them and it's the manner of your voice and the way you talk to them they get scared.' (Indian father)

'When I'm speaking my language they know I'm mad.' (African mother)

There are key determining influences in the implementation of various discipline strategies including context, ethnicity and gender. Black and Asian parents highlighted many fears which were located in the urban environment, but also related to race and racism (Shor, 2000). The implications of this were felt by the children and the parents. A Caribbean mother explained how she had very strict rules to ensure her children's safety. She had become particularly strict as a result of a personal experience when her son went missing for 3 hours following a fight with some older boys in the local park:

'They don't play outside at all. They play in the garden. If they do go out, I go with them because I had a really bad experience a couple of years ago when Stephen went out with his cousins. They were older children, about 12 or 11, and he ran away.' (Caribbean single mother)

Some minority parents expressed dissatisfaction with what they perceived to be over-interference by the state, and felt that their parental authority was undermined by laws that prohibited physical punishment.

'The law says parents mustn't punish the children which is wrong ... If the parents don't punish the children ... punish doesn't mean that we have to get a big stick and start, you know, bashing them up, you know ... no parents would strike their children, you know. But the punishment is maybe a soft slap, you know, just give a soft shout, you know, to control them and the law doesn't allow it.' (Bangladeshi father)

Expressing an incident that echoed the killing of the 10-year-old African boy, Damilola Taylor, in South London, one African father compared the collective responsibility model of African society to the indifferent approach on British streets.

'In Africa it's OK, even a stranger, if they find two children fighting in the street, they pick up a stick and hit them if they are behaving badly. You didn't wait until one is dead and phone the police 999 and say be a witness.' (African father)

DISCUSSION AND CONCLUSION

A challenging task for parents is the decision as to how best to prepare their children for adult life. Although the ways in which parents may choose to transmit this message to their children vary from one set of parents to the other, one of the most commonly recognised messages parents aim to transfer to children cross-culturally, is that children should honour/respect their parents. Beishon et al (1998) reported that Caribbean, South Asian and White families in the UK express greater desire to discipline children in the areas of respect for elders something the white group did not. Our study confirms that both white and minority ethnic parents lamented the loss of respect for older people; however minority ethnic parents expressed this more strongly.

The significance of considering cultural components in approaching situations of parental discipline towards children has been recognised in recent years (Banks, 2001). Difficulties in assessing the adequacy of particular forms of training or control based on restrictions and demands gets increasingly difficult as the same parental behaviour and child responses may have different meanings and interpretations in different cultural contexts (Ghate, 2000; Shor, 2000). Having said that, cross-cultural research including our own has also revealed similarities in the types of punishment used by parents from majority and minority groups (Barn, 2006). Davies' (1996) sample, for instance, which included White, African, and Hispanic parents revealed that 'yelling at' and 'threatening the child' was a widespread form of interacting with children even in public places. Such findings may lead one to believe that there is a commonly used mechanism of child control used by 'ordinary' parents (see also Solomon and Serres, 1999). This said, some other types of parental control over the children have been reported in the literature and have generated a great deal of concern. A clear example is the body of literature on minority ethnic parents and physical punishment. Minority ethnic families have been described as more authoritarian and as engaging in harsher disciplinary practices than other families. While physical punishment is not considered child abuse, per se; social work policy has tended to handle physical punishment with caution. Thus, a minority ethnic mother who openly expresses a preference for physical discipline may be considered as lacking parental skills (Mosby et al, 1999). Such a perspective generally views minority families in isolation and usually from a deficit perspective with an over-reliance on a cultural rationale (Williams and Soydan, 2005, Barn 2007).

While ethnic and cultural factors are perceived to play a significant role in understanding child discipline, other factors have also been found as important in an appreciation of parenting practices. The parental practices observed by Shor (2000), for instance, revealed that the socio-ecological context shaped the nature of parental monitoring and controlling over the children. Indeed, low-income parents in his sample reported that risk in their neighbourhood made them more prone to use 'restrictive methods' in their child rearing practices than those reported among middle income neighbourhood parents. As is evidenced in our study, protective parenting may restrict children's movement in their neighbourhood, especially in areas where there is a perceived feeling of risk for the child. Shor's (2000) research has placed great significance to exploring the rationale behind parent's punitive or disciplinarian practices.

Our study shows that parents employ a range of discipline strategies to deal with their child's perceived or actual bad behaviour (see Barn, 2006). Physical punishment was described by the vast majority of parents as the last resort strategy after other attempts had been tried and failed. Our findings challenge the supposition that physical punishment is more prevalent or harsh in some minority cultures.

In conclusion, it has to be said that in order to enhance our understanding of parenting practices among different ethnic groups, it is crucial that there is a shift in the paradigm of parochialism with its over-emphasis on culture and problematisation. It is important to realise that a perspective that views minority families in isolation with its undue focus on culture will only provide a partial story. In the interests of minority ethnic families who fall prey to the social work 'deficit' lens, a broader approach which attempts to incorporate diversity and difference within the context of wider community and society is a prerequisite. Finally, zero-tolerance to physical punishment of children, in any form, is a laudable goal and should be the ultimate objective for any society in the modern world.

REFERENCES

Banks, N 'Assessing Children and families who belong to Minority Ethnic Groups' in J Howarth (ed), *The Child's World: Assessing Children in Need* (London: NSPCC, Jessica Kingsley Publishers, 2001) 140–149

Barn, R, Sinclair, R and Ferdinand, D *Acting on Principle: An Examination of Race and Ethnicity in Social Services Provision to Children and Families* (London: BAAF, 1997)

Barn, R *Parenting in multi-racial Britain* (London: NCB, 2006)

Barn, R 'Race, Ethnicity and Child Welfare: A Fine Balancing Act, Critical Commentary' (2007) 37 British Journal of Social Work 1425–1434

Beishon, S, Modood, T and Virdee, S *Ethnic Minority Families* (London: PSI, 1998)

Bernard, C and Gupta, A 'Black African Children and the Child Protection System' (2006) 35 British Journal of Social Work 807–821

Brophy, J and Jhutti-Johal, J 'Assessing and documenting child ill-treatment in Ethnic Minority households' (2003) Family Law (October) 756–764

Chand, A 'The Over-representation of Black Children in the Child Protection System: Possible Causes, Consequences, and Solutions' (2000) 5 Child and Family Social Work 67–77

Chand, A 'Do You Speak English? Language Barriers in Child Protection Social Work with Minority Ethnic Families' (2005) 35 British Journal of Social Work 807–821

Channer, Y and Parton, N 'Racism, Cultural Relativism and Child Protection', in *The Violence Against Children Study Group, Taking Child Abuse seriously* (London: Unwin Hyman, 1990)

Davis, P W 'Threats of Corporal Punishment as Verbal Aggression: A Naturalistic Study' (1996) 20 (4) Child Abuse and Neglect 289–304

Day, R D et al 'Parenting and Parent-Child Relations Predicting Spanking of Younger and Older Children by Mothers and Fathers' (1998) 60 (1) Journal of Marriage and the Family 79–94

Department for Education and Skills Statistics of Education: *Referrals, Assessments and Children and Young people on Child protection Registers: Year Ending 31 March 2005* (London: DfES, 2006)

Dutt, R and Phillips, M 'Assessing the Needs of Black Children and their Families' in *Framework for the Assessment of Children in Need and their Families: Practice Guidance* (London: The Stationery Office, 2000)

Ghate, D (2000) 14 Family Violence and Violence Against Children 395–403

Gibbons, J, Conroy, S and Bell, C *Operating the Child Protection System* (London: HMSO, 1995)

Humphreys, C et al 'Discrimination in Child protection Work: recurring Themes in Work with Asian Families' (1999) 4 Child and Family Social Work 283–291

Korbin, J E 'Culture and child maltreatment: cultural competence and beyond' (2002) 26 (6–7) Child Abuse and Neglect 637–644

LeVine, R 'A Cross-Cultural Perspective on Parenting' in M D Fantini and R Cardenes (eds), *Parenting in a Multi-Cultural Society* (New York: Penguin, 1980)

Modood, T et al *Ethnic Minorities in Britain, Diversity and Disadvantage* (London: PSI, 1997)

Mosby, L et al 'Troubles in Interracial Talk about Discipline: An Examination of African American Child Rearing Narratives' (1999) 30(3) Journal of Comparative Family Studies (Summer)

Parton, N 'From Maria Colwell to Victoria Climbié: Reflections on Public Inquiries into Child Abuse a Generation Apart' (2004) 13(2) Child Abuse Review 80–94

Phillips, M and Dutt, R *Towards a Black Perspective in Child Protection* (London: Race Equality Unit, 1989)

Shor, R 'Child Maltreatment: Differences in Perceptions Between Parents in Low Income and Middle Income Neighbourhoods' (2000) 30 British Journal of Social Work 165–178

Solomon, R and Serres, F 'Effects of Parental Verbal Aggression on Children's Self-Esteem and School Marks' (1999) 23(4) Child Abuse and Neglect 339–351

Strauss, C 'Models and Motives', in R D D'Andrade and C Strauss (eds), *Human Motives and Behaviour: Publication for the Society for Psychological Anthropology* (Cambridge: Cambridge University Press, 1992) 1–20

Thompson, A E and Pearce, J B 'Attitudes towards and the Practice of Discipline amongst Parents of Pre-school Children in Nottingham' (2001) 15 Children and Society 231–236

Williams, C and Soydan, H 'When and How Does Ethnicity Matter? A Cross-National Study of Social Work Responses to Ethnicity in Child Protection Cases' (2005) 35 British Journal of Social Work 901–920

Wissow, L S 'Ethnicity, income, and parenting contexts of physical punishment in a national sample of families with young children' (2001) 6(2) Child Maltreatment 118–129

Care proceedings and Minority Ethnic Families

Dr Julia Brophy

Senior Research Fellow

and

Dr Jagbir Jhutti-Johal

Research Associate

Oxford Centre for Family Law & Policy, University of Oxford

SUMMARY OF PAPER

This paper focused on two recent empirical studies undertaken by Dr Brophy and Dr Jhutti-Johal with others.

The data referred to in the paper was drawn from a number of studies, however, in their introduction to this paper Dr Brophy and Dr Jhutti-Johal intended to cover two studies funded by the Ministry of Justice: Significant Harm: child protection litigation in a multi-cultural setting (2003) and Minority ethnic parents, their solicitors and child protection litigation (2005).

It was noted that some aspects of thinking and policy in this area are moving on very swiftly – for example with regard to collecting better data on over- and under-representation of certain groups in 'looked after' populations. In addition, the MacPherson report of 1999 following the murder of Stephen Lawrence highlighted concerns about professionals misunderstanding, misinterpreting or failing to address issues of diversity in their work. There are also concerns about a lack of confidence within ethnic minority communities in relation to the criminal and family justice systems.

Dr Jhutti-Johal dealt with the first study in which documents held in court files were coded according to the range of information they contained regarding issues of language, 'race', religion, ethnicity and cultural diversity. The majority of the documents contained some descriptive information on these issues. Notably, cases were also found to be very similar in terms of levels of complexity; applications were not usually made to the court on the basis of a single issue, rather cases contained multiple allegations of child ill-treatment and multiple allegations of failures of parenting. Common features across all ethnic groups with regard to issues leading to failures of parenting were mental ill-health problems and a refusal of professional help for this, male violence and a refusal to cooperate with health and welfare services. A majority of cases contained expert evidence but the extent to which that evidence contained any information on issues of cultural/religious contexts depended upon the discipline of the expert and the particular ethnic group of the family. Child psychiatrists were, for example, much more likely to refer to diverse contexts than paediatricians.

Dr Brophy dealt with the second study which involved interviews with 45 solicitors in three major cities and 12 minority ethnic parents. Most solicitors interviewed encountered hurdles in getting the parents' stories – some also had anxieties about this. Where parents were newly arrived in the UK a major hurdle was their complete incredulity that the state should be interested in their parenting let alone that the child might be removed from their care on grounds of ill-treatment. An additional hurdle faced was one of resources: additional time for such parents and specific training is necessary to allow solicitors to ensure they get a full story from these parents.

With regard to second/third generation black and Asian British parents, for the most part, solicitors thought that the task of taking instructions was not very different to that involving white British parents. Some solicitors did however express anxiety about raising issues of diverse cultural/religious contexts as they had never been taught to work cross-culturally and might not know what to do with the information they received. They were also concerned that they might be seen as racist for raising these issues.

It was recorded that half of the minority ethnic parents interviewed in this study were dissatisfied with the statements put before the court because diverse cultural contexts were not included or the information in statements was not provided in their words.

The study recorded that none of the parents had experienced anything they considered to be racist at the hands of their solicitor or barrister but three parents reported comments they considered disrespectful and uninformed. Most parents had also not experienced any racism in court but two parents reported comments by a judge which they felt to be unfair and racist.

Interesting elements of this latter study were that while some solicitors had found ways of raising issues of diverse family backgrounds and contexts with parents, many were nervous about raising these issues – fears about issues of racism and a lack of training and knowledge made some solicitors less likely to deal with this area unless it was absolutely necessary. But moreover, minority ethnic parents were no more satisfied with the treatment of these issues when they were 'matched' by ethnic group with a solicitor or indeed an expert.

Dr Brophy reiterated that the study of parents was small and needed repeating with a larger sample. However, there was no evidence arising from either study that the threshold criteria needed to be reassessed in relation to children from minority ethnic backgrounds. The studies do reveal serious gaps in dialogue between parents and professionals which need to be addressed along with the need to consider what it takes for a parent from a diverse culture to feel heard and understood by courts.

THE PAPER

Introduction

In the UK a concern about the relevance of differences of belief, values and practices for care proceedings has been made more complex by several factors – not least a lack of hard evidence. In the 1990s researchers raised concerns about the representation of minority ethnic children in looked-after populations. There were also concerns about whether professionals routinely misunderstood or misinterpreted certain cultural mores/nuances in minority ethnic families when investigating child maltreatment.

An international review of research comparing values, attitudes and practices noted considerable methodological problems with much of the research. However, there was evidence of some agreement both within and between cultures about child maltreatment, although there were also variations (Brophy, 1999; 2005).

Issues of racism were also put centre stage[1] by Sir William Macpherson (Macpherson, 1999) following the murder of Stephen Lawrence and a failure by the police to achieve a prosecution. The Report expressed concerns about stereotyping, 'colour/culture blindness' and institutional racism in the criminal justice system and a loss of faith by minority ethnic communities. That report refocused attention on the experiences of minority ethnic litigants in all courts (family, criminal and tribunals).

With regard to child maltreatment in minority ethnic families, one of the findings from the international review was that discussions in this field come from very different groups with little history of interdisciplinary dialogue or research. Broadly speaking this is because one group – the family law specialists – is generally seen as too deeply embedded in a legal discourse which others find difficult to penetrate. Others, for example, cultural anthropologists, transcultural psychiatrists and psychologists have explored cultural contexts to childhood and parenting, but this work was seldom located within a framework about thresholds of harm/risks to children. In other words, some groups have not engaged sufficiently with 'law' while others are too deeply embedded in law (Brophy, 2007).

That background coupled with an increasingly diverse population presents family courts with several challenges. A major challenge has been to try to get the right balance between respect for different styles of parents and cultural norms (guarding against inappropriate inroads into lifestyles and belief systems), and protecting all children from serious harm/risks. Recent pressure on family courts to be more transparent about decision-making generally (DCA, 2006; MoJ, 2007) may also mean that the system will need to be able to better demonstrate how that balance is achieved and that diverse backgrounds and cultural/religious contexts have been 'heard and understood'. It is arguably also necessary to demonstrate that expert evidence is dynamic and open to change, as child welfare knowledge itself develops to meet the challenges posed by increasingly diverse communities.

Two recent empirical studies on care proceedings concerning children from minority ethnic families addressed these issues (Brophy, Jhutti-Johal and Owen, 2003a; 2003b; Brophy, Jhutti-Johal and McDonald, 2005). The first study provides baseline information on whether/how issues of race, ethnicity, culture, religious and linguistic diversity were addressed in proceedings and whether the threshold criteria for a care order required reassessment. In the second study interviews with solicitors and minority ethnic parents explored some of the 'silences' and gaps in information identified in the first study and whether parents had a fair hearing, were 'heard and understood' by courts – and experts – and whether they experienced any racism in the process.

SIGNIFICANT HARM AND INFORMATION ON 'DIVERSITY' IN COURT FILES

In addressing questions of 'focus and relevance', among other methods[2] the study analysed the written information available to courts on issues of 'race', ethnicity, culture, religion and

---

[1] Various bodies examining evidence have endorsed the view that minority ethnic litigants perceive and experience the criminal justice system as unfair. This evidence is reviewed by Hood et al *Ethnic Minorities in the Criminal Courts: Perceptions of fairness and equality of treatment* (DCA (now, Ministry of Justice): London, 2003) 1–6.

[2] Twenty-five judges, magistrates and legal advisers were interviewed, 36 hearings were observed (chapters 5 and 6, Brophy et al, 2003).

linguistic diversity. In a sample of 182 applications stratified by ethnic group[3] all documents in court files were read and coded according to whether they contained descriptive and substantive information on any aspect of diversity.[4]

Findings were better than might have been predicted. Most cases (over 80%) began with some descriptive information on diversity.[5] However, the degree of substantive treatment of this information was lower at most key stages in proceedings (ranging from 50–83%). Moreover, these findings were based on a composite picture of all the evidence available at each of four key stages in cases thus some documents contained relevant information – others none at all.

GROUNDS FOR APPLICATIONS

The grounds for applications, attention to issues of cultural/religious diversity and any evidence of 'cultural conflicts' between professionals and parents, were explored. Cases concerning minority ethnic children were very similar in terms of complexity to those concerning white British children; most contained multiple allegations of child maltreatment[6] and multiple failures of parenting. Many issues contributing to failures of parenting were common to all groups; these included mental ill-health problems (and refusal of professional help for this), male violence, refusal to cooperate with health and welfare agencies, difficulties in controlling children/young people, substance abuse, and accommodation problems.[7]

There were no 'single issue' cases where allegations of *significant harm* rested unequivocally on behaviours/attitudes argued as culturally acceptable by a parent but as unacceptable by professionals.

'Cultural conflicts'

Evidence of conflict grounded in diverse norms/values/practices was more common in cases concerning parents of South Asian and African origin (compared with cases concerning parents of African-Caribbean origin). However, such conflicts were seldom pivotal by the time cases reached a pre-trial review, and a contested threshold hearing was a rare event.

Two related issues – familiar to lawyers but less so to parents – go some way to explaining this. First, as indicated above, is the sheer range of concerns leading to failures of parenting: one-off events of ill treatment (with the possible exception of sexual abuse and serious non-accidental injury of a baby), are unlikely to reach the court. Second, cases do not necessarily 'go to threshold' on all concerns/allegations; rather the focus will be on those which, if parties cannot agree, the applicant is most likely to obtain a finding of fact from the court.

This 'filtering' process often excluded examples of 'cultural conflicts' between professionals and parents, for example, about whether a child is considered old enough to be left home alone, in charge of siblings, allowed some personal freedom and views about discipline and punishment.

---

3   These comprised 61 black children (African, African Caribbean and other black groups), 42 children of South Asian origin (Indian, Bangladeshi and Pakistani), 32 children of mixed heritage and 46 white British children (182 children in 100 cases – Table 1.1, Brophy et al, 2003).

4   Descriptive information may specify 'ethnic group' (eg Indian), 'religion' (Sikh), 'Language' (Punjabi/English). However, a statement may then explain the significance of these descriptions for lifestyles, childcare values/practices, notions of health/illness, etc for the particular family/parent.

5   Some 56% of cases started and completed in the Magistrates' Family Proceedings Court, and 80% of those completed in higher courts began with some information (Brophy et al, 2003: 82–83).

6   That is, two or more categories (from sexual abuse, physical abuse, neglect or emotional ill treatment). Emotional maltreatment and neglect was the most common combination (Table 4.4, Brophy et al, 2003).

7   Table 4.5, Brophy et al, 2003.

Equally, issues of motivation and context to physical ill treatment although important in understanding a parent's perspective, were not pivotal in establishing whether a child had suffered *significant harm*.

The study also indicated most families who are subject to proceedings share certain socio-economic and psychosocial characteristics despite diverse backgrounds and contexts. How welfare and health professionals address these issues may be as important as some of the cultural/religious differences between groups.

Addressing 'diversity': expert reports and parents' statements

Most cases in care proceedings contain expert evidence (Brophy 2006: Brophy et al 1999). In this sample 89% contained expert reports and these varied in their coverage of diverse cultural/religious/linguistic backgrounds according to the discipline of the expert, and the ethnic group of the family. Paediatric and other medical reports[8] almost never contained any information on diversity. Reports from child and adolescent/family psychiatrists[9] were more likely to contain some information – but this varied according to the ethnic group of the family. For example, two-thirds of reports assessing families of South Asian origin contained descriptive and some substantive information – compared with under half of reports on black families. No reports based on families of African-Caribbean origin contained both categories of information.

Over a third of cases (35%) contained adult psychiatric reports; almost all these reports were based on mothers. In cases concerning mothers of South Asian origin, 48% contained adult psychiatric reports. There was, however, little evidence of substantive attention to cultural/religious diversity in reports. This was rather surprising given the literature on the intersections between 'race', culture and mental health, and the emphasis on the need for appropriate services for minority ethnic patients.[10]

Some minority ethnic parents saw state intervention in parenting practices as a complete anathema – especially those originating from countries with no child welfare services and corrupt state institutions. Nevertheless most parents did participate in proceedings. Overall, more mothers than fathers filed statements and statements demonstrated some fathers were especially resistant to interventions in families.

Many parents' statements conformed to a 'rebuttal' mode in terms of format. Coverage of lifestyles, belief systems and child-rearing values and practices was variable. For example, all mothers of African and Bangladeshi origin and fathers of African and Pakistani origin referred to diverse cultural or religious contexts compared with few parents of Caribbean origin or those in mixed partnerships.

A second study explored these findings with a sample of solicitors and parents.[11]

---

[8]   Filed in 35% of cases (Table 6.2, Brophy et al, 2003).

[9]   For all types of reports – filed in 47% of cases (Table 6.2, Brophy et al, 2003).

[10] This literature was extensively reviewed in Brophy (2000) and published in Brophy (2005) with a subsection in Brophy et al (2003) 232) but see, eg, Fernando *Mental Health in a Multi-ethnic Society: a Multi-disciplinary Handbook* (1995); Falkov *Crossing Bridges: training resources for working with mentally ill parents and their children* (1998) 131–137.

[11] This is a qualitative study; 45 solicitors and 12 respondents in families were interviewed. The samples were drawn from three diverse urban areas in England. Interviews were in-depth, semi-structured, taped and fully transcribed. The strengths and weakness of the samples are outline in Appendix 1 of Brophy, Jhutti-Johal and McDonald (2005).

ADVISING AND REPRESENTING MINORITY ETHNIC PARENTS

Getting a parent's story and explaining law to parents

Some solicitors identified difficulties in getting a parent's story and broaching diverse backgrounds and contexts. This is partly because neither the solicitor nor the parent begins this exercise with much of a 'script': solicitors may not know what to ask a parent; parents may not know what they need to tell their solicitor.

Two *broad* client groups determined approaches: parents who are relatively newly arrived in Britain, and second/third generation black and Asian British. With the former group, a major hurdle to be overcome before getting a parent's story was often a parent's incomprehension at state intervention in parenting practices.

With regard to black British and Asian British parents, solicitors tended to make assumptions about knowledge of welfare and legal systems and integration into British society. With certain exceptions, the solicitor's task was therefore often viewed as little different to that involved with white British parents. However, explaining law and procedures to *all* parents was difficult; language and terms were said to be complex and solicitors often felt they were not terribly skilled at explaining things; parents tended to agree.

'Capturing the client': values, family lifestyles and parenting

Solicitors were divided about responsibility for broaching backgrounds and potential differences in values and practice with parents. Some solicitors were extremely cautious about initiating discussions where they had little knowledge or training and were unsure how a parent viewed issues. There was some concern about being viewed as racist simply by raising the topic. Other solicitors however have developed methods of introducing the issue – precisely because they felt parents simply would not raise it 'uninvited'.

Conversely, some parents were not always clear about why their solicitor had wanted to discuss their background and childhood; others said solicitors had not ventured much beyond discussing the specific allegations – and parents had felt unable to initiate a wider discussion.

Most solicitors were highly critical of a 'rebuttal mode' as a format for parents' statements. However, the issue of including information on backgrounds and 'cultural/religious contexts' raised concerns about 'best strategy' and whether information would assist their case. Nevertheless, the final decision was said to rest with parents. Other solicitors argued the importance of 'capturing the client' and would therefore include information which although 'culturally important, may not be legally relevant'.

However, half the parents in this sample were dissatisfied with their statements *because* diverse cultural/religious backgrounds were not covered or were not in a parent's own words or things were said differently.

'Ethnic matching' did not resolve issues: some minority ethnic solicitors said parents had unrealistic expectations of them, while some parents were disappointed with 'matched' solicitors. Parents had anticipated their solicitor would understand certain issues in families and include them in a statement. When this did not happen, parents felt let down but equally had not felt any more able or empowered to take the initiative by raising issues themselves.

Views about the relevance of diverse backgrounds

Some solicitors said that while *some* minority ethnic parents do mention 'cultural differences' in values and practices in bringing up children compared with white British parents, others do not. For example, some parents have argued physical 'punishment' is sanctioned by their cultural/religious traditions. But equally others have said they do not consider it acceptable to hit or beat children.

Most minority ethnic parents in this study identified differences between their values and practices regarding child rearing and those of white British parents they know. Some parents generalised their views to an ethnic group, others distanced themselves from what they felt were stereotypes of parents of South Asian and African origins – especially with regard to the use of physical punishment. Some stereotypes also emerged about white British parents – as over-liberal with children.

ATTENDING FAMILY COURTS

Most parents in all groups were reported as frightened and anxious about attending court. There are, however, some differences; those minority ethnic parents with no knowledge or experience of state involvement in defining adequate parenting express incredulity that courts should in any way be interested in their parenting. For some parents notions of pride and honour remain important; courts are associated with crime and punishment: attendance – even at a 'family' court – is a source of shame and dishonour with competing impacts on parents' responses to proceedings.[12]

Dedicated family courts were felt to prove a better experience for most parents than those undertaking a mixture of work. Care centres were also likely to be better than most family proceedings courts – although this could depend on the particular judge. Some judges were regarded as particularly good with minority ethnic parents but in one region certain judges were avoided because approaches were thought to be racist, dismissive or disrespectful.

Overall, however, solicitors said judges were generally good or excellent with most parents; judges with problematic attitudes could be dismissive and disrespectful of parents regardless of ethnic group. Some magistrates were also described as excellent with certain minority ethnic parents, others less good.

EXPERIENCES OF RACISM, A FAIR HEARING, AND FEELING 'HEARD AND UNDERSTOOD'

Most parents, in this sample at least, had not experienced racism from solicitors or barristers, but three reported disrespectful and uninformed comments. Most parents also said they had not experienced any racism in court. However, two parents felt the court had been unfair and racist following a judge's comments prior to hearing their evidence. The parents felt they were being pre-judged because 'in Britain people think African parents are violent towards their children'.

Most solicitors said minority ethnic parents probably did get a fair hearing. Nevertheless they had substantial concerns about the *process*. Factors said to influence parents' experiences were

---

[12] Solicitors said some parents will agree to anything in order to get their children returned before knowledge of proceedings becomes known in wider communities, others will 'fight [the threshold] tooth and nail to the bitter end' since conceding the threshold can have enormous ramifications for a parent's position within a family/community.

the attitude of some judges, whether courts received a full picture of a parent's background and cultural contexts, whether parents instructed a Children Panel solicitor, and the attitude of some experts to issues of diversity (see below).

Most parents' views about unfair treatment focused on a lack of court time and judges, long waiting periods then feeling proceedings were rushed once in court, and not being allowed to speak in court. Thus, while some minority ethnic parents were indeed dissatisfied with treatment by courts, in this sample at least most did not put this down to racism/discrimination – they felt most parents suffered similar insensitive and disrespectful treatment.

Some solicitors in all regions were doubtful that minority ethnic parents felt 'heard and understood' by courts. The response of some courts to the detail of diverse cultural contexts was likely to be responsible for this – *some* judges and magistrates do sometimes fail to understand issues and thus misinterpret aspects of behaviour/attitudes. For example, courts sometimes failed to comprehend the complexities of domestic violence for some mothers of South Asian origin and their limited parameters of action. Overall, however, most solicitors felt there had been substantial improvements in recent years.

Some parents felt judges had not understood diverse backgrounds – either because the court simply did not get this information or because judges failed to understand the information provided, and they did not talk directly to parents about these issues. Other parents simply did not know if they had been 'heard and understood' (the judge had not spoken to them in court and statements were a poor source of information) others felt the judge probably did understand them – even though they disagreed with his/her view.

Expert assessments

Solicitors felt issues of diversity were probably not relevant for the work of paediatricians but highly pertinent for psychiatrists, psychologists and family centre assessments. There were concerns about experts who were not prepared to consider that people from other cultures might live and understand their lives differently.

Most solicitors had not seen improvements in the focus on diversity in core assessments following changes to framework and guidance (DoH, 2000a; 2000b).[13] It was argued a lack of resources and experienced social workers meant that the assessment process is failing parents in all groups. Some solicitors also argued the Protocol for Judicial Case Management (DCA, 2003) failed to address the fact that many social workers have neither the time nor expertise to undertake the in-depth parenting assessments required.

Parents' views about whether they felt 'heard and understood' by experts depended on whether the expert had raised potentially different cultural/religious frameworks. Parents had not felt able to raise these issues themselves; they were unsure if/how it might be relevant and they did not want to be seen as 'foreign' or 'exotic'. Parents were especially critical of some psychologists. In all regions solicitors also expressed concerns about the validity of psychometric testing on some minority ethnic parents.

---

[13]   In some regions 34% of cases begin proceedings without a core assessment (Brophy et al, 2003).

CONCLUSIONS AND QUESTIONS

The threshold criteria

Studies indicate that 'significant harm' as a threshold for assessing harm/risks to children in different cultural/religious contexts was about right. There was no suggestion that findings of fact had been fundamentally unfair/unjust for parents from minority ethnic groups/cultures. Equally, evidence to date indicates cases did not usually 'turn' on issues of cultural/religious variation.

Question 1

(a) Are there cases investigated under Part III of the Act which do 'turn' issues of cultural/religious diversity which are successfully resolved – and what lessons could be drawn from such cases?

(b) Will the Pre Proceeding Protocol be supported by additional resources to social workers to ensure a better focus on these issues? And will procedures under the PLO ensure transparency in attention to these issues in cases that result in proceedings?

Gaps and 'silences'

There were some gaps in attention to issues of diversity in some reports and statements, and also some 'silences' in dialogue with parents. Some solicitors were anxious about initiating discussions about diverse backgrounds and contexts with parents. Lack of training, fears of 'getting it wrong', of offending a parent or being seen as racist has constrained some practices.

It is somewhat bizarre that the very behaviour most practitioners wished to avoid (racism and stereotyping of parents) could result in an avoidance of discussions some parents wanted – but which they too felt unable to initiate.

A balance has to be struck between too much emphasis on cultural/religious diversity so that a parent feels inappropriately 'singled out' on grounds of 'race' or culture, and ignoring issues unless they are obvious or unavoidable. These findings arguably require a multidisciplinary response.

Question 2

What are the key issues for training, and where/how could this best be addressed and delivered in legal and clinical training? (eg Children Panel training, CPD training, RCPCH/NSPCC/ALSG Level I/II (Safeguarding Children) – Recognition and Responses in Child Protection Training Packages, etc).

Improving parents' experience of court proceedings

Many solicitors and some parents focused on the need for training to increase knowledge, understanding and confidence in addressing diverse backgrounds and contexts, along with innovative case management to enable judges to demonstrate to parents that they are indeed 'heard and understood'.

Solicitors and parents also felt it would help parents enormously if courts engaged directly with parents, welcomed them in court, and explained issues and decisions to them. Some parents wanted the option of being able to speak to the judge.

Judges, solicitors and parents identified the need for more judges and improved listings in care centres to reduce those areas where parents experience insensitive and disrespectful treatment.

Solicitors and parents also wanted a reduction in jargon, outdated terminology and lengthy statements; parents wanted information from courts in languages and terms they could understand and to which they can refer.

Observations of hearings and interviews highlighted variation in styles of what might be called 'judge craft'. Most judges are excellent with parents; solicitors and parents wanted an extension of that approach – first to improve the experience of parents so that they *feel* understood and fairly treated, second because conceding the threshold means that most parents will not get an opportunity to speak to the judge.

Question 3

Can some courts improve some parents' experiences in court without diminishing the gravity and importance of proceedings, or jeopardising the independence of the judiciary? And if so, what resources/structural changes are necessary to assist that exercise, and how can courts then assess any changes in this field?

Interpreting services for family courts

Both studies highlight problems with interpreters. Judges and solicitors were unclear about whether interpreters receive training for care proceedings or whether family law generally is a mandatory topic in training portfolios.

REFERENCES

Brophy, J 'Child maltreatment in diverse households: Challenges to child care law, theory and practice' in Meuwese, S, Detrick, S and Jansen, S, et al (eds) *100 years of Child Protection* (The Netherlands: Wolf Legal Publishers, 2007)

Brophy, J *Care Proceedings under the Children Act 1989: A Research Review*, Research Series 5/06 (London: DCA, 2006)

Brophy, J 'Building bridges in changing worlds: messages from international child maltreatment research' (2005) 17 (2) *Representing Children* 116–130

Brophy, J 'Child maltreatment and cultural diversity: A critical review of "race" and culture in clinical writing and research' (London: Research Report for the Nuffield Foundation, 2000)

Brophy, J, Jhutti-Johal, J and McDonald, E *Minority ethnic parents, their solicitors and child protection litigation*, Research Series 5/05 (London: DCA, 2005)

Brophy, J, Jhutti-Johal, J and Owen, C *Significant Harm: child protection litigation in a multi-cultural setting* (London: Lord Chancellor's Department, 2003)

Brophy, J, Jhutti-Johal, J and Owen, C 'Child ill-treatment in minority ethnic households' [2003] *Family Law*, October, 756–764

Brophy, J, Bates, P, Brown, L, Cohen, S and Radcliffe, P *Expert Evidence in Child Protection Litigation: Where do we go from here?* (London: The Stationery Office, 1999)

Department for Constitutional Affairs *Confidence and confidentiality: Improving transparency and privacy in family courts* (London: DCA, 2006)

Falkov, A *Crossing Bridges: training resources for working with mentally ill parents and their children* (Brighton: Pavilion Publishing for the Department of Health, 1998)

Fernando, S *Mental Health in a Multi-ethnic Society: a Multi-disciplinary Handbook* (London: Routledge, 1995)

Hood, R, Shute, S and Seemungal, F *Ethnic Minorities in the Criminal Courts: Perceptions of fairness and equality of treatment*, Research Series 2/03 (London: DCA (now, Ministry of Justice), 2003) 1–6

Macpherson, W R, Rt Hon the Lord *The Stephen Lawrence Inquiry* (London: The Stationery Office, 1999)

Ministry of Justice *Confidence & confidentiality: Openness in family courts – a new approach* (London: HMCS, 2007)

Culture and Physical Punishment

Dr Bode Adesida

INTRODUCTION

Child maltreatment has occurred throughout history and it cuts across cultural and national boundaries (Korbin, 1991). There is however, no universal standard for child rearing or for child abuse and neglect. The dominant culture in any society sets the prevailing child rearing standards.

Conflicts can therefore arise when there is great divergence in childcare practices and beliefs between the dominant cultural group and other ethnic or culturally different groups. How do we resolve these potential conflicts? How do we face the challenge of balancing universality and pluralism, and preserve an authentic response to individual/cultural difference?

If we adopt a relatively cultural stance, giving every cultural practice equal status, we might justify a lesser standard of care for some children (Korbin, 1991; Korbin, 1997; Maitra, 1996). However, ignoring a cultural perspective might mean imposing the dominant culture's ethnocentric views about child rearing.

In this paper, I focus on the issue of culture and physical punishment, in particular, the practice in African and Afro-Caribbean communities, because it is a common area of misunderstanding between professionals and families from those communities. I will highlight some 'cultural' issues and offer potential solutions.

PHYSICAL PUNISHMENT

Physical (corporal) punishment is the use of physical force with the intention of causing a child to experience pain, but not injury, for the purpose of correction or control of the child's behaviour (Strauss, 1994). It includes a gamut of practices ranging from an occasional spanking to customary, daily, harsh and intense use of physical force.

There are significant concerns about the use of physical punishment, most notably the association and progression to physical abuse. It is considered that physical abuse often occurs within the context of a physical discipline episode (Whipple and Richey, 1997; Fontes, 2005).

Parents who employ punitive child-rearing practices are believed to use authoritarian means of control. They are convinced that physical punishment is the way to correct perceived child misconduct (Greven, 1990; Smith and Mosby, 2003). Scolding, ridicule and verbal abuse are also used as complementary measures. Parents who fail to mete out 'adequate' punishment to erring children are often seen as permissive.

The authoritarian style of parenting is biased in favour of parent's needs; children's self-expression and independence are suppressed. It is, however, important to note that some studies suggest that an authoritarian style, where parents set rules and enforce them without discussion with their children, may be more beneficial for children in high-risk settings.

Physical punishment has also been associated with negative consequences (Greven, 1990) which include anger, anxiety, fear, lack of empathy and apathy, depression, obsessiveness and rigidity, ambivalence, disassociation, paranoia, sadomasochism, delinquency and criminality and domestic violence.

The use of corporal punishment as a discipline technique by parents and other adults, has at different times being legally and socially sanctioned in all societies (Whipple and Richey, 1997; Smith and Mosby, 2003; Nikapota, 1991; Campbell, 2005; Dietz, 2000; McIntyre and Silva, 1992). The roots for the use of force as a discipline technique are to found in our religious and legal institutions as well as well ingrained in the socio-cultural foundations (Greven, 1990).

THE PROBLEM OF PHYSICAL PUNISHMENT AND CULTURE: THE AFRICAN AND AFRO-CARIBBEAN EXPERIENCE

All 'cultures' use methods of controlling and shaping children's behaviour. The range of disciplinary methods varies from physical punishment, to restriction of privileges, to encouragement, praise and rewards.

In African and Afro-Caribbean communities, the use of physical punishment is not uncommon. A number of observers (Mejiuni, 1991; Smith and Mosby, 2003) however have commented on the extent and prevalence of harsh disciplinary measures in African and Afro-Caribbean child rearing practices. In those communities, it is felt that physical punishment is socially sanctioned and encouraged. Parents and parent surrogates are allowed to use physical punishment in dealing with their children.

There have been specific forms of ill-treatment linked to physical punishment that have also been associated with these communities: facial scarring (Oyetade, 1993, Renteln, 2004); anal/genital insertions (Koramoa, Lynch and Kinnair, 2002); exorcism of children believed to be possessed or to practise witchcraft (Stobart, 2006); using soap to wash out the mouth of the child, kneeling on bare knees or use of a 'prayer' closet (Fontes, 2005).

Okeahialam (1984) has commented on the inaccurate impression that child abuse does not occur in traditional African society. This is felt to be fostered by the sociological concept of the extended family as a system, which provides profound love, protection, security and care.

These traditional and sanctioned practices/forms of physical punishment conflict with the legal system in the UK. Physical punishment, especially when it causes bodily harm is against the laws in the UK. What is acceptable is the use of 'reasonable chastisement'.

BLIND TO CULTURE

Immigrants of African and Afro-Caribbean origin appear to be overrepresented among parents charged with physical abuse and convicted of child abuse and neglect. Over representation of African and Afro-Caribbean children in child abuse and neglect statistics has led to inquiries in factors responsible for this disproportionality (Brophy et al, 2005; Derezotes, Poertner and Testa 2005), especially as there are no significant differences in the overall child maltreatment rates.

Culture/race affecting decision making about children has been posited as an explanation for this disproportionality. Does this mean lack of equal protection for all cultures under the law?

Should all parents or carers regardless of cultural background be expected to conform to UK standards? The disproportionality has also been explained as due to people from those communities experiencing more risk factors associated with child maltreatment.

Ethnic minority status can be a stressor. Ethnicity and culture are significant parameters in understanding psychological and social processes before delivering services (Tharp, 1991). Children of families in changing cultural contexts are often at risk for maltreatment (Roer-Strier, 2001). This is because such families may experience social, cultural and economic change and a loss of their support networks. Stress factors include migration, acculturation, intergenerational conflicts, and discrimination. The risks increase when children are exposed to systems with conflicting socialisation goals and with contradictory definitions of desirable childcare or supervision frameworks.

Raising children is a time-consuming task, and a number of ethnic minority parents feel the constraints of not having the support of the extended family especially with regards childcare and domestic tasks (Oyetade, 1993). Sometimes parents, because of other competing priorities, e g heavy economic burden, either leave their children in their homeland or send them to private foster carers. This practice makes it difficult to build a secure attachment relationship. Problems emerge when the parents and children are reunited because of the lack of a bond.

Sometimes when parents are questioned about their use of corporal punishment, they see it as an attack on their culture and traditions. They feel they are been told to reject the way they were brought up by their parents. They find it difficult to take on the notion that not all cultural practices are supportive of a child's emotional development.

Sometimes misunderstandings have arisen because of language interpretation. It might not be clear what is meant by physical chastisement. Many times, I have come across the confusion of beat with smacking or of the word 'beat' with 'bit' because of a particular accent.

There are also concerns that because of possible differences in help-seeking, there may be cross-cultural differences in parental and community concerns and help-seeking behaviour, which reflects perception of need (Nikapota, 1991; Edwards and Kumru, 1999). In developing countries, difficult behaviour is not construed as requiring help or treatment but rather as a situation requiring advice or discipline. Children with learning disorders can be seen as lazy or disinterested in study.

BLINDED BY CULTURE

Though ethnicity and culture can be significant factors in how we bring up our children, ethnic culture is not the only determinant of parenting. Exploration of family dynamics (Nikapota, 1991; Dietz, 2000; Fong, 2004; McGoldrick, Giordano and Garcia-Preto, 2005; Johnson-Powell 1997; and Canino and Spurlock, 2000) reveal significant stress, family dysfunction and interrelationship difficulties – attachment difficulties, younger parents, lower educational achievement, intergenerational conflict, social isolation, scapegoating, and psychosocial disadvantage.

The cultural background of immigrant families has historically been seen as an explanation for abusive behaviour; relating to different conduct or other aspects of family life to culture and thus granting it acceptance (Jordan, 2002, Korbin, 1981). It can be used to explain apparently irrational or abusive behaviour. This has led to problem of leaving some children unprotected.

DISCUSSION

Consideration of cultural issues is widely accepted in the field of child maltreatment (Smith and Mosby, 2003; Campbell E T, 2005; Maitra, 1999). All children, from whatever culture, should be protected from harm.

Koramoa, Lynch and Kinnair (2002) in their exploration of a the West African culture advise that

> ... professionals working in a multicultural society must be sensitive to diverse cultural approaches to child-rearing and be able to distinguish between those traditions that can cause harm and ones which positively enhance the child's cultural identity. (415)

Professionals, parents and policy-makers need to accept that child rearing traditional practices can be neutral, facilitating or harmful to the socio-emotional well-being of children. The practice of physical chastisement is one that many societies consider inimical to the well-being of our children.

Although we do not have definitive studies of the negative consequences of physical punishment, there is appreciable evidence of probable associated harm. I therefore advocate banning of all forms of physical chastisement of children. It is puzzling that it is unacceptable to hit a spouse but acceptable to hit a child. We have banned the hitting of servants and prisoners and we seem to be against children hitting other children.

I do not however agree that because a child has been physical chastised, it is necessary for the child to be removed from the parents. There are definitely families, either of the dominant cultural group or of the ethnic minority groups, who can be considered abusive or neglectful of their children. In these cases, there would be ample evidence of acts of omission or commission and maltreatment risk factors – mental illness, substance misuse, personality disorders, chaotic lifestyles, history of ill-treatment of parents in childhood, etc – to help one reach a conclusion of ill-treatment.

The dilemma is usually in cases where one has adequate or even excellent parents in other ways, where their authoritarian-style and corporal punishments exist side-by-side with high levels of intimacy and support (Fontes 2005). In these families, corporal punishment may occasionally slip to levels that are considered abusive. I am worried when the children in such families are removed that they will never return to the care of their parents.

The countries of origin of many African and Afro-Caribbean families use corporal punishment. It should therefore not be surprising if these families get into conflict with professionals because of the way they discipline their children. It is important to note that despite the overrepresentation of children from those communities in the statistics, research does not support the view that immigrants and members of ethnic minority groups are more likely to be physically abusive than those from the dominant culture.

I will therefore advocate consideration of cultural factors at all the levels of contact between child welfare professionals and African and Afro-Caribbean families. It is not because of a higher risk of physical ill treatment but rather because preventative efforts are more likely to be effective if they are tailored to the needs of those families. There are also concerns because of their overrepresentation in the statistics.

There are no concrete solutions but by being culturally competent we might be able resolve the dilemma faced by professionals and parents and their children. A culturally competent person exhibits socially adaptive and respectful behaviour in cross-cultural settings. They should also be ready to explore with the families and tactfully challenge their beliefs and values. It will also be important that the professionals have specific awareness of varying forms of discipline and the rationale given for them. Cultural competence has to be seen as ongoing and a multilayered process that involves personal, interpersonal and organisational levels.

We need to understand the systemic stresses that weigh upon many ethnic minority families, often contributing to disciplinary encounters and violence. We should, however, not make the assumption about the families' use of corporal punishment or the possible presence of physical abuse based on the family's ethnic/cultural identity.

The framework and guidelines for intervention should follow the suggestions of 'unpacking the cultural variable' (Korbin 2002). This is because we have to understand culture in context. Culture is not monolithic or static but variable and dynamic. It is not uniformly distributed and does not have uniform impact on all members. Lumping individuals and families together does not reflect cultural reality and may in fact, mask rather than illuminate culture (Abney, 2002; Korbin 2002).

Kuper (2000) warns that there are no pure cultures, distinctive and enduring. Every culture draws on diverse sources, depends on borrowings, and is in flux. Human beings are very much alike, and every culture is rooted in a universal human mentality. He goes on to emphasise that appeals to culture can offer only a partial explanation of why people think and behave as they do, and of what causes them to alter their ways.

The potential stresses for ethnic minority families, which therefore need to be 'unpacked', include the following (Fontes, 2005; Johnson-Powell, 1997; Fong, 2004; and Canino and Spurlock, 2000):

- immigration difficulties;

- cultural conflicts and acculturation stress;

- changes in education and socio-economic status;

- language proficiency;

- disrupted social network and social isolation;

- experiences with prejudice, rejection and discrimination;

- role reversal leading to spousal or intergenerational tensions; and

- inaccessibility of health care.

Increasing professionals' cultural competence is important but equally important is raising the awareness of ethnic minority families (and the general population). They need to know what the law states with regards physical chastisement and clarify the notion of 'reasonable chastisement'. There must be emphasis on the impact of physical punishment on children and the need to adopt alternative non-physical means of punishment. This can be done through the media; positive parent education programmes; and using professionals already involved with families, especially those families with specific risk factors, eg health visitors.

We need to target ethnic communities in every possible way. Professionals who work in those communities need to facilitate relationships. It is crucial to collaborate with community leaders and agencies that are already trusted by their ethnic communities, and to build on efforts that make sense within the ethnic context (and keeping within the legal context).

Professionals should facilitate focus groups and set up child abuse awareness weeks. I am sure it will be easier for parents to cooperate if they attend groups where they can speak in their native language. It will also be important to advertise in ethnic community meeting places, eg ethnic supermarkets, bathrooms of religious institutions, nail salons and beauty parlours. We should not forget the media – ethnic TV stations, local radio stations and newspapers.

For parents who need to or want to change, working towards an authoritative style of parenting is most likely to be beneficial because it is most likely to foster the optimal development of children. We need to make choices that would be more nurturing, loving and life enhancing. In addition, if we hope to make a true difference in the lives of these families, we must be ready for a long-term commitment and engagement.

REFERENCES

Abney, V D 'Cultural Competence in the Field of Child Maltreatment' in Myers et al (eds), *The APSAC Handbook on Child Maltreatment* (Sage Publications, 2002)

Brophy, J, Jhutti-Johal, J, McDonald, E *Minority ethnic parents, their solicitors and child protection litigation* (Department of Constitutional Affairs (DCA) Research Series, October 2005)

Canino, I A and Spurlock, J *Culturally Diverse Children and Adolescents: Assessment, Diagnosis and Treatment* (The Guildford Press, 2nd edn, 2000)

Dietz, T L 'Disciplining Children: Characteristic Associated with the Use of Corporal Punishment' (2000) 24 *Child Abuse and Neglect* 1529–1542

Edwards, C P and Kumru, A 'Culturally Sensitive Assessment' (1999) 8(2) *Child and Adolescent Psychiatric Clinics of North America* 409–424

Fong, R *Culturally Competent Practice with Immigrant and Refugee Children and Families* (The Guildford Press, 2004)

Greven, P *Spare the child: The religious roots of punishment and the psychological impact of physical abuse* (New York: Knopf, 1990)

Johnson-Powell, G & Yamamoto *Transcultural Child Development: Psychological Assessment and Treatment* (John Wiley & Sons Inc, 1997)

Koramoa, J, Lynch, M A, and Kinnair, D 'A Continuum of Child Rearing: Responding to Traditional Practices' (2002) 11 *Child Abuse Review* 415–421

Korbin, J E 'Cross-cultural perspectives and research directions for the 21st century' (1991) 15(1) *Child Abuse and Neglect* 67–77

Korbin, J E 'Culture and Child Maltreatment' Chapter 2 in M E Helfer, R S Kempe and R D Krugman (eds), *The Battered Child* (The University of Chicago Press, 1997)

Korbin, J E 'Culture and child maltreatment: cultural competence and beyond' (2002) 26 *Child Abuse and Neglect* 637–644

Kuper, A *Culture: The Anthropologists' Account* (Harvard University Press, 2000)

Maitra, B 'Child Abuse: A universal 'diagnostic' category? The implication of culture in definition and assessment' (1996) 42(4) *International Journal of Social Psychiatry* 287–304

McGoldrick, M, Giordano, J and Garcia-Preto, N *Ethnicity and Family Therapy* (The Guildford Press, 3rd edn, 2005)

McIntyre, T and Silva, P 'Culturally Diverse Childrearing Practices: Abusive or Different?' (1992) 4(1) *Beyond Behaviour* 8–12

Mejiuni, C O 'Educating adults against socio-culturally induced abuse and neglect of children in Nigeria' (1991) 15 *Child Abuse and Neglect* 139–145

Mohler, B 'Cross-cultural Issues in Research on Child Mental Health' (2001) 10(4) *Child and Adolescent Psychiatric clinics of North America* 763–776

Nikapota, A D 'Child Psychiatry in Developing Countries' (1991) 158 *British Journal of Psychiatry* 743–751

Okeahialam, T C 'Child Abuse in Nigeria' (1984) 8 *Child Abuse and Neglect* 69–73

Renteln, A D *The Cultural Defence* (Oxford University Press, 2004)

Smith, D E and Mosby, G 'Jamaican child-rearing practices: the role of corporal punishment' (2003) *Adolescence*, Summer

Sprott, J E 'One person's "spoiling" is another's freedom to become: overcoming ethnocentric views about parental control' (1994) 38 (8) *Social Science Medicine* 1111–1124

Stobart, E 'Child Abuse Linked to Accusations of "Possession" and "Witchcraft"', Research Report RR750 (Department for Education and Skills. DfES Publications, 2006)

Strauss, M A *Beating The Devil Out Of Them: Corporal Punishment in American Families* (Lexington Books, 1994)

Tharp, R G 'Cultural Diversity and Treatment of Children' (1991) 59 (6) *Journal of Consulting and Clinical Psychology* 799–812

Whipple, E E, and Richey, C A 'Crossing the line from physical discipline to child abuse: How much is too much?' (1997) 21 (5) *Child Abuse and Neglect* 431–444

Integrating Diversity into Paediatric Thinking Practice: Messages for the Family Justice System

Dr Neela Shabde

Consultant Paediatrician, North Tyneside General Hospital

with Dr Julia Brophy

Senior Research Fellow, Oxford Centre for Family Law and Policy, University of Oxford and Dr Kate Ward, Consultant Paediatrician, Airedale General Hospital

SUMMARY OF THE PAPER

Dr Neela Shabde introduced her paper by emphasising its context; there have been a number of recent high-profile cases which have resulted in eminent paediatricians being pilloried. Consequently, paediatricians are anxious and worried about doing child protection work. A 2004 survey by the Royal College of Paediatrics and Child Health (RCPCH), which explored levels of complaints about paediatricians, revealed that only a very small number of complaints were referred to the GMC and a very small number of those were upheld. While the anxiety may, therefore, be irrational among paediatricians it is nonetheless very real.

Paediatricians face various challenges in their work, one of which is contributing to issues of diversity. It is important that paediatricians do not overlook these issues as traditionally the domain of psychologists, psychiatrists and social workers. Life is so not simple for a case of accidental injuries to be only that.

Dr Shabde noted that many paediatricians are already undertaking holistic assessments in the exercise of their duties and in the caring approach they adopt. In this area, medicine is not just science, it is also art. It is not simply a question of looking at physical diagnosis but also how to communicate concerns to families in a way that makes them feel heard and understood. Dr Shabde considered that diversity issues also have implications for health. For example, failure to thrive could be the result of a mother's poor nutrition and without an understanding of the relevant background an assessment could be flawed from the outset. However, increasingly questions of cultural competence are being addressed in the training of paediatricians.

Dr Shabde concluded the introduction to her paper by highlighting her own strong belief that paediatric assessments should include cultural, religious and diversity issues whether the assessment is for the purposes of a report to the court or for assisting parents in dealing with the implications of health issues.

THE PAPER

Introduction – current debates

Several issues have focused attention on paediatricians in the child protection arena. A number of child deaths, the discredited evidence of certain experts and concerns about the impact of paediatricians contributed to a survey of members by the RCPCH in 2004 exploring levels of complaint about paediatricians and any impact on future willingness to work as expert witnesses.

These developments have overshadowed existing concerns about shortages of paediatricians (generally and as expert witnesses). And while the RCPCH survey revealed complaints upheld against paediatricians were small (3% of the 14% subject to a complaint)[1] the ramifications may be more widespread partly because they exacerbate existing anxieties about court work and gaps in training.

This is the climate in which we address the relevance of cultural, religious and linguistic diversity for paediatric assessments and reports for courts. Some paediatricians have already raised concerns about services for minority ethnic families. Work in Bradford identified a high prevalence of certain genetic disorders in Pakistani communities but local paediatricians argue overloaded teams have no time to do research and develop new approaches to working with families (eg Corry, 2003 and see Maitre, 2005).

Other paediatricians (Bhopal, 2001, 2000; Webb, 2005, 2003, 2002, 2000; Webb and Sergison, 2003; Shah et al, 1996; Smith, 2000; Ingleby, 1995; Moghal et al, 1995) highlight the importance of attention to issues of racism and cultural diversity and the need for training and research to improve services. However, little attention has focused on issues of 'diversity' in paediatric reports for courts.

This article aims to start that debate; it sets out the contexts in which paediatricians work and through which concerns about child maltreatment may arise, along with new training initiatives. It outlines research findings on attention to diverse backgrounds/contexts in reports and summaries the views of key professionals regarding the relevance of these factors.

It is developed against substantial changes in the organisation of a safeguarding agenda for children and the training of paediatricians. These follow the abuse and murder of Victoria Climbié, a black child from the Ivory Coast, the subsequent Inquiry and Report (Laming 2003, Part III – Health), and the government's response (DfES 2004 – *Every Child Matters*; DfES 2006 – *Working Together to Safeguard Children*).

---

[1]   The survey reported 14% of members had been subject to a formal complaint. Most complaints (79%) were dealt with locally; on available data, few (8%) went to independent review, while 11% were serious enough for referral to the GMC. Of those complaints dealt with *locally* most (76%) were dropped, 21% were found unproven; 3% were upheld (8% ongoing). Of the 11% referred on to the GMC, where outcome is known, 41% were dropped, 59% were found not proven. Of the 14% subject to a complaint, 29% were less willing to become involved in child protection work. Thus, a relatively small number of paediatricians have been subject to a formal complaint, most were resolved at a local level and just 3% were upheld at that level. None of those referred to the GMC were upheld. Data does not support the view that there are numerous complaints about expert witnesses – although these have risen (from fewer than 20 in 1995 to over 100 in 2003) (RCPCH, 2004). Qualitative work with a sub-sample of 70 paediatricians has also been undertaken (Turton and Haines, 2006).

INSTITUTIONAL SETTINGS, POSTS AND TRAINING FOR PAEDIATRICIANS

There is a range of specialisms within paediatrics and child health and several avenues through which paediatricians may become involved in cases where there are child protection concerns – either as a treating doctor or as an expert witness.

For example, with regard to institutional settings, a clinician may be involved in general paediatric work at District General Hospital level, working on a ward with responsibility for managing and delivering acute paediatric services[2] including neonatal and services for children with chronic diseases (eg asthma, allergies, diabetes, chronic arthritis, chronic renal diseases and oncology). An acute unit may accept referrals from primary care teams (including GPs, health visitors and others), Accident and Emergency Departments, Community Paediatric Teams, and other hospitals. Some hospitals have a dedicated Children's 'A & E' Department.

There are also community paediatric services where consultant-led teams provide locally based services and in some cases, district-wide specialist services. So, for example, a portfolio of services in a community service may include services for children with physical and learning disabilities, visual and hearing problems and neurological problems (eg cerebral palsy and degenerative conditions, and also autistic spectrum disorder, attention-deficit hyperactivity disorder and other significant emotional and behavioural difficulties). Also, 'Looked-after' children and 'Children in need' have increased and unmet needs which bring them into contact with community paediatric services.

Paediatricians specialising in community aspects also undertake developmental assessments, focusing on children with growth and complex developmental disorders as well as some emotional and behavioural problems. A significant number of paediatricians with appropriate training may also undertake some child mental health work and may work closely with Child and Adolescent Mental Health Teams (CAMHS).

In addition, paediatricians also work in child public health and preventative medicine (eg addressing obesity). There are also specialisms within paediatrics, for example, cardiology, endocrinology, respiratory and renal medicine where clinicians working at a tertiary (specialist) level are experts in their field and may be called on to provide an assessment and opinion in the context of child protection concerns.[3]

With regard to training on child protection issues, historically this has been limited and somewhat variable. However, following the Laming Report (2003) – and subsequent consultations and recommendations following the government's response to that Report[4] – there are substantial training initiatives.[5]

The focus here is on training for Consultants, Specialist Registrars and Senior House Officers (now called Speciality Trainees collectively). There are other career grades and associate grades[6]

---

[2] A range of services can be provided including a neonatal unit, a paediatric day assessment unit, paediatric Accident and Emergency, children's home care team, outpatient clinics and inpatient services.

[3] Plus a range of surgical specialisms.

[4] DfES *Keeping Children Safe and Safeguarding Children* (2003); DfES *Every Child Matters – Changes for Children in Health Services* (2004).

[5] For example, the RCPCH/NSPCC/ALSG (2006) Training Package – Level I, Safeguarding Children – Recognition and Response in Child Protection: An Educational Programme for Paediatricians in training. This is a one-day intensive course run by experienced trainers. Additionally, materials are available on an interactive CD-ROM and accompanying RCPCH (2007) Child Protection Reader.

[6] For example, junior grades such as staff grade, associate specialist, and clinical/teaching fellows.

where people have acquired experience through direct clinical work (eg where a child presents with bruising or a urinary tract infection which may raise child protection concerns).

As already argued (Shabde, 2006) child protection work within paediatric services and the safeguarding agenda requires not only a range of clinical competences but also confidence, courage, and support in developing appropriate attitudes and feelings. Thus, the aim of the RCPCH Level I training package is to raise awareness and better equip paediatricians with the knowledge and skills to recognise and respond to safeguarding issues competently and confidently at a level appropriate to levels of training and responsibility. It is also hoped that prior to specialist level all trainees will have undergone child protection training and will be expected to maintain their skills and competences at regular intervals. The learning objectives include understanding attitudes and feelings, increasing background knowledge on abuse and neglect and outcomes for children and the duties of paediatricians in safeguarding children.

The course addresses the fact that doctors' responses to child maltreatment may reflect their attitudes, beliefs and values and that unchallenged, these can be an impediment in recognising and responding to maltreatment. We want to take this a step further when thinking about work with minority ethnic families. Our aim is not to pose families as 'other', but rather to argue that cultural competence and reflective practice should be an integral and transparent part of the 'picture building' exercise in assessments.

RESEARCH FINDINGS

Paediatric evidence in care proceedings

The majority of cases contain expert evidence, and paediatric reports are filed in about 35% of cases; this figure has remained stable over several years (Brophy, 2006; Brophy, Wales and Bates, 1999).[7] There is, however, evidence that patterns may differ between ethnic groups. A recent study found that in cases concerning children of South Asian origin there was a high use of all the major types of expert reports.[8] For example, paediatric reports were filed in 52% of such cases, compared with 32% of cases concerning Black children and 26% of cases concerning White British children (Brophy, Jhutti-Johal and Owen, 2003: 81).

The focus on 'diversity' in paediatric reports

In the above study of 182 applications, an examination of the focus on diversity in expert reports revealed considerable variation in the degree to which reports addressed these issues. Coverage varied according to the discipline of the expert and the ethnic group of the child/parents. For example, paediatric reports seldom contained any information on diverse backgrounds/ contexts.

---

[7] The national survey of cases involving experts concerned just under 1,000 children in 557 cases – see Brophy, Wale and Bates, 1999.

[8] The four categories providing the vast majority of expert evidence are: child psychiatrists, paediatricians, adult psychiatrists and psychologists; other disciplines are instructed but in very much smaller numbers (Brophy, 2006: 26).

Views of judges, magistrates and legal advisers in care proceedings

A further study of the views of 25 judges, magistrates and legal advisers included questions about the quality and relevance of information on diverse cultural/religious backgrounds and contexts in determining harm to children and failures of parenting (Brophy, Jhutti-Johal and McDonald, 2005).

Respondents were divided as to whether clinicians were helpful in determining these issues – mostly because it was felt cases did not usually 'turn' on 'cultural conflicts or misunderstandings'.[9] Some judges are sceptical about whether diversity contexts had any relevance for paediatricians; much discussion at this point focused on physical injury. Most respondents also argued that responsibility for addressing these issues lies with the parties; courts have no independent way of knowing if they are relevant in the absence of written evidence. The onus of responsibility was thus placed very firmly with advocates and experts.

The views of solicitors representing parents and minority ethnic parents

Childcare solicitors[10] also tend to think issues of diversity are probably irrelevant for paediatricians; discussions again tended to focus on physical injury. Moreover, some solicitors were extremely cautious about raising diverse backgrounds and lifestyles with some minority ethnic parents.

Interviews with a small sample of parents explored views about the relevance of diverse lifestyles and values and whether solicitors and experts had discussed these issues with them. Some parents expressed concern that neither solicitors nor experts broached this area – but equally parents felt unable to raise issues (Brophy, Jhutti-Johal and McDonald, 2005).

In summary, research identifies a lack of attention to issues of diversity in paediatric reports and some judges, magistrates and lawyers felt diverse contexts were unlikely to be relevant for paediatricians. Some experts and solicitors may not broach this area with parents but that was a discussion some parents clearly wanted.

Finally, below we give some examples from the work of paediatricians in circumstances where an understanding of ethno-cultural contexts was central.[11]

Case 1

A 9-month-old Pakistani child was admitted with meningitis. She responded to treatment and made good progress. During her stay the nursing staff noted that the mother did not visit regularly and stayed only for a few minutes. She did not speak good English and had limited communication with doctors and nurses.

The nursing staff raised concerns regarding parents' infrequent visiting and brought it to the attention of doctors. They agreed that a referral to the Children's Social Care (formerly Social Services) should be made in view of possible neglect. A newly appointed paediatric registrar who spoke the same language as the family offered to speak to the mother. It transpired that the family with two children aged 3 and 4 years, ran a corner shop and had no support whatsoever.

---

[9]   See Brophy et al, 2005: 223.
[10]   Interviews were undertaken with 45 childcare lawyers and 12 parents/carers in three urban areas.
[11]   Cases are based on real scenarios; some details have been changed to ensure anonymity but without losing the gist of messages.

The mother felt that her daughter was in the best hands and was getting better. She also shared her guilt for not spending enough time with her daughter but was under tremendous pressure to run the shop and look after two young children. Social services were then involved to offer support to the family.

This synopsis illustrates:

- a need for paediatricians to engage directly with parents about their background and their language and cultural needs before coming to a decision about whether there are child protection concerns;

- lack of an appropriate interpreter could have led to an unnecessary child protection referral to Children's Social Care when in practice, understanding the need for appropriate support was necessary.

Case 2

An 11-month-old Iraqi girl of an asylum-seeking family was admitted with friction burns on her left foot near the toes. A detailed history was unobtainable due to the language barrier. An interpreter was arranged, who was delayed. The parents were anxious and demanded the girl's discharge. A further detailed history revealed she had a diagnosis of birth asphyxia after an emergency caesarean section and the parents had concerns about her overall development. A multi-disciplinary meeting was set up and cerebral palsy diagnosed with subsequent care packages initiated.

The parents stated that the girl had caught her foot under a sofa and a thin rough carpet in their lounge caused the friction burn. They had requested rehousing due to the poor condition of the house and its unsuitability for a child. The paediatrician felt this reason for the girl's injury was not inconsistent. She had already been referred to Children's Social Care by the ward staff. No concerns were found on enquiry and the parents happily accepted 'Child in Need' services. The family are coping well with support and awaiting a decision from the Home Office regarding application for asylum in the UK.

This synopsis illustrates:

- for some minority ethnic parents, poor cooperation may be due to a range of issues including anger, fear, and lack of trust and communication barriers;

- food interpreting services coupled with cultural understanding is imperative;

- improved decision making for this child occurred once the family circumstances were fully understood.

Case 3

A 13-year-old girl from Pakistan was referred to a paediatrician and a CAMHS team by the school nurse because of inappropriate behaviour in school. Sexual abuse was suspected. Her schoolwork had deteriorated and she often ran out of class, was self-harming by cutting her arms, and had developed daytime wetting. She spoke to the school counsellor of her unhappiness at home, but made no disclosures.

She was admitted to the paediatric unit after an overdose of paracetamol and disclosed to a CAMHS worker that she had been sexually abused for several years by her grandfather and uncle.

Her mother was informed of the disclosure. Initially she was supportive, but after speaking to her husband, she disowned her daughter saying she was telling lies. Members of the community pressurised the girl to retract her allegations. While the Children's Social Care Department was preparing to instigate care proceedings her family removed her from the ward and arranged for her immediate relocation to Pakistan.

This synopsis illustrates:

• professionals did not fully appreciate the implications of the girl's allegations for the 'honour' of her family and 'shame' on the community as a whole, over-riding her parents' responsibility to protect her;

• professionals were impotent in protecting her once the family took control and removed her from the country;

• a greater understanding of the potential effects of disclosure on the family and community would have led to earlier proceedings and removal to a place of safety.

Case 4

This case concerned a Bangladeshi family in which there were three children with a degenerative disorder affecting their mobility, feeding, swallowing and cognitive function.

The oldest child sadly died from complications of a gastrostomy carried out because of feeding problems and weight loss. His maternal aunt had been the interpreter.

The parents separated but the aunt supported the mother with the two remaining daughters along with minimal support from care services. The aunt went to Bangladesh for several months and during this time the girls' school attendance deteriorated, they missed physiotherapy and paediatrician's appointments and they became more unkempt.

Care proceedings on grounds of neglect were instigated when the paediatrician with an interpreter recommended a gastrostomy for one of the girls because of her weight loss and because the mother refused to cooperate with welfare and health agencies. The paediatrician had been unaware that she was a single parent and her supportive sister was abroad.

On the return of the child's aunt, it transpired that the interpreter had not communicated with the mother adequately (the mother spoke Bengali, the interpreter Urdu). The mother's understanding of English had been overestimated. She was fearful that this daughter too would die from the gastrostomy. She felt that accepting help implied she couldn't cope. Care proceedings were abandoned once a suitable interpreter was found and the mother understood her child's condition and the implications.

This synopsis illustrates:

• a failure of professionals to understand that adequate interpreting and an understanding of socio-cultural issues – including mother's fears and unresolved bereavement issues – were imperative;

- the need to consider language and communication barriers when assessing uncooperative and neglectful behaviour.

Case 5

An 18-month-old boy joined his father in the UK as a refugee from Zimbabwe. His mother was left behind. Staff at his nursery reported multiple incidents of bruising, thought to be accidental. However, on one occasion the child was extremely drowsy and unresponsive and had a bite mark on his cheek.

Medical examination revealed 17 bite marks, positioned symmetrically on the body over the shoulders, nipples, buttocks and thighs leaving permanent scars. A forensic odontologist identified the mechanism of injury as simultaneous biting and sucking.

The father identified as the perpetrator, began to speak of spirits being involved and the 'Muti' being responsible. An expert appointed to advise on the significance of the spirit world in this culture explained that in traditional beliefs the 'Muti' (spirits) do not influence children.

In spite of the cultural implications of the father's beliefs about the 'Muti', the child was considered to have suffered actual harm in his father's care and the injuries were the result of maltreatment. Initially made the subject of a care order, he was placed with his mother on her arrival in the UK after an assessment was completed. His parents separated at this time.

This synopsis illustrates:

- challenges to paediatricians because the injuries were so unusual and the father spoke of a spirit world in terms that were unfamiliar to their culture;

- the child had suffered serious harm. Seeking an expert opinion established that the father's actions were neither representative nor acceptable in his culture.

CONCLUSIONS

Cases illustrate the importance of a holistic assessment by paediatricians that includes physical, psycho-social and socio-cultural aspects of child rearing where a full family history includes ethno-cultural contexts. As already argued (Webb and Sergison, 2003), this is not about equipping doctors with 'encyclopaedic' knowledge of diverse cultures. As argued elsewhere (eg Brophy, 2003) that is to misunderstand the challenge. While research demonstrates enduring religious and cultural traditions framing family life, it also demonstrates groups are not homogeneous and 'culture' is a not static phenomenon.

Rather this is about integrating cultural competence and anti-racism practice into everyday work. Assumptions about motivation for behaviours and 'non-cooperation', a reluctance to seek help and mistrust of agencies places parents on an early collision course with health professionals. Independent, highly skilled interpreters are central but not sufficient. Paediatricians must develop cultural competence within an anti-racist framework where 'reflective practice' informs thinking and questions for parents and is integral to understanding responses.

Most paediatricians do far more than diagnose physical injury and they increasingly practise in diverse communities where services have been slow to understand and meet the needs of some minority ethnic families. Thus, 'reflective practice' is not simply the task of paediatricians but should underscore all interagency, multidisciplinary work (both in pre-proceedings protocol and during proceedings).

REFERENCES

Bhopal, R 'Race and ethnicity as epidemiological variables. Centrality of purpose and context' in H Macbeth (ed), *Ethnicity and Health* (London: Taylor and Francis, 2000) 21–40

Bhopal, R 'Racism in Medicine' (2001) 322 BMJ 1503–1504

Brophy, J *Care Proceedings under the Children Act 1989: A Research Review, Research Series 5/06* (London: Ministry of Justice (MoJ), 2006)

Brophy, J 'Diversity and child protection' [2003] Family Law (September) 674–678

Brophy, J, Jhutti-Johal, J and McDonald, E *Minority ethnic parents, their solicitors and child protection litigation, Research Series 5/05* (London: MoJ, 2005)

Brophy, J, Jhutti-Johal, J and Owen, C *Significant Harm: child protection litigation in a multi-cultural setting* (London: MoJ, 2003)

Brophy, J, Jhutti-Johal, J and Owen, C 'Child ill-treatment in minority ethnic households' (2003a) Family Law (October) 756–764

Brophy, J, Wale, C and Bates, P *Myths and Practices: A national survey of the use of experts in care proceedings* (London: BAAF, 1999)

Corry, P 'Bradford has a long tradition of welcoming incomers' (2003) Newsletter – Child Development and Disability, Special Issue – Cross Cultural Issues in Child Disability, issue 7 (March) 3–4 (British Association for Community Child Health)

Laming, Lord *The Victoria Climbié Inquiry* (London: TSO, Cm 5730, 2003)

Department for Education of Skills *Working Together to Safeguard Children: A Guide to inter-agency working to safeguard and promote the welfare of children* (2006) available at www.everychildmatters.gov.uk/resources-and-practice/IG00060

Department for Educational and Skills *Every Child Matters – Changes for Children in Health Services* (2004) available at www.everychildmatters.gov.uk/publications/

Department for Education and Skills Keeping Children Safe and Safeguarding Children – Government's response to the Victoria Climbié report and the Joint Chief Inspector's report Safeguarding Children (2003) available at www.everychildmatters.gov.uk/publications/

Ingleby, D 'Psychosocial problems among children of migrants, in Child health for migrants and refuges', Annual conference of the European Society of Social Paediatrics (Rotterdam: Stichting Ouder en Kindzorg, 1995) 40–46

Maitra, B 'Culture and child protection' (2005) 15 Current Paediatrics 253–259

Moghal, N E, Nota, I K and Hobbs, C J 'A study of sexual abuse in an Asian Community' (1995) 72 Archives of Disease in Childhood 346–347

Royal College of Paediatrics and Child Health (RCPCH) *Report of the Survey on Child Protection* (2004) available at www.rcpch.ac.uk/publications

Royal College of Paediatrics and Child Health *Child Protection Reader* (plus interactive DVD-ROM) (London: RCPCH, 2007)

RCPCH, NSPCC and ALSG Training Package – Level I, Safeguarding Children: Recognition and Response in Child Protection: An Educational Programme for Paediatricians in Training (London: RCPCH, 2006)) (contact neela.shabde@nhct.nhs.uk)

Shabde, N 'Child protection training for paediatricians' (2006) 91 Archives of Disease in Childhood 639–641

Shah, L, Thomas-Ramuset, A, Webb, E *Equal rights, equal access-improving the health care of disabled and chronically ill children from minority ethnic communities: training pack* (Department of Child Health, University of Wales College of Medicine, Cardiff, 1996)

Smith, L 'So who's teaching whom?' (2000) 320 BMJ 323

Turton, J and Haines, L *An investigation into the nature and impact of complaints made against paediatricians* (London: RCPCH, 2006)

Webb, E 'Stereotypes and semaphore, leave them coming back for more, pieces missing, nothing fitting, complications galore' (2005) 90 Archives of Disease in Childhood, Education and Practice Edition 11–14

Webb, E 'The impact of migration and dislocation on family and child mental health. Issues of multiculturalism for families and practitioners' (London: NAGALRO Conference: Protecting Children in a Changing World, 2003)

Webb, E 'Health services: who are the best advocates for children?' (2002) 87 Archives of Disease in Childhood 175–177

Webb, L 'Health Care for Ethnic Minorities' (2000) 10 Current Paediatrics 184–190

Webb, L and Sergison, M 'Evaluation of cultural competence and anti-racism training in child health services' (2003) 88 Archives Disease in Childhood 291–294

PLENARY 6

FAMILY PLACEMENT AND CULTURE

Transracial Placements: What Psychological Issues Should be Considered in Placing Black and Mixed 'Race' Children with White Carers?

Dr Nick Banks

Chartered Consultant Clinical Psychologist, Child & Family Psychological Assessment Services

INTRODUCTION

Due to the limitations on word length I am going to focus on psychological issues of assessing white carers as prospective adopters, rather than consider in any detail the psychological implications of black children in transracial placements. I should also say that I am, in this paper, only considering children of African-Caribbean and mixed 'race' background, although it may be that there can be some generalisations to other ethnic groups. Furthermore, this paper, due to the prescribed available length, will only seek to address the placement of black children with white prospective adopters and will not consider the placement of white children with black adopters, as is sometimes the case, but tending to happen much less often.

It will be clear from the title that the thrust of the argument in this paper will offer no absolutist objection in principle to placing black and mixed 'race' children with white carers. However, as will become apparent, additional issues of white prospective adopter suitability need to be thoroughly considered before white prospective adopters could be seen as suitable to care for a black or mixed 'race' child. Many agencies and professionals involved in adoption placement have moved on from an absolutist or fundamentalist view that transracial placements should not happen at all. This is not to say that such a view was fundamentally flawed in the 1980s and 1990s. Resistance to transracial placements acted, at least in part, as an attempt to promote and protect the specific needs of black children who may have been placed in white families without the necessary attention being given to whether such a placement was suitable or viable. However, there were clearly, in my view, fundamental flaws in what I refer to as the 'absolutist or fundamentalist position', that transracial placements should never take place as white people were 'instinctively/inherently unable to meet the needs of black children' or so the argument usually proceeds. This argument, by implication, would also suggest that white women, even in intact mixed 'race' relationships, would be unable to care for mixed 'race' children. The fundamentalist view would also, by implication, tend to invite the involvement of Social Services in mass assessments of white women with mixed 'race' children. This would clearly be a nonsense.

In considering the white prospective adopters' ability to meet the needs of black children, one will need to ask what the prospective adopters' knowledge and attitudes to 'race' and culture are. It will not be unusual to find that a frequent answer will be 'I don't see colour, I see the child'. Such a response may be seen as adopting a 'colour blind' position. Individuals providing this response often do so in the belief that they wish to see beyond colour, not fully able to comprehend that whereas they may have altruistic values, wider white society may not.

It is always necessary to ask how will white prospective adopters equip themselves to deal with the specific needs of a black child growing up in white racist society? For those readers who sense an emotional reaction in themselves to the assertion that white society is racist, we already have some intrapersonal subjective evidence of the need to assess one's understanding, personal position and reaction to issues of 'race' and culture.

For individuals who assume that 'race' and culture are secondary to other issues in determining whether white adopters can meet the needs of a black child, then one immediately reaches a position where one is likely to be accused of having a lack of understanding of the particular needs of a black child living in a predominantly white society.

Before considering the psychological assessment of capacity to meet a black child's family placement needs, it is worthwhile looking briefly at some of the issues and arguments which were given as to why transracial placement should happen. It has been known for some time that black children are over-represented in the care and adoption statistics (Banks, 1995; Barn, Sinclair and Ferdinand, 1997). This in itself is not a valid reason for arguing the case for transracial adoption. Placement matching from a psychological perspective is important to carefully consider and carry out, and children should not be placed in the next available 'slot'. Adoption of white children with complex needs into white families involves complex and difficult decisions. Transracial placement involves even more difficult decisions being taken, involving various contradictions and problems that many workers find themselves ill-equipped to consider and deal with. I would suggest that workers and agencies need to demonstrate how transracial adoption within a particular family can be shown to be a viable and enduring long-term placement option for black children. There is more to the placement process in transracial adoption than embarking on naive, colour-blind social engineering. White prospective adopters need to be skilfully assessed and prepared to meet the particular needs of any black child in their care.

Returning to some of my earlier assertions about the particular needs of black children, one may ask what these are? Indeed, if one needs to ask this question, then one already has some indication that issues of diversity, 'race' and culture are not well understood and/or have not been directly experienced. The Minnesota Department of Health and Human Services Workers' Assessment Guide suggests that:

> In addition to the qualities necessary to enhance the normal development of any child in placement, these (particular needs of black children, sic) are:
>
> - to live in an environment that provides the child an opportunity to participate in positive experiences with their culture, religion and language;
> - for association with the same 'race', adult and peer role models and relationships, on an ongoing basis;
> - for environmental experiences that teach survival, problem solving and coping skills which give the child a sense of racial and ethnic pride;
> - a parent who can understand and relate to the child's life and daily relationship, to racial and cultural differences and who can respond to those experiences with acceptance, understanding and empathy;
> - for a parent who accepts and can help the child accept the child's racial and cultural ancestry and can comfortably share knowledge and information about the child's racial and cultural ancestry with the child;
> - for the child to have adults around them who understand what it feels like for the child to look different from the parent;
> - to have a parent who has knowledge of special dietary, skin, hair and health care needs.

It is my view that some of these particular needs could be effectively taught through a specialist parenting skills training programme. Others have to do with attitudes and an existing psychological set that may prove much more difficult to shift and maintain change in a way that may not be initially easily recognised.

It would appear to be a nonsense to say that no black children should be transracially adopted by any white family; however, one needs to make an assessment as to whether it would be suitable for a particular black child to be raised by a specific white prospective adopter. There are a number of different placements scenarios that may arise when a black child is being considered for adoption. First, the child may be in a position where they have been with a white substitute family for a significant period of time. Here, one needs to balance the existence and potential severance of an attachment against the prospective adopters' long-term capacity to meet the child's needs. There may also be a scenario where white extended family members put themselves forward to adopt a child of mixed ethnic background. The third, much less common (in terms of my own direct experience of being asked to provide assessments), is the scenario of an unknown white family being put forward for potential placement with a black child.

The Minnesota Department of Health and Human Services Workers' Assessment Guide (Crumbley, 1999) and Banks (1995) suggest that prospective transracial adopters should possess specific capabilities, these being:

- understanding of their own sense of personal history and how that helped form their values and attitudes about racial, cultural and religious similarities and differences;

- an understanding of racism and whether life experiences have given them an understanding of how racism works and how to minimise its effects;

- life experiences and personal history which have given them a capacity or ability to parent cross-racially/culturally;

- commitment to, and capacity of demonstrating empathy with the children's family of origin, regardless of the socio-economic and lifestyle differences between them and the child's family;

- capacity and commitment to provide the child with positive racial and cultural experiences and information and knowledge of their 'race' and culture;

- capacity for preparing the child for an active participation in or return to the child's racial and cultural community;

- adequate support from those significant to them in their decision to parent cross-racially/culturally;

- residence in a community that provides the child with the same 'race', adult and peer role models and relationships on an ongoing basis;

- tolerance and ability to deal appropriately with the questions, ambiguity or disapproval which arise when people see that the child is the applicant's birth child;

- willingness to incorporate participation in cross-racial/cultural activities into their lifestyle and participate in 'race'/cultural awareness training;

- acknowledgement that interracial/intercultural parenting makes their family an interracial/intercultural family which will have an impact on all family members (including extended family relations) and that a decision to adopt interracially will make the family interracial forever;

- acknowledgement of and preparedness to deal positively and effectively with the fact that as an interracial family, they will experience discrimination similar to other minority families;

- the skills, the capacity, interests and commitment to learn parenting skills necessary to parent children to understand and accept their 'race' and racial identity, and to work to change the feelings of children who deny their racial identity;

- the capacity and interest to learn the skills to meet the children's special dietary, hair and health care needs and appreciation of the child's uniqueness and, at the same time, helping the child to have a sense of belonging and full family membership.

Again, some of above is related to the need for education and guidance whereas some is perhaps related to a more fundamental psychological set of how cultural difference and opportunity discrepancy shape and determine attitudes.

Of interest is that the academic research on transracial adoption (Simon and Alstein, 2002; Vroegh, 1997; Griffith and Adams, 1990; Griffith and Silverman, 1995; and Burrow and Finley, 2004) tends to support that black children can thrive and may develop robust racial identities when nurtured in families with white parents. The findings tend to support the view that transracially adopted children do well on measures of self-esteem, cognitive development and educational achievement. However, the measurement of what is often seen as a 'strong racial identity' is often debated in the literature between black academics (NABSW, 1972 and 1991) and white academics, where black academics argue the case that the measures are weak, biased and therefore inconclusive. The topic of transracial adoption tends to generate a considerable amount of emotion in both white and black discussants, with the NABSW arguing, in its position paper, that transracial adoption was 'a blatant form of racial and cultural genocide'. However, this position was reviewed in 1994 when the NABSW believed that adoption should be a last resort, only after a documented failure to find a home with black parents. The NABSW argued strongly for the prioritisation of same 'race' placements, believing that transracial placements would allow adoption agencies to avoid equal treatment of prospective black adopters. The view was that there would be a double discrimination placing a black child in a white family and, discrimination during the selection process against prospective black families. It is still fair to say that tension in placement practice remains.

Kennedy (2006) has argued the point, in specifically considering foster carer suitability, that psychological assessment has merits. The current practice in selecting foster carers or prospective adopters, is not empirically based and tends to be more a focus on legal and pragmatic requirements. 'Matching' is a questionable term/process, based more on opinion and availability than any empirically based analysis. Goodness of fit in even non-transracial adoptive placements is therefore a matter of faith or professional experience and skill at best. Kennedy believes that selection processes involved in foster care selection could be improved by using psychometric tests to assess suitability. If this is true with foster carers, then the case may be argued to be even stronger with prospective adopters. Kennedy takes the view that the current informal processes involved in carer selection are vulnerable to the biases and errors that affect us all. Certainly, in considering the suitability of prospective transracial adopters, the case for specific psychological assessment may be even stronger. Of interest is, in the White Paper, *Adoption: A New Approach*, December 2000, it was noted that the review mechanism for those applying to adopt was seen as unfair and not impartial.

Given figures that suggest one in ten adoptions are likely to break down (Fitzgerald, 1983) then it would seem clear that action to reduce break down by assessing prospective adopter suitability as part of the matching process, or the particular needs for any child going through the adoption process, seems necessary. What information is available, suggests that there is a growing trend in adoption disruption with increasing age at time of placement ranging from 5% of infants to 30% to 50% with children over the age of 11 years. Sellick, Thoburn and Philpot (2004) suggest that on average, one in five places from care with adoptive parents or permanent foster carers, not known to the child, breaks down within 5 years' of placement. However, the figure needs to be considered in the overall context of the age that the child was placed, together with the characteristics of the child and, as this paper is arguing, the characteristics of the adult carers. A finding of the Sellick et al study, was that there was no difference in break down rates between adoptive placements and placements with permanent foster families. The study also suggested that children of mixed racial heritage were most likely to experience placement breakdown than either black or white children. Thoburn, Norford and Rashid (2000) found, when age at placement of black and Asian children and mixed 'race' children was held constant, there was no difference in the incidence of placement break down, with those placed with a two or single white carer family and placements which could be seen as 'ethnically matched'. Of interest was that break down rates for matched placements of boys were higher than for transracial placements with the converse being the case for girls. Thoburn's research found that most of the new parents made clear efforts to ensure that the young person had a strong sense of ethnic identity and pride, however, white families had more obstacles to overcome in achieving this than families where children were ethnically matched. More of the transracially placed children, less than half, felt some discomfort about their ethnicity.

The present writer (Banks, 1999) has suggested a framework by which the assessment of potential prospective adopters may be made more objective in their capacity to meet the needs of a black child in a transracial placement. This framework is based on the work of Janet Helms (1990).

The purpose of this paper is not to discuss the specific assessment process in detail, but to introduce the general notion of the value of an assessment in considering prospective white adopters' ability to meet the placement needs of a black child. Helms suggests an empirically based theoretical model for the assessment of white racial identity development. Here there is a six stage model empirically derived. Helms' model is based on the view that the greater extent that racism exists and is denied in the white individual, then the less possible it is to develop a positive white identify. She posits three types of racism:

1. individual or personal attitudes and beliefs and behaviours, designed to convince oneself of the superiority of white people;

2. institutional, meaning social policies, laws and regulations, whose purpose it is to maintain the economic and social advantage of white groups; and

3. cultural or the societal beliefs and customs that promote the assumption that the products of white culture, eg language, traditions and appearance, are superior.

Racist attitudes can either be overt or covert, or direct or indirect. The view is that each of the different types of racism is inherent in the cultural milieu and can become part of the white person's racial identity or consciousness. Helms takes the view that in order to achieve, what she refers to as a 'healthy white identity', defined in part as a non-racist identity, white individuals must overcome one or more of these aspects of racism. In addition, she suggests that the white individual must accept their own whiteness, the cultural implications of being white and define a view of self as a racial being that does not depend on perceived racial superiority. Helms originally proposed a five stage white identity developmental model, although this was expanded to include a six stage. These will be briefly summarised.

STAGE 1 – CONTACT

As soon as the white person encounters the idea or actuality of black people, they enter the contact stage of identity. This will either be a naive curiosity and trepidation about black people, with some superficial and inconsistent awareness of being white. When one is in the contact stage, if one exhibits individual racism, it will be exhibited in a weak and unsophisticated form. Helms suggests that the person in the contact stage may experience less intra-personal challenge being a racist than those at the other stages, as they have not had to confront the moral dilemmas resulting from such an identification. In this stage, the white person uses the black person to teach them what other 'black people are like' in general, and often uses societal stereotypes of black people as the standard against which the black person is evaluated. Comments such as 'You don't act like a black person' or 'I don't notice what "race" a person is' are likely to be made by white people in the Contact stage. It is suggested that the time a white person spends in the Contact stage depends upon the type of experiences that they have with black and white people in the context of racial issues. When the person in the Contact stage begins to acquire insight that there are differences in how black and white people are treated, and when these experiences penetrate the white person's identity system, they may enter the next stage.

STAGE 2 – DISINTEGRATION

Entry into this stage implies consciousness through conflicted acknowledgement of one's whiteness. There is a recognition of the moral dilemmas associated with being white. The individual experiences a conflicted white identification with a questioning of racial realities that the person has previously been socialised to believe. The white person, very much for the first time, comes to see themselves as caught between two racial groups. Helms notes that self-actualisation personality theorists, such as Carl Rogers, suggest that emotional discomfort or what is often referred to as 'incongruence', comes about when one has to alter one's real self in order to be accepted by others in one's environment. Feelings of guilt, depression and helplessness are experienced. This is accompanied by a conflicted view of white self and a questioning of the racial realities the person has been taught to believe. Here, it is suggested that the person first comes to realise that despite social pretence, black people are not considered equals and negative consequences (to them as a white person) can result from a white person not respecting social inequalities. Also the white person, in this stage, comes to realise that the social skills they have used in interacting with black people are superficial.

STAGE 3 – REINTEGRATION

In this stage, the white person consciously acknowledges a white identity. The Reintegration Stage tends to confirm the belief in white racial superiority. Racial similarities tend to be minimised or denied. Any residual feelings of guilt and anxiety are transformed into fear and anger towards black people. Feelings may not be overtly expressed but may lie just below the surface of the person's awareness, with a threat to the white person's sense of self, tending to unleash such feelings. Beliefs and feelings may be expressed either passively or actively. Passive expression involves deliberate removal of oneself or avoidance from environments where they may encounter black people. Honest discussion of racial matters tends to occur among same 'race' peers who share, or are believed to share, a similar world view. Such behaviour would be consistent with a well-known paradigm in psychology, referred to as 'cognitive dissonance' (Festinger, 1957), where when dissonance is present, a person will attempt to reduce this and also take steps to avoid situations and information that are likely to increase dissonance.

STAGE 4 – PSEUDO INDEPENDENT

This is seen as the first stage of redefining a positive white racial identity. Here the person actively begins to question the proposition of black inferiority. Here the person begins to acknowledge personal responsibility and white societal responsibility for racism. The individual is no longer comfortable with a racist identity and begins to search for new ways to redefine their white identity. The redefining process may take the form of intellectual acceptance and curiosity about black people. Helms suggests that this stage is primarily a stage of intellectualisation. Nonetheless, although the individual is attempting to abandon the belief in white superiority, they may still behave in ways that unwittingly perpetuate this belief system. The individual may seek greater interaction with black people, although this may involve helping black people to change themselves so they function more like white people on white criteria for success and acceptability, rather than considering that such criteria might be inappropriate or too narrowly defined. The white individual in this stage may still look to black people rather than white people to explain racism and seek solutions for it in hypothetical perceived black cultural dysfunctionalities. Individuals considering transracial placement may abound in this stage, believing that they can rescue black children from black cultural dysfunctionalities.

STAGE 5 – IMMERSION/EMERSION

Here, it is argued that redefining a positive white identity requires the person to replace white and black myths and stereotypes with accurate information about whiteness. The individual in this stage searches for the answers to the questions 'Who am I racially?' and 'Who do I want to be?' Often the individual will immerse themselves in biographies and autobiographies of white people who have made similar identity process journeys. They may participate in white consciousness raising groups whose purpose is to help the person discover their own individual racism. Changing black people is no longer the focus of their activities but rather the goal of changing white people becomes salient. Helms believes that emotional as well as cognitive restructuring can happen during this stage.

STAGE 6 – AUTONOMY

The internalising, nurturing and applying the new definition of whiteness involved in the earlier stages, are major goals of the Autonomy Stage. In this stage, the individual no longer feels the need to oppress, idealise or denigrate people on the basis of racial group membership. 'Race' no longer symbolises a threat to the individual since they no longer react out of rigid world views. One finds the autonomous individual actively seeking opportunities to learn from other cultural groups. Helms suggests that this stage should not be seen as a 'fixed level', but should be seen more as an ongoing process where the individual is continually open to new information and new ways of thinking about racial and cultural issues. One may also, in my view, see this stage theory as offering the possibility of different levels at each stage, where the individual may, at particular times of emotional and cognitive threat and/or challenge, go back to earlier stages of thinking, where higher levels of a stage have not yet been consolidated.

Now, one needs to consider how the prospective white adopters' position/level at any stage, can be assessed. Here lies the psychological skill. Helms has suggested an initial tool which has begun to attract psychometric characteristics in the development, of what she terms, a White Racial Identity inventory. However, the application of this to a British population has not been tested. I take the view, from my own experience, that a psychometric tool, in isolation, would not be wholly suitable to rely upon. One would also need qualitative information obtained from an individual's response to, for example, case study material. Such an approach has some existing foundation as suggested by the New York State's Coalition for Children, who have proposed a workers' assessment guide for families adopting cross racially/cross culturally. Here, several case scenario examples are given to allow prospective white adopters to consider their response. An example of such a scenario is as follows.

You are at a shopping centre with your (black adopted infant). You notice several people looking at you. Two men seem to walk by you several times and finally one seems to purposefully bump into you (or your partner). He then looks at his friend, laughs and makes some remarks about you or your partner's morals. He uses several derogatory terms about your child's ethnic heritage, together with a lot of profanity. Although he is talking to his companion, it is obvious that the remarks are intended for you to hear.

How would you feel? Would you respond to the remarks? How will you deal with such remarks when your child is old enough to understand them?

Another scenario for prospective white transracial adopters would be the following.

Your family has known the Smiths for years and are good friends and your children grew up together. As the children were growing up they always played together, participated in activities together and were close friends. Your (black adopted son) is now 16, as is the Smiths' oldest daughter. Your son asks their daughter to go to a party with him as his date. She tells your son she can't go with him because he is not white. Your son comes to you asking why he could be her friend all these years but can't take her to a party because of his 'race'.

What would you tell your son? How would you feel as a parent? How would this affect your relationship with the Smiths?

One can see from this how, using the Helms model to analyse responses to these example scenarios, that one may be enabled to gain a detailed picture of where an individual is at the time of assessment. One may then structure training programmes to help people progress on during the adoption selection and training process and, at the end of such a process, attempting, through the use of other similar case scenarios, to gauge the shift in the individuals' ability to meet the long-term needs of any black children placed in their care. At the moment there is no structure or framework or even guidelines for determining whether white prospective adopters could meet the needs of black children with assessments and conclusions likely to be much as Rowe (1990) suggests, stemming from individuals' own 'race', preferred bias, and social environments. The specific assessment of racial attitudes is of value for considering the needs of black children and the capacity of prospective white adopters, to meet the needs of black children and, for that matter, to be further considered for the placement of white children, if their attitudes are shown to be so intractably racist that they would socialise any white children in their care with such views.

CONCLUSION

Given the disproportionate numbers of black children who wait for family placement where, with younger children, adoption may be preferred to fostering, and gives the opportunity for better outcome, a fundamentalist view against transracial placement may be hard to support. One may be better off, from a child centred perspective, to consider what psychological awareness prospective white transracial adopters need to have, in order to meet the long-term needs of a black child. Research needs to be carried out in this area based on the framework I have suggested, in order to advance current thinking, practice and policy.

REFERENCES

Adoption: Performance and Innovation Unit Report (July 2000)

Banks, N, 'Transracial Placements and the Assessment of White Carers' (1999), 16(3) *Education & Child Psychology*

Banks, N, 'Children of Black and Mixed Parentage, and their Placement Needs' (1995) 19 *Adoption and Fostering* 19–24

Barn, R, Sinclair, R and Ferdinand, D *Acting on Principle: An Examination of 'race' and Ethnicity in Social Services Provision for Children and Families* (London: BAAF, 1997)

Burrow, A L and Finley, G E 'Transracial, Same "race" Adoptions and the Need for Multiple Measures of Adolescent Adjustment' (2004) 74 *American Journal of Orthopsychiatry* 577–583

Crumbley, J *Transracial Adoption and Foster Care, Practice Issues for Professionals and Carers* (Child Welfare League of America, 1999)

Festinger, L *A Theory of Cognitive Dissonance* (Stanford: Stanford University Press, 1957)

Fitzgerald, J *Understanding Disruption* (BAAF, 1983)

Griffith, E E H and Adams, A 'Public Policy and Transracial Adoptions of Black Children' in E Sorel (ed), *Family, Culture and Psychobiology* (Ottawa, Canada: Legas Press, 1990) 211–233

Griffith, E E H and Silverman, I L 'Transracial Adoptions and the Continuing Debate on the Racial Identity of Families' in H W Harris, H C Blue and E E H Griffith (eds), *Racial Ethnic Identity: Psychological development and creative expression* (New York: Routledge, 1995) 95–114

Helms, J *Black and White Racial Identity* (Greenwood Press, 1990)

Kennedy, B 'Selecting Foster Carers: Could personnel psychology improve outcome?' (2006) 30 (3) *Adoption & Fostering* 29–38

National Association of Black Social Workers, *Position Statement of Transracial Adoptions* (September 1972)

National Association of Black Social Workers *Position Statement: Preserving African American Families* (Detroit, MI, 1994)

Rowe, J 'Research, "race" and Child Care Placements' (1990) 14 *Adoption & Fostering* 7–9

Sellick, C, Thoburn, J, Philpot, T *Works and Adoption and Foster Care* (Barnardo's Policy and Research Unit, 2004)

Simon, R J and Alstein, H *Adoption, 'race' & Identity; from infancy to young adulthood* (New Brunswick, NJ: Transaction Publishers, 2002)

Thoburn, J, Norford, L and Rashid, S *Permanent Family Placement for Children of Minority Ethnic Origin* (London: Jessica Kingsley, 2000)

Vroegh, K S 'Transracial Adoptees: Developmental Status after seventeen years' (1997) 67 *American Journal of Orthopsychiatry* 568–575

Zeitlin, H 'Adoption of Children from Minority Groups' in K Dwivedi and V Varma (eds), *Meeting the Needs of Ethnic Minority Children: A handbook for professionals* (London: Jessica Kingsley, 1996) 63–78

Factors Contributing to the Over Representation of Black and Mixed Race Looked After Children

Dr Aggrey Burke

Consultant Psychiatrist and Senior Lecturer, St Georges University, London

SUMMARY OF THE PAPER

Dr Aggrey Burke introduced his paper by considering issues relating to how a group moves from one stage in society or a period in history and the challenge this presents. His aim was to achieve a sense of how colonisation continues to impact on society. Dr Burke considered the theories of Albert Memmi, a North African, who has studied the issues surrounding those who are colonised and their colonisers.

The coloniser, after entering a land and colonising it, will find that his plantations are doing well. His status is bestowed by being white; he usurps the position of the people in the new environment. The colonised find they are losing money and losing their land. The colonised cannot be equal because the coloniser is white. The question is how can the colonised move from this stage?

The independence of the colony is an important turning point; the position changes dramatically. However, the coloniser remains despite the change. Families are disrupted in slavery and after. There are forced labour migrations, sexual exploitation of women is rampant and there is no morality at all. There are shortfalls in provisions to meet basic survival needs. The important point is that this position is similar to that which is witnessed on housing estates in Britain today. Living on such estates can present similar ecological risks.

Dr Burke considered that one of the most interesting aspects of the research which considers the racial make-up of the looked after children population is that Asian groups represent half the proportion they could have done based on the overall make-up of society. Black and mixed race black children, however, are over-represented.

Dr Burke noted the known predictors indicating that a parent may perpetrate physical child abuse to be:

- *being looked after by the local authority;*

- *an unhappy childhood;*

- *poor support from spouses;*

- *being diagnosed with anti-social personality disorder;*

- *being violent to others.*

With these predictors in mind, Dr Burke considered individual cases in which he had involvement that raise questions about what issues are truly important in care cases.

The first case involved a shaken baby with blindness. The mother was white and had herself been looked after as a child, the father was black and had a violent history. There were lots of professionals and lots of reports in this case. The questions to be considered included how to overcome stereotypes and how to be impartial to race.

The second case involved sexual abuse. The child came from a single mother household. The perpetrator was the mother's partner, he was a drug abuser. Dr Burke raised the question: what are the considerations in this case? For example, were the parents white? Does this matter? Do we need to think about race within this scenario? Can sexual abuse ever be 'cultural'?

The next case involved issues of child abuse and race when domestic violence and child abuse are seen together. The young mother had a history of being sexually abused in childhood. The child presented as malnourished and had bruises. What are the cultural issues in a case such as this? Has domestic violence become part of human culture as common to all ethnic groups?

In the third case, the father had killed the mother of the children and it was necessary to examine the effects of this upon the children. This case raised the cultural issue of whether it is inappropriate to attribute Asian fathers with the trait of 'pathological jealousy'.

Dr Burke considered that the explanatory models give insight into the problem of overrepresentation of black and mixed race children. Importantly, the cycle of being looked after is no less of an issue than the cycle of violence. Societal indifference or, in other words, institutional racism, is part of the explanation. In particular, there is indifference to the high numbers of black children in prison. Dr Burke acknowledged, however, that these issues of racism and social exclusion are difficult and fraught.

Dr Burke concluded by considering the solutions to the problems his paper highlights. In his view, family support is an important part of the possible solution. In particular, efforts should be made to promote migration of complete family units. It is also necessary to examine ways of reducing the effects of institutional racism. Finally, removal of children from parental homes should be prevented if at all possible.

Dr Burke noted that more training and diversity conferences, like this one, are also important in the package of solutions needed to address the problem of overrepresentation of black and mixed race children in the care system.

THE PAPER

Introduction

Children taken away from home following abuse/neglect are more likely to suffer mental health problems than those remaining.[1] Placement stability and disruption contribute to the outcome[2] but adoption is not always successful.[3] Here in Britain every third child is a vulnerable with one-tenth of vulnerables being a child in need; one-fifth of those in need will be looked after (LA).[4]

---

[1]   Brand and Brinich, 1999.
[2]   Leathers, 2006; Rubin et al, 2007.
[3]   Miller et al, 2000.
[4]   DfES, 2003.

Compared to white children, black and mixed-race (BMR) children are over-represented on Child Protection Registers,[5] as children in need and those to be looked after.[6] Vulnerable BMR children are more likely to be excluded from services[7] partly because of the racial attitudes/stereotypes of professionals.[8]

Racism may contribute to the excess of black British children in child protection[9] and in court proceedings.[10] In one US county racial disproportionality increased at each stage, from reporting to exiting the childcare system, for African-American and native-American children.[11] Race influences decision making, restricts access[12] and determines service allocation.[13]

The Victoria Climbié inquiry understated the complexity of motivations leading to migration from poor countries and the tortuous route in finding a 'home' in the new society. Victoria's death was one of about 100 annual maltreatment cases in the UK.[14] The inquiry focused on worker/system failure,[15] but did not highlight environmental factors[16] and the extent of carer inadequacy[17] and disturbance.[18]

In modern society abuse is viewed as an evil; its elimination a legitimate aim/pursuit. It is argued that the abusive carer has failed society; therefore the child should be rescued. In extreme circumstances child migrants have been sent away from Britain to Canada and elsewhere[19] without monitoring their welfare. Many child migrants suffered 'hardship and emotional deprivation'[20] because of prior abuse/neglect or the trauma of removal and being looked after.[21] Chater and Le Grand (2006) believe that professionals contribute to the structural bias against looked after children and the disadvantage and stigma they suffer.

Looked after children are more likely to suffer conduct disorders[22] and incur high costs long-term.[23] Poor selection in removing children from home[24] may reflect the difficulty of identifying risk factors of taking a child away to be looked after.[25]

---

[5] DfES, 2006a.

[6] Southwark Analytic Hub, 2006.

[7] Hurlburt et al, 2004.

[8] Barth et al, 2006.

[9] Chand, 2000.

[10] Abbas, 2004.

[11] King County Coalition, 2004.

[12] Hill, 2006.

[13] Hampton & Newberger, 1985.

[14] The UN Children's Fund, 2003.

[15] Laming, 2003.

[16] Child Poverty Action Group, 2004.

[17] Crittenden, 2006.

[18] Brown et al, 1998.

[19] Buti, 2002.

[20] House of Commons, 1998.

[21] Kendall-Tackett, 2002.

[22] Meltzer and others, 2003.

[23] Scott et al, 2001.

[24] Barber et al, 2001.

[25] Johnson et al, 2006.

DISTRIBUTION OF LOOKED AFTER CHILDREN BY RACE/ETHNICITY (ENGLAND)

There were 234,700 children in need among 11,132,900 children aged 0–17 in a sample week in February 2005 (21 per 1,000). BMR children are markedly over-represented in both children in need categories.[26]

During the 5-year period 2002–2006 the distribution of looked after children by race/ethnicity showed: a decrease in the number of white children; mixed-race no change; increases among Asian and black.[27] Table 1 shows the distributions of looked after children in March 2006, throughout that year, and adoptions in that year.

Table 1: Ethnicity of looked after children and adoptions (2006)

Race Ethnicity	National Census (2001) %	Looked after on 31/03/06 %	Looked after started in 2006 %	Adoptions in 2006 as % Looked after on 31/03/06
Black	2.0	8	11	1.8 (90)
Mixed-race	1.2	8	7	7.4 (370)
Asian	4.0	3	6	2.5 (50)
Other minority	0.7	2	4	2.7 (30)
White	92.1	78	72	6.6 (3,100)
Total	100 (58.7m)	99 (60,300)	100 (24,200)	21 (3,640)

Percentage Distributions (N= Total Population)

The findings show:

• marked over-representation of BMR children;

• decreases in the white distribution from census to looked after in year;

• the adoption rate is low (the 5-year trend shows no change);

• adoption rates among mixed-race and white are appreciably higher than Asian and black using the annual looked after population for calculation;

• using census data adoption rates per 100,000 are: black, 78; mixed-race, 546; Asian, 21; white, 57; other, 63 (assuming same 'race' placements).

Outcome indicators confirm the relatively poor prognosis of LA children;[28] many under-achieve,[29] become delinquent and are permanently excluded from school.[30] Marked excesses of BMR children among permanently excluded may be partly related to these findings.

The aims of the present paper are:

1. to describe the circumstances of mothers presenting in court proceedings aimed at determining whether their child should be looked after or not;

---

[26] DfES, 2006b.
[27] DfES, 2007.
[28] DfES, 2006c.
[29] DfES, 2006d.
[30] DfES, 2006e.

2. to carry out an analysis of risk factors leading to a child being looked after;

3. to examine possible causes for the over-representation of BMR children in the LA population. There are three possible explanations for the excesses. First, that the characteristics of the looked after population are common to all ethnicities but are more highly distributed in specific sectors of society (social exclusion model); second, racial stereotypes and attitudes of society lead to higher rates of looked after children among BMR groups (institutional racism model); third, a combination of the two sets of factors.

THE BACKGROUND

The black population includes groups linked together by race, history and geography. Asylum seekers and migrants from Africa are diverse in origin. Mixed-race ethnicity suggests a greater degree of interaction among others who are from mixed-parentage than others and assumes that black-white unions were not extensive pre-migration. Racial groups are not true ethnicities and have limited application for research.[31]

The origins of the Caribbean people are complex and largely based on a slave tradition. African slaves were stripped of name, tribe, language, culture and religion; the group was socialised to be British (and French in the Eastern Caribbean). Indentured (slave replacement) labour, mainly from 'India' (20% of total population; 50% in Trinidad & Tobago and Guyana) retained name, religion, family and culture; they were given land and had the right to return home. Native American Indians were largely destroyed before British arrival in the 17th century.

It is unlikely that Africans experienced meaningful family life in slavery. At emancipation a minority of children/mothers were evicted or ran away; the vast majority remained on former estates. 'Masters' maintained the practice of illicit relationships with African women initiated in slavery. A caste system based on skin colour ensured white dominance.[32] Following slavery many men worked away from home; boys stayed away from school at crop time. The single mother household prospered during that period.[33]

The early migration of colonial Caribbean people is described as serial migration; initially, one parent migrated, family members followed thereafter.[34] The migration was selective with few privileged. Though 'truly British in make-up' Caribbean migrants were disadvantaged by race and at greater risk of social exclusion (SE) than other migrants and matched whites.

FINDINGS FROM A RETROSPECTIVE COURT SAMPLE

In childcare practice it is important to identify children likely to benefit from being looked after and those likely to lose out. The approach in the present study is to use evidence from court decisions on being looked after to identify risk factors.

The study population is a consecutive series of assessments over a 10-year mean period. Ethical approval was obtained for a retrospective case note analysis of 470 carers and their children. Material was collected on the carer's early life and present circumstances including psychiatric information. Two investigators extracted information. The outcome of proceedings was ascertained in each case from social workers. Statistical calculations were carried out using the

---

[31] Bradby, 2003.
[32] Patterson, 1967.
[33] Brown and Innis, 2005.
[34] Smith et al, 2004.

SPSS 14.0 package. Fathers (a quarter), and the few carers from Asian/other minority groups, have been excluded. The remaining sample includes almost 400 BMR or white carers (85%) and potential (15%) female carers.

THE CIRCUMSTANCES OF MOTHERS IN FAMILY COURT PROCEEDINGS

When material on the family backgrounds of carers is compared with findings among a control group of potential carers (mainly kinship), younger than 45, similarities were found by ethnicity, migrant status, family disruption experience, extended family upbringing, in-care experience and parental history of disorder (mental illness, substance abuse and crime).

In Britain minority groups are more likely to live in areas of SE.[35] In the present study total scores on six variables are used to describe the circumstances of carers (Box 1).

Box 1: variables used to describe social exclusion in the present study**

- Receiving income support

- Untrained (semi/unskilled)

- No examination passes

- Not owner occupier

- Unemployed

- 'Lone parent'

** Each variable scored 0 or 1

These six variables are correlated with each other. A score of four or more (carers 80%; controls, 50%) characterises vulnerable carers. The median score among carers is five and is the cut-off point for defining high and low SE groups. SE among carers (55%) is three times greater than controls. Box 2 shows childhood risk factors of SE.

Box 2: childhood risk factors of social exclusion (findings in present study)

- Feels unloved/unwanted***

- Runs away from home***

- Repeatedly violent***

- 'Looked after'***

*** Group differences highly significant statistically

SE is not associated with ethnicity in the present study.

---

[35]   Gordon et al, 2000; Levitas et al, 2007.

PREDICTIVE FACTORS OF THE DECISION TO REMOVE A CHILD FROM HOME

This section of the study includes almost 300 mothers identified in care proceedings (African 22%; Afro-Caribbean 52%; Mixed Race 7%; Irish 3%; White British 16%). The age range is 15 to 54 with 5% being 45 or older. Background characteristics were similarly distributed among BMR and white groups; white mothers were more likely to be married/cohabiting (75% vs 25%) but less likely to be migrant (15% vs 57%).

Outcome groups were defined according to the court decision regarding parental capacity to provide care and the best interests of the child:

- Poor outcome – children removed and looked after – three-quarters;

- Good outcome – children remain with carer – one-quarter.

Factors which predict the child's removal are shown in Table 2.

Table 2: Risk factors for child being looked after**

Carer – In-care in childhood
Carer – No examination passes at school
Carer – History of physical violence/crime
Carer – Suffers from psychotic mental illness
Carer – Suffers from drug abuse disorder
Carer – Previous child looked after
Child – Exposed to repeated or/and severe abuse/neglect
Child – Eldest child younger than 7 years

** Multiple regression analysis

Case-note evidence of child physical abuse by a carer was not predictive of outcome. The category 'repeated or severe' abuse/neglect (57% of total) predicts outcome and was more prevalent among black mothers (56% vs 42%).

No one individual risk factor in Table 2 predicts outcome with any certainty. White mothers were more likely to be diagnosed with personality disorder (78% vs 50%) but less likely to be psychotic (24% vs 47%). When these two diagnoses co-exist in any carer the outcome for children is poor; outcome is not associated with one diagnosis without the other.

There were differences by race among those psychotic patients (half of all carers with this condition) with co-existing personality disorder or substance abuse disorder and those with a poor prognosis for 'recovery'. Invariably children were removed from home in these circumstances.

Only a few children were removed from home only because of difficulties presented by the carer's partner and race had no bearing on outcome among them.

OPINION

The study population may be representative of carers presenting to the family court. The sample was retrospective with few children coming to the attention of authorities because of sexual abuse by a carer. Only BMR and white mothers were studied. Two outcome groups were defined by children being looked after (poor) or remaining at home (good) following court proceedings.

National statistics suggest that the distribution of looked after children increases in areas of multiple deprivations. In the present study it has been shown that the multi-dimensional aspects of SE provide an appropriate framework for studying parents of looked after children. Many of these parents (almost half of British born) have passed through the care system suggesting a cycle of looked after carers and their children.

The case example of Victoria Climbié is pertinent to the present debate. She was one of many children in need and of SE who are unregistered and not receiving any service. Her death[36] highlights the difficulty of managing the childcare system.[37] As Victoria and her grand-aunt fell through the net in France and Britain this suggests SE because of race in both societies. The escalation of abuse/neglect once they moved in with the grand-aunt's lover suggests that the causes of personality disorder among her carers should have been considered.

The excess of looked after black children is true whatever the broad grouping (African, Caribbean, and mixed). One simple explanation would be that institutional racism is pervasive and operates at every stage of the process. Here the findings suggest that only a fifth of mothers in this sample could be identified by psychiatric findings as a poor outcome group. Professionals highlight the damage to child development caused by abuse/neglect but do not balance this argument with negative evidence regarding rescue efforts.[38]

Here three in four mothers suffered childhood abuse (physical, sexual, parental domestic violence). Abused mothers can be categorised by their experience of having been in care in childhood. An analysis of findings among around 120 British born abused mothers, half were looked after in childhood. These mothers were five to six times more likely to run away, become repeatedly violent and permanently excluded than others. This confirms the hazard of being looked after and highlights cycles of violence[39] and inadequate parenting.

Asian children are infrequently removed from their families, whatever the extent of material hardship suggesting that family structure and support are protective factors.[40] Black mothers are more likely to be employed[41] and single, but these are not risk factors.

The circumstances of carers of looked after children may be explained by the multi-dimensional aspects of SE. Here all six variables used to describe SE are similarly distributed by race. In the general population, black groups are in excess on each of these six variables[42] suggesting that SE contributes to the excess of looked after children.

The marked excesses of black and white mothers with psychosis[43] and personality disorders respectively did not have a direct bearing on the rates of child removal. Admission to mental hospital was similarly distributed by race suggesting that the diagnostic process is racially biased. Among hospital patients this diagnostic tendency is upheld. Response to treatment and take up of services are important considerations in assessing parenting potential in hospital

---

[36]   Cooper et al, 2001.
[37]   Hirst, 2001.
[38]   Harder, 2005.
[39]   Dodge, 1990.
[40]   Taussig, 2002.
[41]   Reynolds, 2001.
[42]   Mayor of London, 2002.
[43]   Healthcare Commission, 2007.

patients. The small numbers suffering from one or other condition cannot account for the disproportional numbers of BMR looked after children. The child's emotional/ behavioural state did not predict outcome in the present study.

Two factors – a mother's experience of being looked after and severe abuse/neglect experienced by a child – predict a poor outcome and are associated with race. Other possible explanations for this looked after excess include social stress and social support (similar ethnic distributions and not associated with outcome). Migrant status frequently found among African and Caribbean populations is not associated with outcome or child abuse.

Severe abuse/neglect was 50% over-represented among BMR carers. Few children (6%) were exposed to cruel abuse/neglect by virtue of criminal proceedings against their carers. Invariably the victims were removed and looked after. The recognition, substantiation and selection of cases for court proceedings suggest that racial factors may be at play in defining thresholds of abuse/neglect or severe abuse/neglect. These factors are unlikely to account for the 400% BMR excess among looked after children.

The therapeutic implications of working with black carers and their children[44] may not have led to any change in practice[45] but initiatives prosper.[46] It is of considerable concern that rates of looked after children among BMR sectors of the population are 400% greater than expected with few adopted. Year on year additions to this vulnerable population is bad news for society, a tragedy for the individuals involved and a basis for the continued exclusion of these groups.

The present findings suggest three explanatory models for the over-representation of BMR looked after children:

- the cycle of being looked after (cumulative);

- societal indifference (institutional racism);

- SE of BMR populations (historical).

The indications from this retrospective study are that probably only a third of looked after placements can be described as 'in the best interest of the child'. If this is true it would suggest some urgency in rectifying this problem.[47]

SUMMARY

The findings of a retrospective study of mothers and children in family court proceedings are described. An attempt is made to describe the circumstances (SE) leading to children being removed from home and being looked after. The results indicate that three-quarters of carers are deemed to be unfit to care for their children (poor outcome). Variables predicting poor outcome are likely to be associated with the over representation of BMR looked after children to include a history of the mother being looked after in childhood (a cycle) and evidence that a child suffered severe abuse/neglect. A psychiatric diagnosis of mental illness of poor prognosis or coexisting with personality disorder or substance abuse disorder predicts that the child will be removed. It is concluded that the ethnic over representation results first from the greater likelihood of SE; second, the inherent racial bias of the system; and finally, the cycle of being looked after.

---

[44] Bean et al, 2002; Baptiste Jr et al, 1997; Foner, 1997; Thrasher and Anderson, 1988.
[45] Williams and Soydan, 2005.
[46] Thoburn et al, 2004.
[47] Harder, 2005; Berrick, 1998.

178 *Integrating Diversity*

REFERENCES

Abbas, T '"Race" ethnicity and the courts: a review of existing and ongoing research' (2004) *Internet Journal of Criminology*

Armstrong, D, et al 'Children, risk and crime: the On Track Youth Lifestyles Surveys' (2005) *Home Office Research Study* 278

Baptiste, D A, et al 'Family therapy with English Caribbean Immigrant Families in the United States: Issues of Emigration, Immigration, Culture and Race' (1997) 19(3) *Contemporary Family Therapy* 337–359

Barber J G, et al 'The Predictors of unsuccessful transition to foster care' (2001) 42(6) *J Child Psychol Psychiatry* 785–790

Barn, R 'Improving services to meet the needs of minority ethnic children and families' (2006) *Research and Practice briefings: Children and Families. Every Child Matters*

Barth, R P, et al 'Placement into foster care and the interplay of urbanicity, child behaviour problems, and poverty' (2006) 76 (3) *Amer J Orthopsychiat* 358–366

Bean, R A, et al 'Developing culturally competent marriage and family therapists: Treatment guidelines for non African American therapists working with African-American families' (2002) 28(2) *Journal of Marital and Family Therapy* 153–164

Berrick, J D 'When children cannot remain home: foster family care and kinship care' (1998) 8(1) *Protecting Children from Abuse and Neglect* 72–87

Bradby, H 'Describing ethnicity in health research' (2003) 8(1) *Ethnicity and Health* 5–13

Brand A E and Brinich, P M 'Behaviour problems and mental health contacts in adopted, foster, and non adopted children' (1999) 40(8) J Child Psychol Psychiatry 1221–1229

Brown J, et al 'A longitudinal analysis of risk factors for child maltreatment: findings of a 17-year prospective study of officially recorded and self-reported child abuse and neglect' (1998) 22(11) *Child Abuse and Neglect* 1065–1078

Brown, L and Innis, T 'The slave family in the transition to freedom: Barbados, 1834–1841' (2005) 26(2) *Slavery and Abolition* 257–269

Buti, A 'British Child Migration to Australia: History, Senate Inquiry and Responsibilities' (2002) 9(4) *Murdoch University Electronic Journal of Law*

Cabinet Office 'Reaching Out: Progress on Social Exclusion' (London, 2007)

Chand, A 'The over-representation of black children in the child protection system: Possible causes, consequence, and solutions' (2000) *Child and Family Social Work* 51, 66–77

Chater, D and Le Grand, J 'Looked after or overlooked? Good parenting and school choice for looked after children' (London: The Social Market Foundation, 2006)

Child Poverty Action Group 'Ensuring that every child matters' (London, 2004)

Cooper R S, et al 'Relationship between premature mortality and socioeconomic factors in black and white populations of US metropolitan areas and its Public' (2001) 116(5) Health Rep 464–473

Crittenden, P M 'Why do inadequate parents do what they do?' in O Mayseless (ed), *Parenting representations: theory, research, and clinical implications* (Cambridge: Cambridge University Press, 2006) 388–433

DfES 'Every child matters: The consultation process' (2003) Cm 5860

DfES 'Outcome indicators for looked after children: twelve months to 30 September 2004, England' (2005)

DfES 'Statistics of Education: Referrals, assessments and children and young people on child protection registers: year ending 31 March 2005' (2006)

DfES 'Children in Need in England 2005' (Internet Only, 2006)

DfES 'Statistics of Education: Outcome Indicators for Looked after children. Twelve months to 30 September 2005, England' (2006)

DfES 'Ethnicity and Education: the Evidence on Minority Ethnic Pupils aged 5-16' (2006)

DfES 'Exclusion of Black Pupils: Priority Review. Getting it right' (2006)

DfES 'Children looked after by Local Authorities, Year Ending 31 March 2006 (Internet only, 2007)

Dodge, K A, et al 'Mechanisms in the cycle of violence' (1990) 250 (4988) *Science* 1678–1683

English D J, et al 'Defining maltreatment chronicity: are there differences in child outcomes?' (2005) 29(5) *Child Abuse and Neglect* 575–595

Foner, N 'The immigrant family: cultural legacies and cultural changes' (1997) 31 (4) Int Migr Rev 961–974

Fontes, L Aronson 'Child abuse and culture: working with diverse families' (London: Guildford Press, 2005)

Gordon, J, et al 'Poverty and Social Exclusion in Britain' (Joseph Rowntree Foundation, 2000)

Hampton, R L and Newberger, E H 'Child abuse incidence and reporting by hospitals: significance of severity, class and race' (1985) 75 (1) Amer J Public Health 56–60

Harder, J 'Prevention of child abuse and neglect: an evaluation of a home visitation parent aide program using recidivism data' (2005) 15(4) *Social Work Practice* 1246–1256

Harman, J S, et al 'Mental health care utilization and expenditures by children in foster care' (2000) 154 Arch Pediatr Adolesc Med 1114–1117

Healthcare Commission 'Count me in: results of national census of inpatients in mental health' (2007)

Hill, R B 'Synthesis of research on disproportionality in child welfare: an update' (Casey-CSSP Alliance for Racial Equity in the child welfare system, 2006)

Hirst, J 'Another crumbling public service' *New Statesman* 22 January 2001

House of Commons 'Health – Third Report: The welfare of former British child migrants. UK' (1998)

Hurlburt, M S, et al 'Contextual predictors of mental health service use among children open to child welfare' (2004) 61(12) Arch Gen Psychiatry 1217–1224

Johnson, J G et al 'Parenting behaviours associated with risk for offspring personality disorder during adulthood' (2006) 63(5) Arch Gen Psychiatry 579–587

Kendall-Tackett, K 'The health effects of childhood abuse: four pathways by which abuse can influence health' (2002) 6/7 *Child Abuse and Neglect* 715–730

King County Coalition 'Racial Disproportionality in the Child Welfare System in King County, Washington' (Clegg and Associates/Wanda Hackett Enterprises, 2004)

Laming Lord 'The Victoria Climbié Inquiry: Summary and Recommendations' (2003)

Leathers, S J 'Placement disruption and negative placement outcome among adolescents in long-term foster care: the role of behaviour problems' (2006) 30(3) *Child Abuse and Neglect* 307–324

Levitas, R, et al 'The multi-dimensional analysis of social exclusion: A Research for the Social Exclusion Task Force' (Cabinet Office, 2007)

Mayor of London 'London Divided: Income inequality and poverty in the capital: summary' (Greater London Authority, 2002)

Meltzer, H, et al 'The Mental Health of Young People Looked after by Local Authorities in England' (DOH: National Statistics, 2003)

Miller, B C, et al 'Comparisons of adopted and non adopted adolescents in a large, nationally representative sample' (2000) 71(5) *Child Development* 1458–1473

Patterson, O *The Sociology of Slavery: An Analysis of the Origins, Development and Structure of Negro Slave Society in Jamaica* (London: Cambridge University Press, 1967)

Reynolds, T 'Black mothering, paid work and identity' (2001) 24(6) *Ethnic and Racial Studies* 1046–1064

Rubin, D M 'The impact of placement stability on behavioural well-being for children in foster care' (2007) 119(2) *Pediatrics* 336–344

Scott, S, et al 'Financial cost of social exclusion: follow up study of antisocial children into adulthood' (2001) 323 *British Medical Journal* 191

Smith, A, et al 'Serial migration and its implications for the parent-child relationship: a retrospective analysis of the experiences of the children of Caribbean immigrants. Cultural diversity and ethnic minority' (2004) 10(2) *Psychology* 107–122

Social Exclusion Unit 'Improving services, Improving Lives: Evidence and Key Themes' (London, 2005)

Southwark Analytical Hub 'Ethnicity Needs Audit: Health and Social Care' (London Borough of Southwark, 2006)

Taussig, H N 'Risk behaviours in maltreated youth placed in foster care: a longitudinal study of protective and vulnerability factors' (2002) 26(11) *Child Abuse and Neglect* 1179–1199

The United Nations Children Fund 'A league table of child maltreatment deaths in rich nations' (2003) Innocenti Report Card, Issue No 5

Thoburn, J, et al *Child Welfare Services for Minority Ethnic Families: The Research Reviewed* (Jessica Kingsley Publishers, London, 2004)

Thrasher, S and Anderson, G 'The West Indian family: treatment challenges' (1988) 69(3) *Social Casework* 171–176.

Webb, E, et al 'Effectively protecting Black and minority ethnic children from harm: overcoming barriers to the child protection process' (2002) 11 *Child Abuse Review* 394–410

Williams, C and Soydan, H 'When and How Does Ethnicity Matter? A Cross-National Study of Social Work Responses to Ethnicity in Child' (2005) 35 *British Journal of Social Work* 901–920

PLENARY 7

CONFERENCE ACTION POINTS

Conference Resolutions

NEITHER BLIND TO CULTURE NOR BLINDED BY CULTURE

1. This Conference adopts the proposition that there are no homogeneous cultures. We must understand culture in context as it is not monolithic or static but variable and dynamic. The Conference recommends that in dealing with individual cases all professionals involved in Family Justice do receive appropriate training to enable them to elicit culturally related information that is relevant.

2. This Conference believes that if the Family Justice System is to improve its approach to diversity more time is needed to prepare and investigate individual cases. This Conference fears that this may not be possible given the imminent public funding changes.

3. This Conference advocates that families must be able to access culturally sensitive support and services to prevent court intervention.

4. This Conference seeks a review of policy to enable every child to have access to care, education and medical services regardless of immigration status.

5. The expectation of this Conference is that Independent Reviewing Officers will fulfil their duty to ensure the welfare of children regardless of immigration status.

6. This Conference strongly recommends review of current practices of deportation and incarceration of children and young adults who do not have the automatic right to remain in this country.

7. This Conference believes that children who are born as a result of egg or sperm donation are entitled to information about their genetic identity but the provision of this information should not automatically give rise to any parental entitlement to the donor.
    (a) This Conference invites a re-examination of the concept and definition of Parental Responsibility to reflect diverse and complex family relationships.
    (b) This Conference recommends that there be an amendment of the welfare checklist so that s 1(3)(d) of the Children Act 1989 reads 'his age, sex, background, including his *racial, religious, cultural and linguistic background* and any other characteristic of his, which the court considers relevant'.
    This Conference notes that making changes to primary legislation is a lengthy process and therefore recommends that, as an interim measure, a practice direction should be issued, the purpose of which would be to indicate that the wording highlighted above is already implicit within the existing legislation and that consideration of those matters to which it refers would be appropriate and proper, notwithstanding that the wording is not yet explicitly contained within primary legislation.

8. This Conference recommends that in cases where parental learning disability is a significant factor, save in exceptional circumstances, the local authority should only bring cases before the Court where, having complied with their obligations under the Disability Discrimination Act 2005, the children's needs have nevertheless not been met.

(a) This Conference advocates as good practice the nationwide use of a model akin to the Cornish Special Parenting Service.

(b) This Conference recognises that there needs to be more uniform awareness of the *Good Practice Guidance on Working with Parents with a Learning Disability* (2007) and the work of the Disability Rights Commission. It recommends to the Judicial Studies Board and CAFCASS in England and Wales that it should form part of the basic training for all levels of judiciary and for Children's Guardians doing public law work to ensure the provisions of the Guidance upon local authorities are complied with when cases involving learning disabled parents are litigated.

9.   This Conference highlights the need for good quality interpreters and agrees that the current mixed quality of the interpreters available to the Courts and professionals is a cause for concern. We encourage long-term investment in training and accreditation of interpreters to achieve high professional standards and a uniform good service throughout the country.

10. This Conference recommends that all experts, including paediatricians, should address relevant issues of diversity in their assessments and reports.

11. This Conference believes that physical abuse as a form of discipline of children is unacceptable and transcends class, race, cultures and religion.

12. This Conference recommends the wider dissemination of discussions arising from Dartington Conferences to ensure the spread of the valuable information. For example, by way of regular articles in practitioners' publications such as *Family Affairs, Family Law, Resolution Review,* etc.

13. This Conference recommends that there be improved training and support for alternative carers, including family members to enhance the child's sense of belonging and identity.

14. This Conference requests that research be commissioned for the purpose of ascertaining the accurate demography of children, in particular minority ethnic children, in the Family Justice System and Looked After children system across England and Wales.